Praise for the 1st edition of *White by Law*

As Ian F. Haney López shows in *White by Law: The Legal Construction of Race*, immigrants recognized the value of whiteness and sometimes petitioned the courts to be recognized as white. Through an analysis of the 'prerequisite cases' in the 19th and 20th centuries, López argues for the centrality of law in constructing race."
—*Village Voice Literary Supplement*

"This book is remarkable for sheer information value, but draws its analytic power from the emphasis on Whiteness to make sense of racial oppression. . . . Haney López convincingly demonstrates that the United States is ideologically White not by accident but by design. . . . a provocative and worthwhile volume, highly recommended for graduate students and faculty."
—*Choice*

"Haney López shares with us an historical narrative, one that few contemporary Americans know. It is a narrative about citizenship and racism. . . . Those who want to pretend that racism is nothing but a ghost from a distant past must ignore history. The work of legal historians like Haney López and books like *White by Law* make it harder to indulge in this delusion of a color-blind society. This alone makes the book a worthy read."
—*Buffalo Law Review*

"Haney López has written a great book. *White by Law: The Legal Construction of Race* deserves the highest praise that his colleagues in the academy can give a scholarly study: sympathetic readers and reviewers may be prompted to say, 'I wish I'd written that.' Haney López's book is perhaps one of the finest works yet produced by the Critical Race Theory (CRT) movement."
—*Asian Law Journal*

"Demonstrating the complexities of race relation is where *White by Law* begins, not ends. . . . Haney López has blazed a trail for those exploring the legal and social constructions of race in the United States."
—*Berkeley Women's Law Journal*

White by Law

Critical America
General Editors: RICHARD DELGADO and JEAN STEFANCIC

White by Law: The Legal Construction of Race by Ian Haney López, originally published in 1996, was the inaugural book in the Critical America series. For a complete list of titles in the series, please visit the New York University Press website at www.nyupress.org.

White by Law

The Legal Construction of Race

Revised and Updated
10th Anniversary Edition

Ian Haney López

NEW YORK UNIVERSITY PRESS
New York and London

NEW YORK UNIVERSITY PRESS
New York and London
www.nyupress.org°

Library of Congress Cataloging-in-Publication Data

Haney López, Ian.
   White by law : the legal construction of race / by Ian Haney
López.—
      Rev. and updated, 10th anniversary ed.
         p. cm.—(Critical America)
      Includes bibliographical references and index.
      ISBN-13: 978-0-8147-3698-2 (cloth : alk. paper)
      ISBN-10: 0-8147-3698-X (cloth : alk. paper)
      ISBN-13: 978-0-8147-3694-4 (pbk. : alk. paper)
      ISBN-10: 0-8147-3694-7 (pbk. : alk. paper)
      1. Race discrimination—Law and legislation—United States.
   2. Whites—Legal status, laws, etc.—United States.   I. Title.
   II. Series.
   KF4755.H36 2006
   342.7308'73—dc22
   2006010913

New York University Press books are printed on acid-free paper,
and their binding materials are chosen for strength and durability.

Manufactured in the United States of America

To my family
Terrence Eugene Haney
Maria Daisy López de Haney
and
Garth Mark Haney
with love.

Then, what is white?
        —*Ex parte Shahid*

Contents

Preface to the Revised
and Updated Edition

The son of a White father from the United States and a brown-skinned mother from El Salvador, I grew up in Hawaii, a place that found my mixed identity unproblematic, indeed almost typical. It was not until I arrived in St. Louis, Missouri, for college that I encountered on a sustained basis racial dynamics troubled by my identity. I was struck first, though, not by the question of my own location in mainland racial patterns, but by the patterns themselves. Never had I seen an environment so starkly segregated between White and Black. Even more startling, I could scarcely believe just how natural and commonplace such extreme segregation seemed to virtually all of my White peers and professors. No one ever talked about the overwhelming Whiteness of our academic world, or the Blackness of those doing menial work in our midst or populating the decaying city to the campus's east—our Manichean world was, literally, unremarkable.

It was this seemingly natural order that my identity disturbed, for I moved at the margin between White and non-White. There were some curious incidents, and a few ugly episodes as well—the double-take from professors when they first called roll and I raised my hand, a door slammed in my face to the yell of "go back where you came from" (and believe me, I wanted nothing more than to return to Hawaii). But on the whole I was treated well. Or rather, as I would eventually come to understand, I was treated White.

This understanding that I was being offered a White identity came first not from my peers and teachers but from the police. On half a dozen occasions during my university years, I was stopped and questioned by the police while walking in White areas—on campuses, in adjoining neighborhoods, in a city I was visiting. In each case but one, my educated accent, self-confidence, and university ID cards defused the initial hostility of the confrontation. With each iteration, though, the basic contours of this treacherous dance became clearer. Stopped for being non-White and hence suspicious and out of place, my exact enunciation and university affiliations combined to re-racialize me in the officers' eyes, rendering me safely White: innocent, entitled to be there, and deserving of deference.

Only figuratively rather than literally policing racialized spaces, the students and professors I encountered in my classes were less aggressive in their initial suspicions of my presence. But many of them too seemed to follow the same script, questioning my identity and then resolving their doubts in favor of a presumption of Whiteness. Most sought to understand and accept me by erasing those parts of me that coded as non-White, and by assuming that in extending to me a White identity they were according me friendship and equal respect. To make my Latino identity less easy to disregard, I changed my name by following Hispanic custom and adding my mother's family name to my own. Though I had grown up as Ian Haney, in graduate school I started to go by Ian Haney López. The first paper I turned in under that new name came back ungraded, with the question: "Is English your first language?" On the cusp between White and non-White, it turned out that achieving a marginalized, suspect identity was surprisingly easy.

One interaction, at the intersection of encounters with the police and responses by my White peers, particularly influenced my intellectual engagement with race and law. In a confrontation that my educated accent and elite bravado did not neutralize, a cop on the University of Virginia campus, where I was visiting a friend, took up the shotgun he had rested on the hood of his patrol car and ordered me to back away when I stepped forward to proffer my Harvard Law School student ID. He ordered me to toss my identification forward; he copied down the particulars; he threatened that if any crimes were reported that evening he would personally come looking for me; and finally he dismissed me with the order to get back to Boston. That episode sticks graphically in my mind, though not principally because of the intense fear-then-anger engendered by the encounter. I know well that I have remained privileged and insulated from the full violence and physical humiliation often inflicted by police on minorities, brutal beat downs that I have seen, heard about from friends, and studied, but to which I have never been subjected. Instead, I remember that stop, in my third year of law school, because my Virginia friend responded skeptically to my outrage. How did I know, she queried, that I had been singled out because I was a Latino? After all, she correctly pointed out, it was night, I'm not that dark, and (OK, I admit it) I was dressed like a typical preppy college kid, even down to the blue LL Bean windbreaker. My outrage turned against her, her Whiteness and (relatedly) her unwillingness to accept what to me seemed so obviously true. Only later did the question really sink in. How did I know that the police were stopping me because of race?

I took this question with me when I began my academic career. You can see the rudiments of an answer in my first law review article: "The Social Construction of Race: Some Observations on Illusion, Fabrication, and Choice."[1] There I explored race as something constructed through social processes, built on physical features, yes, but only superficially; I located the main action instead in the social dynamics that defined everything from racial categories to the criteria used to assign people to putative races to the characteristics supposedly borne by racial groups. And then you can see a more focused effort to grapple with this question in my next major piece, *White by Law: The Legal Construction of Race.* Here I further refined my thinking on the social construction of race, but much more importantly I turned directly to the question of how law participates in racial formation. I argued—and correctly, I still believe—that law constructs race at every level: changing the physical features borne by people in this country, shaping the social meanings that define races, and rendering concrete the privileges and disadvantages justified by racial ideology.

But as I look back on *White by Law* from a decade's remove, I see now that it does not fully respond to how and why police stops should be seen in terms of racial dynamics, rather than, say, merely as affronts to civil liberties, or even the praiseworthy vigilance of a protective police force. *White by Law* addresses what might be termed the *formal* legal construction of race—that is, the way in which law as a formal matter, either through legislation or adjudication, directly engages racial definitions. This has become a burgeoning field, with studies aimed at uncovering legal productions of race in the contexts of slavery, the postbellum South, the census, OMB Directive 15 on federal racial categories, contemporary immigration laws, and so on. But today race is legally constructed principally indirectly by legal institutions that produce and bolster deleterious racial ideologies without forthrightly engaging the categorical debates that so preoccupied race law through the early twentieth century. Like police conduct, the overwhelming bulk of law currently constructs race *informally,* not by directly addressing conceptions of race, but by relying on, promulgating, and giving force (often enough literal physical force) to particular ideas about the nature of race, races, and racism. It would take a second book, *Racism on Trial: The Chicano Fight for Justice*, for me to fully engage the questions concerning the informal legal construction of race raised for me in Virginia. It is in that volume that I examine directly how the law today relies on and produces racial ideas.[2]

Taking it on its own terms, though, I would offer two revisions to *White by Law*. My main concern when I wrote this book was with the constructedness of race, its plasticity and malleability. Thus, the definition I offered focused on race as "the historically contingent social systems of meaning that attach to elements of morphology and ancestry." Though dissecting the construction of race is crucial to understanding contemporary race relations, today I would shift my emphasis to the instrumental function of race and its material consequences. I noted in *White by Law* the remark of a businessman who in 1909 preferred Chinese over Japanese immigrants because "we find the Chinese fitting much better than the Japanese into the status which the white American prefers them to occupy—that of biped domestic animals in the white man's service." I commented as well on how the economic position of immigrants from Armenia and Japan diverged sharply when the former but not the latter were declared legally White. These, it seems to me, are key aspects of the prerequisite cases, and of the legal construction of race, that I failed to sufficiently emphasize in the original volume. Race and racism are centrally about seeking, or contesting, power. They have their origins in efforts to rationalize the expropriation and exploitation of land and labor, and they remain vibrant today only because racial hierarchy remains in the material interest of very many in our society. True, race is not simply, or always, about struggles over group advantage. Instead, race clearly exhibits independent cultural dynamics, informing how people think about and act in the world even when status concerns are not prevalent. Nevertheless, from my current vantage point I think we too often fail to appreciate how important race remains as a system for amassing and defending wealth and privilege. Thus, while I would still define race in terms of morphology, ancestry, and historically contingent social practices, I would add that racial systems use appearances and ancestry as weapons in violent struggles over group position in material and social status.

In a related vein, I would clarify what I meant when I first wrote in *White by Law* that Whites should work to deconstruct White identity. For someone mixed-race like me, "choosing not to be White" might entail assuming a socially intelligible not-White identity (as brown, Latino, angry minority, or so forth). It may seem that I am asking Whites to do the same, to opt out of Whiteness, which has prompted the rejoinder that this is impossible for a person whose identity is socially constructed consistently and thoroughly as White. For a U.S. citizen of European descent with fair features and an Anglo name, for example, there is no available not-White identity, for she or he cannot simply step outside of race entirely, at least not in our society, not yet, nor for a long time to come. But in calling for Whites to resolve against Whiteness, I did not mean that they should adopt another (non-existent) identity so much as that antiracist Whites should work against White privilege. Connecting this clarification with the shift in emphasis offered above, I would broaden the point further: race remains a social system in which persons from different positions in the racial hierarchy seek, or contest their exclusion from, social and material status. Justice lies, then, not in embracing Whiteness (that is, advantage), but in seeking to dismantle race as a system that correlates to power and privilege.

These clarifications have not prompted me to make revisions to the text in this new edition. These principal points excepted, my earlier arguments do not seem to have suffered too much with time, perhaps because the main focus was on the legal construction of race prior to the civil rights movement. These concerns have, however, led me to add a new concluding chapter in which I consider the future of race in the United States over the next few decades. This may seem principally a demographic question, and indeed immigration and changing intermarriage patterns play a prominent role in the predictions I offer. It is enormously consequential, after all, that Latinos now outnumber Blacks as the largest minority group and that mixed-race persons are reshaping America's racial imagination, especially among the young. Without slighting demography, however, there is a close connection between our racial future and the legal construction of race. That future will turn on the persistence of race in the United States as a system for allocating and preserving social advantage—which is to say, on the shifting contours and meanings of Whiteness. Here, the legal construction of race will be paramount, not so much in redefining White identity, but in shaping the ideological understandings of race and racism that will undergird any racial evolution. The nation's courts, captured by the racial right, for the last quarter century have been elaborating and proselytizing the racial ideology of our immediate future—colorblindness.

In the new chapter I predict that we are headed toward a reign of what

I term "colorblind White dominance." The era of culturally legitimate expressions of White supremacy is over, defeated by the moral triumph of the civil rights movement. But the dominance of Whites across the range of social, political, and economic spheres continues and indeed over the last couple of decades has intensified. This dominance, in turn, is protected by colorblindness, an ideology that self-righteously wraps itself in the raiment of the civil rights movement and that, while proclaiming a deep fealty to eliminating racism, perversely defines discrimination strictly in terms of explicit references to race. Thus, it is "racism" when society uses affirmative race-conscious means to respond to gross inequalities, but there is no racial harm no matter how strongly disparities in health care, education, residential segregation, or incarceration correlate to race, so long as no one has uttered a racial word. Colorblindness wears its antiracist pretensions boldly but acts overwhelmingly to condemn affirmative action and to condone structural racial inequality. This ideology, which at once claims the mantle of the civil rights movement but preserves the racial status quo, protects the continued privileged position of Whites in our society even as it relegates minorities to continued immiseration, marginalization, and social disdain. I conclude this new edition with the dismal prediction that colorblindness, a legal construction that serves increasingly as the most powerful ideology of race in the United States, will protect continued White racial dominance in the decades to come.[3]

Acknowledgments

Many people helped in this project, and in many different ways. Some contributed through reading and commenting on drafts of this book, others through pushing me to elaborate on ideas included herein, a few through help with research, and untold many simply by listening and responding to my various constructivist theories. I am grateful to all of these people. I particularly thank Neil Gotanda, Beverly Moran, Richard Ford, Robert García, Ann Althouse, Robert Correales, Michael Morgalla, Jean Stefancic, Rey Rodríguez, Chris Smith, Bill Whyman, and Juan Zúñiga. My thanks also to Angela Miller, Michael Risher, and Michael Van Sistine for their first-rate research and editorial assistance. Three individuals deserve special recognition: Richard Delgado, who provided the initial impetus for this book; Miguel Méndez, for his support and encouragement while I was at Stanford; and Deborah Drickersen Córtez, for her help with the ideas behind this project, and more, for her companionship.

I must thank some institutions and institutionalized practices as well. This book greatly benefited from the commentary and questions offered in response to presentations at the University of Wisconsin Law School, the Sixth Annual Critical Race Theory Workshop, the Stanford Anthropology Department, the Stanford Humanities Center, Boalt Hall School of Law, the University of Southern California Law Center, and Stanford Law School. I also very much appreciate the support given to me in the form of research grants and writing time by the University of Wisconsin Law School, the Rockefeller Foundation, and the Stanford Humanities Center.

Without the invaluable assistance of these friends, students, colleagues, and institutions, this book would not have been possible. Of course, all errors, conceptual or factual, are my responsibility alone.

A Note on Whiteness

This book examines a series of cases from the first part of this century in which state and federal courts sought to determine, and thereby partially defined, who was White enough to naturalize as a citizen. It thus concerns the legal construction of White racial identity. Yet, "White" as a category of human identity and difference is an enormously complex phenomenon. Races are not biologically differentiated groupings but rather social constructions. Race exists alongside a multitude of social identities that shape and are themselves shaped by the way in which race is given meaning. We live race through class, religion, nationality, gender, sexual identity, and so on. Whether one is White therefore depends in part on other elements of identity—for example, on whether one is wealthy or poor, Protestant or Muslim, male or female—just as these aspects of identity are given shape and significance by whether or not one is White. Moreover, like these other social categories, race is highly contingent, specific to times, places, and situations. Whiteness, or the state of being White, thus turns on where one is, Watts or Westchester, Stanford University or San Jose State; on when one is there, two in the afternoon or three in the morning, 1878 or 1995; on the immediate context, applying to rent an apartment, seeking entrance into an exclusive club, or talking with a police officer. Being White is not a monolithic or homogenous experience, either in terms of race, other social identities, space or time. Instead, Whiteness is contingent, changeable, partial, inconstant, and ultimately social. As a descriptor and as an experience, "White" takes on highly variegated nuances across the range of social axes and individual lives.

The usage in this book reflects an understanding of Whiteness as a complex, falsely homogenizing term. "White" is capitalized to indicate its reference to a specific social group, but this group is recognized to possess fluid borders and heterogenous members. Here, "White" does not denote a rigidly defined, congeneric grouping of indistinguishable individuals. It refers to an unstable category which gains its meaning only through social relations and that encompasses a profoundly diverse set of persons.

Notwithstanding this rich diversity, however, it remains the case that in the social elaboration of Whiteness, trends can be discerned and some commonalities persist in recognizable form. In this book I attempt to unearth and elaborate some of the perduring, seemingly fundamental characteristics of Whiteness, particularly as these have been fashioned by law. Nevertheless, I seek to talk about the legal construction of White racial identity in a manner that remains true to the argument that, however powerful and however deeply a part of our society race may be, races are still only human inventions.

1

White Lines

In its first words on the subject of citizenship, Congress in 1790 restricted naturalization to "white persons."[1] Though the requirements for naturalization changed frequently thereafter, this racial prerequisite to citizenship endured for over a century and a half, remaining in force until 1952.[2] From the earliest years of this country until just a generation ago, being a "white person" was a condition for acquiring citizenship.

Whether one was "white," however, was often no easy question. As immigration reached record highs at the turn of this century, countless people found themselves arguing their racial identity in order to naturalize. From 1907, when the federal government began collecting data on naturalization, until 1920, over one million people gained citizenship under the racially restrictive naturalization laws.[3] Many more sought to naturalize and were rejected. Naturalization rarely involved formal court proceedings and therefore usually generated few if any written records beyond the simple decision.[4] However, a number of cases construing the "white person" prerequisite reached the highest state and federal judicial circles, and two were argued before the U.S. Supreme Court in the early 1920s. These cases produced illuminating published decisions that document the efforts of would-be citizens from around the world to establish their Whiteness at law. Applicants from Hawaii, China, Japan, Burma, and the Philippines, as well as all mixed-race applicants, failed in their arguments. Conversely, courts ruled that applicants from Mexico and Armenia were "white," but vacillated over the Whiteness of petitioners from Syria, India, and Arabia.[5] Seen as a taxonomy of Whiteness, these cases are instructive because they reveal the imprecisions and contradictions inherent in the establishment of racial lines between Whites and non-Whites.

It is on the level of taxonomical *practice*, however, that these cases are most intriguing. The individuals who petitioned for naturalization forced the courts into a case-by-case struggle to define who was a "white person." More importantly, the courts were required in these prerequisite cases to articulate rationales for the divisions they were creating. Beyond simply issuing declarations in favor of or against a particular applicant, the courts, as exponents of the applicable law, had to explain the basis on which they drew the boundaries of Whiteness. The courts had to establish by law whether, for example, a petitioner's race was to be measured by skin color, facial features, national origin, language, culture, ancestry, the speculations of scientists, popular opinion, or some combination of these factors. Moreover, the courts also had to decide which of these or other factors would govern in the inevitable cases where the various indices of race contradicted one another. In short, the courts were responsible for deciding not only who was White, but *why* someone was White. Thus, the courts had to wrestle in their decisions with the nature of race in general and of White racial identity in particular. Their categorical practices in deciding who was White by law provide the empirical basis for this book.

How did the courts define who was White? What reasons did they offer, and what do those rationales tell us about the nature of Whiteness? What do the cases reveal about the legal construction of race, about the ways in which the operation of law creates and maintains the social knowledge of racial difference? Do these cases also afford insights into White racial identity as it exists today? What, finally, *is* White? In this book I examine these and related questions, offering a general theory of the legal construction of race and exploring contemporary White identity. I conclude that Whiteness exists at the vortex of race in U.S. law and society, and that Whites should renounce their racial identity as it is currently constituted in the interests of social justice. This chapter introduces the ideas I develop throughout the book.

The Racial Prerequisite Cases

Although now largely forgotten, the prerequisite cases were at the center of racial debates in the United States for the fifty years following the Civil War, when immigration and nativism were both running high. Naturalization laws figured prominently in the furor over the appropriate status of the newcomers and were heatedly discussed not only by the most respected public figures of the day, but also in the swirl of popular politics.

Debates about racial prerequisites to citizenship arose at the end of the Civil War when Senator Charles Sumner sought to expunge *Dred Scott,* the Supreme Court decision which had held that Blacks were not citizens, by striking any reference to race from the naturalization statute.[6] His efforts failed because of racial animosity in much of Congress toward Asians and Native Americans.[7] The persistence of anti-Asian agitation through the early 1900s kept the prerequisite laws at the forefront of national and even international attention. Efforts in San Francisco to segregate Japanese schoolchildren, for example, led to a crisis in relations with Japan that prompted President Theodore Roosevelt to propose legislation granting Japanese immigrants the right to naturalize.[8] Controversy over the prerequisite laws also found voice in popular politics. Anti-immigrant groups such as the Asiatic Exclusion League formulated arguments for restrictive interpretations of the "white person" prerequisite, for example claiming in 1910 that Asian Indians were not "white," but an "effeminate, caste-ridden, and degraded" race who did not deserve citizenship.[9] For their part, immigrants also participated in the debates on naturalization, organizing civic groups around the issue of citizenship, writing in the immigrant press, and lobbying local, state, and federal governments.[10]

The principal locus of the debate, however, was in the courts. From the first prerequisite case in 1878 until racial restrictions were removed in 1952, fifty-two racial prerequisite cases were reported, including two heard by the U.S. Supreme Court. Framing fundamental questions about who could join the citizenry in terms of who was White, these cases attracted some of the most renowned jurists of the times, such as John Wigmore, as well as some of the greatest experts on race, including Franz Boas. Wigmore, now famous for his legal treatises, published a law review article in 1894 asserting that Japanese immigrants were eligible for citizenship on the grounds that the Japanese people were anthropologically and culturally White.[11] Boas, today commonly regarded as the founder of modern anthropology, participated in at least one of the prerequisite cases as an expert witness on behalf of an Armenian applicant, whom he argued was White.[12] Despite the occasional participation of these accomplished scholars, the courts struggled with the narrow question of whom to naturalize, and with the categorical question of how to determine racial identity.

Though the courts offered many different rationales to justify the various racial divisions they advanced, two predominated: common knowledge and scientific evidence. Both of these rationales appear in the first prerequisite case, *In re Ah Yup,* decided in 1878 by a federal district court in California.[13] "Common knowledge" rationales appealed to popular, widely held conceptions of races and racial divisions. For example, the *Ah Yup* court denied citizenship to a Chinese applicant in part because of the popular understanding of the term "white person": "The words 'white person' . . . in this country, at least, have undoubtedly acquired a well settled meaning in common popular speech, and they are constantly used in the sense so acquired in the literature of the country, as well as in common parlance."[14] Under a common knowledge approach, courts justified the assignment of petitioners to one race or another by reference to common beliefs about race.

The common knowledge rationale contrasts with reasoning based on supposedly objective, technical, and specialized knowledge. Such "scientific evidence" rationales justified racial divisions by reference to the naturalistic studies of humankind. A longer excerpt from *Ah Yup* exemplifies this second sort of rationale:

> In speaking of the various classifications of races, Webster in his dictionary says, "The common classification is that of Blumenbach, who makes five. 1. The Caucasian, or white race, to which belong the greater part of European nations and those of Western Asia; 2. The Mongolian, or yellow race, occupying Tartary, China, Japan, etc.; 3. The Ethiopian or Negro (black) race, occupying all of Africa, except the north; 4. The American, or red race, containing the Indians of North and South America; and, 5. The Malay, or Brown race, occupying the islands of the Indian Archipelago," etc. This division was adopted from Buffon, with some changes in names, and is founded on the combined characteristics of complexion, hair and skull. . . . [N]o one includes the white, or Caucasian, with the Mongolian or yellow race.[15]

These rationales, one appealing to common knowledge and the other to scientific evidence, were the two core approaches used by courts to explain their determinations of whether individuals belonged to the "white" race.

As *Ah Yup* demonstrates, the courts deciding racial prerequisite cases initially relied on both rationales to justify their decisions. However, beginning in 1909 a schism appeared among the courts over whether common knowledge or scientific evidence was the appropriate standard. Thereafter, the lower courts divided almost evenly on the proper test for

Whiteness: six courts relied on common knowledge, while seven others based their racial determinations on scientific evidence. No court used both rationales. Over the course of two cases, heard in 1922 and 1923, the Supreme Court broke the impasse in favor of common knowledge. Though the courts did not see their decisions in this light, the early congruence of and subsequent contradiction between common knowledge and scientific evidence set the terms of a debate about whether race is a social construction or a natural occurrence. In these terms, the Supreme Court's elevation of common knowledge as the legal meter of race convincingly demonstrates that racial categorization finds its origins in social practices.

The early prerequisite courts assumed that common knowledge and scientific evidence both measured the same thing, namely, the natural physical differences that divided humankind into disparate races. Courts assumed that typological differences between the two rationales, if any, resulted from differences in how accurately popular opinion and science measured race, rather than from substantive disagreements about the nature of race itself. This position seemed tenable so long as science and popular beliefs jibed in the construction of racial categories. However, by 1909 changes in immigrant demographics and in anthropological thinking combined to create contradictions between science and common knowledge. These contradictions surfaced most directly in cases concerning immigrants from western and southern Asia, such as Syrians and Asian Indians, dark-skinned peoples who were nevertheless uniformly classified as Caucasians by the leading anthropologists of the times. Science's inability to confirm through empirical evidence the popular racial beliefs that held Syrians and Asian Indians to be non-Whites should have led the courts to question whether race was a natural phenomenon. So deeply held was this belief, however, that instead of re-examining the nature of race, the courts began to disparage science.

Over the course of two decisions, the Supreme Court resolved the conflict between common knowledge and scientific evidence in favor of the former, but not without some initial confusion. In *Ozawa v. United States,* the Court relied on both rationales to exclude a Japanese petitioner, holding that he was not of the type "popularly known as the Caucasian race," thereby invoking both common knowledge ("popularly known") and science ("the Caucasian race").[16] Here, as in the earliest prerequisite cases, science and popular knowledge worked hand in hand to exclude the applicant from citizenship. Within a few months of its decision in *Ozawa*, however, the Court heard a case brought by an Asian Indian, Bhagat Singh Thind, who relied on the Court's earlier linkage of "Caucasian" with "white" to argue for his own naturalization. In *United States v. Thind*, science and common knowledge diverged, complicating a case that should have been easy under *Ozawa*'s straightforward rule of racial specification. Reversing course, the Court repudiated its earlier equation and rejected any role for science in racial assignments.[17] The Court decried the "scientific manipulation" it believed had ignored racial differences by including as Caucasian "far more [people] than the unscientific mind suspects," even some persons the Court described as ranging "in color . . . from brown to black."[18] "We venture to think," the Court said, "that the average well informed white American would learn with some degree of astonishment that the race to which he belongs is made up of such heterogenous elements."[19] The Court held instead that "the words 'free white persons' are words of common speech, to be interpreted in accordance with the understanding of the common man."[20] In the Court's opinion, science had failed as an arbiter of human difference, and common knowledge was made into the touchstone of racial division.

In elevating common knowledge, the Court no doubt remained convinced that racial divisions followed from real, natural, physical differences. The Court upheld common knowledge in the belief that people are accomplished amateur naturalists, capable of accurately discerning differences in the physical world. This explains the Court's frustration with science, which to the Court's mind was curiously and suspiciously unable to identify and quantify those racial differences so readily apparent in the petitioners who came before them. This frustration is understandable, given early anthropology's promise to establish a definitive catalogue of racial differences, and from these differences to give scientific justification to a racial hierarchy that placed Whites at the top. This, however, was a promise science could not keep. Despite their strained efforts, students of race could not plot the boundaries of Whiteness because such boundaries are socially fashioned and cannot be measured, or found, in nature. The Court resented the failure of science to fulfil an impossible vow; it might better have resented that science ever undertook such an enterprise. The early congruence between scientific evidence and common knowledge did not reflect the accuracy of popular understandings of race, but rather the social embeddedness of scientific inquiry. Neither common knowledge nor the science of the day measured human variation. Both merely reported social beliefs about races.

The early reliance on scientific evidence to justify racial assignments implied that races exist as physical fact, humanly knowable but not dependent on human knowledge or human relations. The Court's ultimate reliance on common knowledge says otherwise: it demonstrates that racial taxonomies devolve upon social demarcations. That common knowledge emerged as the only workable racial test shows that race is something which must be measured in terms of what people believe, that it is a socially mediated idea. The social construction of the White race is manifest in the Court's repudiation of science and its installation of common knowledge as the appropriate racial meter of Whiteness.

The Legal Construction of Race

The prerequisite cases compellingly demonstrate that races are socially constructed. More importantly, they evidence the centrality of law in that construction. Law is one of the most powerful mechanisms by which any society creates, defines, and regulates itself. Its centrality in the constitution of society is especially pronounced in highly legalized and bureaucratized late-industrial democracies such as the United States.[21] It follows, then, that to say race is socially constructed is to conclude that race is at least partially legally produced. Put most starkly, law constructs race. Of course, it does so within the larger context of society, and so law is only one of many institutions and forces implicated in the formation of races. Moreover, as a complex set of institutions and ideas, "law" intersects and interacts with the social knowledge about race in convoluted, unpredictable, sometimes self-contradictory ways. Nevertheless, the prerequisite cases make clear that law does more than simply codify race in the limited sense of merely giving legal definition to pre-existing social categories. Instead, legislatures and courts have served not only to fix the boundaries of race in the forms we recognize today, but also to define the content of racial identities and to specify their relative privilege or disadvantage in U.S. society. As Cheryl Harris argues specifically with respect to Whites, "[t]he law's construction of whiteness defined and affirmed critical aspects of identity (who is white); of privilege (what benefits accrue to that status); and of property (what *legal* entitlements arise from that status)."²² The operation of law does far more than merely legalize race; it defines as well the spectrum of domination and subordination that constitutes race relations.

Little to date has been written on the legal construction of race. Indeed, the tendency of those writing on race and law has been to assume that races exist wholly independent of and outside law. While the race-and-law literature is too extensive to summarize quickly, two of the best-known works on the subject illustrate this point. Consider A. Leon Higginbotham, Jr.'s classic study, *In the Matter of Color: Race and the American Legal Process: The Colonial Period* (1978) and Derrick Bell's equally classic casebook, *Race, Racism, and American Law* (3rd edition, 1992). Both works provide exhaustive, meticulously researched, and invaluable studies of the legal burdens imposed on Blacks in North America over the last few centuries. Yet, in both works, "Black" and "White" are treated as natural categories rather than as concepts created through social, and at least partially through legal, interaction between peoples not initially racially defined in those terms. The discussions in both books of the arrival of the first Africans in colonial North America exemplify this tendency. Higginbotham writes: "In 1619, when these first twenty blacks arrived in Jamestown, there was not yet a statutory process to especially fix the legal standing of blacks."²³ For his part, Bell quotes the following passage from the Kerner Commission: "In Colonial America, the first Negroes landed at Jamestown in August, 1619. Within forty years, Negroes had become a group apart, separated from the rest of the population by custom and law. Treated as servants for life, forbidden to intermarry with whites, deprived of their African traditions and dispersed among Southern plantations, American Negroes lost tribal, regional and family ties."²⁴ These passages are striking because of the manner in which "blacks," "Negroes," and "whites" seem to exist as prelegal givens, groups that interacted socially and legally but that in all significant respects possessed identities not dependent on their social and legal interaction.

In Higginbotham's study, those African men who were forced onto American shores in 1619 disembarked already possessed of a "black" identity. Similarly, in Bell's casebook, the Africans who were brought to Jamestown only a year after the Pilgrims had landed at Plymouth Rock arrived already "Negroes" in a way that attributed to them the same identity as those the passage later terms "American Negroes." Neither work seems to recognize that the very racial categories under examination were largely created by the legal and social relations between the dis-

parate peoples who found themselves for weal or woe on the northeast-
ern shores of the Americas in the first years of the seventeenth century.
This is all the more surprising because the very point of both passages is
that the legal liabilities that would significantly define the relative identity
of Whites and Blacks in North America were not in place in 1619. These
works treat races as natural, pre-legal categories on which the law operates, but which the law does not in many ways create. In this assumption,
they are joined by almost every other examination of race and law.

Nevertheless, the tendency to treat race as a prelegal phenomenon is
coming to an end. Of late, a new strand of legal scholarship dedicated to
reconsidering of the role of race in U.S. society has emerged. Writers in
this genre, known as critical race theory, have for the most part shown an
acute awareness of the socially constructed nature of race.[25] Much critical
race theory scholarship recognizes that race is a legal construction. For
example, a recent article by Gerald Torres and Kathryn Milun examines
the imposition of the legal concept of "tribe" on the Mashpee of Massachusetts.[26] In order to proceed in a suit over alienated lands, the Mashpee
were required to prove their existence as a tribe in legal terms that focused
on racial purity, hierarchical leadership, and clearly demarcated geographic boundaries. This legal definition of tribal identity ineluctably led
to the nonexistence of the Mashpee people, since it "incorporated specific
perceptions regarding race, leadership, community, and territory that
were entirely alien to Mashpee culture."[27] Because the Mashpee did not
conform to the racial and cultural stereotypes that infuse the law, they
could not prove their existence in those terms, and hence did not exist as
a people capable of suing in federal court. The article documents the manner in which Mashpee legal identity—and more, their existence—depended upon a particular definition of race and tribe, thus unearthing the
manner in which law mediates racial and tribal ontology. This recognition of the role of law in the social dynamics of racial identity arguably
lies near the heart of critical race theory. As John Calmore argues, "Critical race theory begins with a recognition that 'race' is not a fixed term.
Instead, 'race' is a fluctuating, decentered complex of social meanings
that are formed and transformed under the constant pressures of political struggle."[28] Critical race theory increasingly acknowledges the extent
to which race is not an independent given on which the law acts, but
rather a social construction at least in part fashioned by law.[29]

Despite the spreading recognition that law is a prime suspect in the formation of races, however, to date there has been no attempt to evaluate

systematically just how the law creates and maintains races. How does the operation of law contribute to the formation of races? More particularly, by what mechanisms do courts and legislatures elaborate races, and what is the role of legal actors in these processes? Do legal rules construct races through the direct control of human behavior, or do they work more subtly as an ideology shaping our notions of what is and what can be? By the same token, are legal actors aware of their role in the fabrication of races, or are they unwitting participants, passive actors caught in processes beyond their ken and control? These are the questions this book attempts to answer. I suggest that law constructs races in a complex manner through both coercion and ideology, with legal actors as both conscious and unwitting participants. Rather than turning directly to theories of how law creates and maintains racial difference, however, I would like here to explore at greater length what is meant by the basic assertion that law constructs race.

A more precise definition of race will help us explore the importance of law in its creation. Race can be understood as the historically contingent social systems of meaning that attach to elements of morphology and ancestry.[30] This definition can be pushed on three interrelated levels, the physical, the social, and the material. First, race turns on physical features and lines of descent, not because features or lineage themselves are a function of racial variation, but because society has invested these with racial meanings. Second, because the meanings given to certain features and ancestries denote race, it is the social processes of ascribing racialized meanings to faces and forbearers that lie at the heart of racial fabrication. Third, these meaning-systems, while originally only ideas, gain force as they are reproduced in the material conditions of society. The distribution of wealth and poverty turns in part on the actions of social and legal actors who have accepted ideas of race, with the resulting material conditions becoming part of and reinforcement for the contingent meanings understood as race.

Examining the role of law in the construction of race becomes, then, an examination of the possible ways in which law creates differences in physical appearance, of the extent to which law ascribes racialized meanings to physical features and ancestry, and of the ways in which law translates ideas about race into the material societal conditions that confirm and entrench those ideas.

Initially, it may be difficult to see how laws could possibly create differences in physical appearance. Biology, it seems, must be the sole provenance of morphology, while laws would appear to have no ability to regulate what people look like. However, laws have shaped the physical features evident in our society. While admittedly laws cannot alter the biology governing human morphology, rule-makers can and have altered the human behavior that produces variations in physical appearance. In other words, laws have directly shaped reproductive choices. The prerequisite laws evidence this on two levels. First, these laws constrained reproductive choices by excluding people with certain features from this country. From 1924 until the end of racial prerequisites to naturalization in 1952, persons ineligible for citizenship could not enter the United States.[31] The prerequisite laws determined the types of faces and features present in the United States, and thus, who could marry and bear children here. Second, the prerequisite laws had a more direct regulatory reproductive effect through the legal consequences imposed on women who married noncitizen men. Until 1931, a woman could not naturalize if she was married to a foreigner racially ineligible for citizenship, even if she otherwise qualified to naturalize in every respect. Furthermore, women who were U.S. citizens were automatically stripped of their citizenship upon marriage to such a person.[32] These legal penalties for marriage to racially barred aliens made such unions far less likely, and thus skewed the procreative choices that determined the appearance of the U.S. population. The prerequisite laws have directly shaped the physical appearance of people in the United States by limiting entrance to certain physical types and by altering the range of marital choices available to people here. What we look like, the literal and "racial" features we in this country exhibit, is to a large extent the product of legal rules and decisions.

Race is not, however, simply a matter of physical appearance and ancestry. Instead, it is primarily a function of the meanings given to these. On this level, too, law creates races. The statutes and cases that make up the laws of this country have directly contributed to defining the range of meanings without which notions of race could not exist. Recall the exclusion from citizenship of Ozawa and Thind. These cases established the significance of physical features on two levels. On the most obvious one, they established in stark terms the denotation and connotation of being non-White versus that of being White. To be the former meant one was unfit for naturalization, while to be the latter defined one as suited for citizenship. This stark division necessarily also carried important connotations regarding, for example, agency, will, moral authority, intelligence, and belonging. To be unfit for naturalization—that is, to be non-White—implied a certain degeneracy of intellect, morals, self-restraint, and political values; to be suited for citizenship—to be White—suggested moral maturity, self-assurance, personal independence, and political sophistication. These cases thus aided in the construction of the positive and negative meanings associated with racial difference, at least by giving such meanings legitimacy, and at most by actually fabricating them. The normative meanings that attach to racial difference—the contingent evaluations of worth, temperament, intellect, culture, and so on, which are at the core of racial beliefs—are partially the product of law.

Rather than simply shaping the social content of racial identity, however, the operation of law also creates the racial meanings that attach to features in a much more subtle and fundamental way: laws and legal decisions define which physical and ancestral traits code as Black or White, and so on. Appearances and origins are not White or non-White in any natural or presocial way. Rather, White is a figure of speech, a social convention read from looks. As Henry Louis Gates, Jr., writes, "Who has seen a black or red person, a white, yellow, or brown? These terms are arbitrary constructs, not reports of reality."[33] The construction of race thus occurs in part by the definition of certain features as White, other features as Black, some as Yellow, and so on. On this level, the prerequisite cases demonstrate that law can construct races by setting the standard by which features and ancestry should be read as denoting a White or a non-White person. When the Supreme Court rested its decision regarding Thind's petition for naturalization on common knowledge, it participated in the creation of that knowledge, saying this person and persons like him do not "look" White. The prerequisite cases did more than decide who qualified as a "white person." They defined the racial semiotics of morphology and ancestry. It is upon this seed of racial physicality that the courts imposed the flesh of normative racial meanings, establishing the social significance of the very racial categories they were themselves constructing. Only after constructing the underlying racial categories could the courts infuse them with legal meaning. The legal system constructs race by elaborating on multiple levels and in various contexts and forms the meaning systems that constitute race.

Finally, racial meaning systems are complex, containing both ideological and material components. That is, the common knowledge of race is grounded not only in the world of ideas, but in the material geography of social life. Here, too, law constructs race. U.S. social geography has in part been constructed by the legal system. Racial categories are in one sense a series of abstractions, but their constant legal usage makes these abstractions concrete and material. Indeed, the very purpose of some laws was to create and maintain material differences between races, to structure racial dominance and subordination into the socioeconomic relations of this society. It is here that the operation of law effects the greatest, most injurious, and least visible influence in entrenching racial categories. As laws and legal decision-makers transform racial ideas into a lived reality of material inequality, the ensuing reality becomes a further justification for the ideas of race.

In terms of the prerequisite cases, for example, the categories of White and non-White became tangible when certain persons were granted citizenship and others excluded. A "white" citizenry took on physical form, in part because of the demographics of migration, but also because of the laws and cases proscribing non-White naturalization and immigration. The idea of a White country, given ideological and *physical* effect by law, has provided the basis for contemporary claims regarding the European nature of the United States, where "European" serves as a not-so-subtle synonym for White. In turn, the notion of a White nation is used to justify arguments for restrictive immigration laws designed to preserve this supposed national identity. Consider here Patrick Buchanan's views on immigration, offered during his 1992 bid for the Republican presidential nomination: "I think God made all people good, but if we had to take a million immigrants in, say, Zulus, next year, or Englishmen and put them in Virginia, what group would be easier to assimilate and would cause less problems for the people of Virginia? There is nothing wrong with sitting down and arguing that issue, that we are a European country."[34] Buchanan argues as a matter of fact that the United States is a European country, refusing to recognize that this "fact" is a contingent one, a product in large part of identifiable immigration and naturalization laws. Buchanan and others easily confirm their notions regarding the racial nature of the United States, as well as the naturalness of a White citizenry, by looking around and noting the predominance of White people. The physical reality evident in the features of the U.S. citizenry supports the ideological supposition that Whites exist as a race and that this is a White country. Hidden from view, indeed difficult to discern except through extended study, is that Whites do not exist as a natural group, but only as a social and legal creation. What we see in the prerequisite cases is "not the defence of the white state but the creation of the state through white-ness."[35] The legal reification of racial categories has made race an in-escapable material reality in our society, one which at every turn seems to reinvigorate race with the appearance of reality.

On multiple levels, law is implicated in the construction of the contin-gent social systems of meaning that attach in our society to morphology and ancestry, the meaning systems we commonly refer to as race. The legal system influences what we look like, the meanings ascribed to our looks, and the material reality that confirms the meanings of our appear-ances. Law constructs race.

White Race-Consciousness

The racial prerequisite cases demonstrate that race is legally constructed. More than that, though, they exemplify the construction of Whiteness. They thus serve as a convenient point of departure for a discussion of White identity as it exists today, particularly regarding both the way in which those constructed as White conceptualize their racial identity, and in terms of the content of that identity. In this way, the prerequisite cases also afford a basis for formulating arguments concerning the way Whites ought to think about Whiteness. In short, the prerequisite cases offer a useful vehicle for exploring the forms White race-consciousness does and should take.

Race-consciousness, the explicit recognition of racial differences, has recently emerged as a trend in legal scholarship. The vast bulk of race-conscious scholarship is by minority scholars, particularly those writing in the genre of critical race theory.[36] This trend toward race-consciousness takes two forms. First, some scholars have explicitly recognized, and en-couraged the recognition of, races and racial difference. This has often come in response to arguments that the legal system should be "color-blind," that is, that law ought not to notice races.[37] Second, scholars are also increasingly race-conscious in the sense of acknowledging the im-portance of race to personal identity and world view. Scholars now fre-quently discuss the epistemological influence of race in general, or an au-thor's race in particular, positing the existence of subjective, racially me-diated points of view as a rebuttal to the notion of an objective, "race-less" perspective.[38]

For the most part, White scholars have been reluctant either to produce or to engage intellectually this emergent race-based scholarship. Several potential reasons for the silence of White legal scholars suggest themselves. Some minority scholars have asserted a special expertise in the area of race, perhaps suggesting to Whites that they are not welcome to join the critical discourse on race and law.[39] This silence may also result from institutional pressures, where White scholars are directed away from, and minority academics are channeled toward, the relatively marginal discussion of race and law.[40] Or the lack of response may be engendered by racism on the part of some Whites—of a subtle sort that relegates the concerns of minorities to the margins of relevance, or of a more pernicious type that, by disregarding minority voices, seeks to control all discourse about race.[41] Whatever its origins, this White silence has resulted in the accumulation of a body of race-conscious scholarship that focuses almost exclusively on people of color and on the epistemological importance of being a minority. Until recently, this scholarship rarely concerned Whites or addressed the intellectual influence of White identity.

In the last few years, however, this pattern has been broken. Writing in top law reviews across the country, several White law professors have helped place race-consciousness at the forefront of legal academic discourse.[42] These efforts seem to be part of a larger current in which White scholars are increasingly willing to grapple with critical race theory, and they constitute an important contribution to the exploration of the relationship between race and law.[43] Nevertheless, these writings invite critical response. Some of this scholarship maintains Whiteness as the unexamined norm by equating race-consciousness with the conscious recognition of Blackness. Other writings uncritically advocate race-consciousness as a step toward the elaboration of a positive White racial identity, and thus disregard the extent to which a positive White identity already exists, and further, the extent to which such a positive identity may require inferior minority identities as tropes of hierarchical difference.

An article by Alexander Aleinikoff entitled simply *A Case for Race-Consciousness* exemplifies the first error.[44] Responding to arguments in favor of color-blindness, Aleinikoff asserts that law, or more particularly the Supreme Court, should acknowledge the paramount importance of racial differences in our society. Yet, the racial differences Aleinikoff argues the law should recognize are those distinctions that mark Blacks, not Whites. For example, he writes: "Race matters. . . . To be born black is to know an unchangeable fact about oneself that matters every day";[45] and, "race has deep social significance that continues to disadvantage blacks and other Americans of color";[46] and, "at the base of racial injustice is a set of assumptions—a way of understanding the world—that so characterizes blacks as to make persistent inequality seem largely untroubling."[47] It is difficult to take issue with what Aleinikoff writes; indeed, his assertions are insightful and entirely accurate. His error lies in what he omits. Aleinikoff does not explore the implications of consciously recognizing Whites, and thus misses important insights about Whiteness. He does not write, as he might have with powerful effect, that "to be born White is to know an unchangeable fact about oneself that matters every day"; or that "race has deep social significance that continues to advantage Whites"; or that "at the base of racial injustice is a set of assumptions—a way of understanding the world—that so characterizes Whites as to make persistent inequality seem largely untroubling." Instead, and unfortunately, he limits himself to discussing Blacks. For Aleinikoff, as well as for others, race-consciousness seems to mean the conscious recognition of Black difference.[48]

Not all White scholars suffer from the same myopia regarding Whiteness. Indeed, Barbara Flagg introduces her article on White race-consciousness, *"Was Blind, But Now I See": White Race Consciousness and the Requirement of Discriminating Intent,* by criticizing other White authors for their singular focus on Blacks.[49] Importantly, Flagg suggests that the exclusive focus on Blacks is more than an innocent mistake. She argues that it is a contingent, particularly revealing error, a function of the nature of White race-consciousness rather than a fortuitous slip. Flagg fits this myopia into her theory of White race-consciousness by suggesting that there exists a tendency among Whites not to see themselves in racial terms. She identifies this tendency as one of the defining characteristics of being White, and labels this the "transparency phenomenon." "The most striking characteristic of whites' consciousness of whiteness is that most of the time we don't have any. I call this the *transparency* phenomenon: the tendency of whites not to think about whiteness, or about norms, behaviors, experiences, or perspectives that are white-specific."[50] Flagg argues that as an antidote to transparency, Whites must develop "a carefully conceived race consciousness, one that begins with whites' consciousness of whiteness."[51] In this critique and in her prescription for change, Flagg is almost certainly correct. Her article advances the thinking on race-consciousness by placing Whites securely within the parameters of discussion and by identifying transparency as a central hurdle that must be surmounted in the development of White racial self-awareness.

If transparency is a common phenomenon among Whites today, it seems also to have afflicted judges deciding prerequisite cases. Despite the apparent simplicity of the issue before them, the courts hearing prerequisite cases experienced great difficulty defining who was White, often turning for succor to such disparate materials as amici briefs, encyclopedias, and anthropological texts. Even with the assistance of these materials, however, the courts hearing prerequisite cases were slow to develop a defensible definition of Whiteness, instead frequently reaching contradictory results. Though themselves White, judges hearing prerequisite cases could not easily say what distinguished a "white person." More than a few judges expressed considerable consternation over the indeterminacy of the prerequisite language in its reference to "whites." Thus, in a 1913 case, *Ex parte Shahid,* a federal court in South Carolina protested that "[t]he statute as it stands is most uncertain, ambiguous, and difficult both of construction and application."[52] *Shahid* posed in frustration the beguilingly simple question that introduces this book: "Then, what is white?"[53]

The inability of the judges to articulate who was White is a product of the transparency phenomenon. Within the logic of transparency, the race of non-Whites is readily apparent and regularly noted, while the race of Whites is consistently overlooked and scarcely ever mentioned. The first case in North America to turn on race exhibits this tendency. The full report of *Re Davis,* a Virginia case decided in 1630, reads as follows: "Hugh Davis to be soundly whipt before an assembly of negroes & others for abusing himself to the dishonor of God and shame of Christianity by defiling his body in lying with a negro which fault he is to act Next sabbath day."[54] As Leon Higginbotham notes, "Although the full picture can never be reconstructed, some of its elements can reasonably be assumed. . . . [B]ecause Davis's mate was described as a 'negro,' but no corresponding racial identification was made of Davis, it can be inferred that Davis was white."[55] Transparency is a legal tradition of long standing, not something new to the law today or to the prerequisite cases. As a threshold matter, then, defining "whites" taxed the prerequisite courts' abilities not because the question was inherently abstruse, but because through the operation of transparency the judges had never really thought about it.

But why, after they had thought about it, were the judges still unable to define Whiteness? Exploring the origins and maintaining technologies of transparency is useful here. For her part, Flagg ascribes transparency to White privilege. "There is a profound cognitive dimension to the material and social privilege that attaches to whiteness in this society," she writes, "in that the white person has an everyday option not to think of herself in racial terms at all."[56] Yet, the prerequisite cases hint that transparency is not simply a matter of privilege. Privilege explains transparency by positing that those who are constructed as the norm experience difficulty in accurately perceiving their relational position in society exactly because they constitute the norm.[57] But privilege does not seem to fully explain why, when finally jarred into the task of examining White racial identity, the judges in the prerequisite cases could not readily identify the normative boundaries by which they defined themselves—even as late as *Shahid* in 1913, with thirty-five years of precedent to assist them. On this score, the transparency of White identity seems inextricably tied to the naturalization of Whiteness.

The prerequisite cases are literally about the legal naturalization of Whites; they are also figuratively about naturalizing White identity. First, these cases naturalize Whites by treating this grouping as a purely physical phenomenon, an unchanging division of humankind that occurs in nature. Thus, the court in *Shahid,* while frustrated by the ambiguity of the term "white," nevertheless asserted that the phrase "would mean such persons as in 1790 were known as white Europeans, with their descendants, including as their descendants their descendants in other countries to which they have emigrated."[58] The emphasis on descent, repeated three times in a single sentence, transforms Whiteness into a zoetic grouping, a matter of innate, inherited, physical, essential, and, finally, natural being. When Virginia Dominguez observes that "legal disputes over race are nearly always *naturalized,*" she does so in this sense of the term. As Dominguez writes, "[T]here is a willingness to recognize nature as the architect of racial distinctions, and man simply as the foreman who interprets nature's design."[59] This conceptualization of race as a natural phenomenon facilitates transparency by obscuring the contingency of racial demarcation in the language of physicality. By framing race as a physical phenomenon, the courts obviated the need for, and made more difficult, a careful examination of racial typologies. The insistence that "white persons" constitute a natural grouping prohibits at the level of basic assumptions any exploration of the social origins and functions of Whiteness, rendering its socially mediated parameters invisible and impossible to discern correctly.

The definition of Whiteness offered in *Shahid* also indicates a second way in which Whiteness has been naturalized, one which may in fact have a far greater impact in preserving transparency among Whites. *Shahid* used not only the language of descent, but also that of common knowledge, defining Whites in terms of those "known as white."⁶⁰ In this way, *Shahid* anticipated the ruling in *Thind* that a "white person" was a person "the average well informed white American" knew to be White.⁶¹ To grasp how this common knowledge of Whiteness naturalizes Whites, consider an alternate formulation used by the court in *Shahid* to express its holding: "the meaning of free white persons is to be such as would *naturally* have been given to it."⁶² This allusion to natural meaning illustrates the manner in which common knowledge is widely seen as entailing an unmediated (and therefore true) understanding of the world. Locating race in common knowledge suggests that race is part of the external world, and that our perception of race is a matter of its objective existence rather than of its subjective creation. Consequently, races as well as the belief in races are seen as "natural." In the face of this type of naturalization, any effort to interrogate Whiteness becomes a doomed battle against received knowledge. The common-knowledge naturalization of Whites deflects and defeats any inquisition of Whiteness by positing that this grouping is an easily identified, commonly recognized truth. Transparency is established and maintained first in the assertion that Whites are a physical grouping and second in the assertion that everyone knows what White is. More than simply a function of privilege, transparency is also the result of the physical and common-knowledge naturalization of Whiteness.

The prerequisite cases reveal the various levels on which Whiteness has been naturalized. In turn, understanding the physical and common-knowledge naturalization of Whiteness helps explain the persistence of both transparency and the belief in the naturalness of racial differences. Yet, these are not the most important lessons regarding Whiteness to be taken from the prerequisite cases. More important is the light these cases shed on how the construction of Whiteness has given content to White identity.

As a category, "white" was constructed by the prerequisite courts in a two-step process that ultimately defined not just the boundaries of the group, but its identity as well. First, the courts constructed the bounds of Whiteness by deciding on a case-by-case basis who was *not* White. Though the prerequisite courts were charged with defining the term "white person," they did not do so by referring to a freestanding notion of Whiteness. No court offered a complete typology listing the characteristics

of Whiteness against which to compare the petitioner. Instead, the courts
defined "white" through a process of negation, systematically identifying
who was non-White. Thus, from *Ah Yup* to *Thind,* the courts established
not so much the parameters of Whiteness as the non-Whiteness of Chinese, South Asians, and so on. This comports with an understanding of
races not as absolute categories, but as comparative taxonomies of relative
difference. Races do not exist as defined entities, but only as amalgama-
tions of people standing in complex relationships with other such groups.
In this relational system, the prerequisite cases show that Whites are those
not constructed as non-White. This is the significance of the "one drop of
blood" rule of racial descent in the United States.[63] Under this rule, historically given legal form in numerous state statutes, any known African ancestry renders one Black. As Neil Gotanda writes, "The metaphor is one
of purity and contamination: White is unblemished and pure, so one drop
of ancestral Black blood renders one Black. Black is a contaminant that
overwhelms white ancestry."[64] Stated differently, Whites are those with no
known African or other non-White ancestry. In this respect, recall that no
mixed-race applicant was naturalized as "white." Whites exist as a category of people subject to a double negative: they are those who are not
non-White.

The second step in the construction of Whiteness contributes more directly to the content of the White character. After defining Whiteness by
declaring certain peoples non-White, the prerequisite courts denigrated
those so described. For example, the Supreme Court in *Thind* wrote not
only that common knowledge held South Asians to be non-White, but
also that the racial difference marking South Asians "is of such character
and extent that the great body of our people recognize and reject it."[65] The
prerequisite courts in effect labeled those who were excluded from citizenship (those who were non-White) as inferior; by implication, those
who were admitted (White persons) were superior. In this way, the prerequisite cases show that Whiteness exists not only as the opposite of non-
Whiteness, but as the *superior* opposite. Witness the close connection between the negative characteristics imputed to Blacks and the reverse, positive traits attributed to Whites. Blacks have been constructed as lazy,
ignorant, lascivious, and criminal; Whites as industrious, knowledgeable,
virtuous, and law-abiding.[66] For each negative characteristic ascribed to
people of color, an equal but opposite and positive characteristic is attributed to Whites. To this list, the prerequisite cases add Whites as citizens and others as aliens.[67] The prerequisite cases show that Whites fash-

ion an identity for themselves that is the positive mirror image of the negative identity imposed on people of color.

This observation has been made in different contexts and with different language. For example, Richard Ford advances a "psycho-spatial" version of this point:

> [I]n order for the concept of a white race to exist, there must be a Black race which is everything the white race is not (read of course: does not want to be associated with). Thus, the most debased stereotypical attributes of the 'Black savage' are none other than the guilty projections of white society. This white self-regard is at the root of race bigotry in all its forms: it is not a fear of the other, but a fear and loathing of the self; it is not so much the construction of Blackness which matters, it is the construction of whiteness as the absence of those demons the white subject must project onto the other.[68]

By way of comparison, Toni Morrison describes the same oppositional constructivism in the literary fabrication of Whiteness through the depiction of Black ("Africanist") subjects.

> Africanism is the vehicle by which the American self knows itself as not enslaved, but free; not repulsive, but desirable; not helpless, but licensed and powerful; not history-less but historical; not damned but innocent; not a blind accident of evolution, but a progressive fulfillment of destiny.[69]

Whatever the language used, it is clear that White identity is tied inextricably to non-White identity as its positive mirror, its superior opposite.

In this relational system, where White identity is the positive mirror of non-White identity, the question of White race-consciousness is a difficult one. Clearly, some form of racial self-awareness exists among Whites, though this consciousness remains superficially buried by the transparency and naturalization of Whiteness. Whites need to elaborate a more critical racial self-consciousness, if only to overcome the tendency not to see themselves in racial terms. Beyond this, however, in what direction should a White race-consciousness move? Other than bringing White identity into focus, what should be the purpose behind White race-consciousness? One suggestion, offered by Barbara Flagg, is that Whites should develop a new race-consciousness tied to the elaboration of a "positive" self-image. Flagg introduces her article by writing: "Reconceptualizing white race consciousness means doing the hard work of developing a positive white racial identity."[70] She returns to this theme in her conclusion, reiterating the importance of developing "a positive white racial identity, one that comprehends whiteness . . . as just one racial identity among many."[71] But in what sense should White race-consciousness be "positive"? Certainly, Flagg repudiates the idea that White identity should rest on superiority to Blacks, or should otherwise advantage Whites.[72] However, she says little more about her vision of a positive White racial identity.

In a setting in which White identity exists as the superior opposite to the identity of non-Whites, elaborating a positive White racial identity seems at best redundant, and at worst dangerous. Whiteness is already defined almost exclusively in terms of positive attributes. Whites already exist as innocent, industrious, temperate, judicious, and so on, in a series of racial accolades that hardly need burnishing through a program of positive reinforcement. Further, advocating the development of a positive White racial identity disregards the extent to which White attributes rest on the negative traits that supposedly define minorities. All racial characteristics are relational descriptors: innocence can only be established by comparison with guilt, industriousness by reference to indolence, temperance in contradistinction to indulgence. Because identities are relational, inferiority is a predicate for superiority, and vice versa. This implies that there can be no positive White identity without commensurately negative minority identities. Elaborating a positive White racial identity thus runs the high risk of concomitantly fostering deleterious images of non-Whites.

The diacritical relationship between White and minority identities condemns the idea of a positive White race-consciousness and it suggests instead that a deconstructive one is necessary. Because White identity is a hierarchical fantasy that requires inferior minority identities, Whiteness as it currently exists should be dismantled. The systems of meaning that define races revolve primarily around Whites, not non-Whites. The vast, intricate, pervasive belief structures about racial identity, the backdrop against which Whites so easily see non-Whites but not themselves, are predicated on, and indeed are a requirement for, the existence of Whites. The existence of Whites depends on the identification of cultures and societies, particular human traits, groups, and individuals as non-White. Whites thus stand at the powerful vortex of race in the United States; Whiteness is the source and maintaining force of the systems of meaning that position some as superior and others as subordinate. In this violent context, Whites should renounce their privileged racial status. They should do so, however, not simply out of guilt or any sense of self-deprecation, but because the edifice of Whiteness stands at the heart of racial inequality in America. Whiteness in its current incarnation necessitates and perpetuates patterns of superiority and inferiority. To move from society's present injustices to any future of racial equality will require the disassembly of Whiteness. Whites must overcome transparency in order fully to appreciate the salience of race to their identity. They should do so, however, with the intention of consciously repudiating Whiteness as it is currently constituted in the systems of meaning known as races, in the interest of social justice.

The argument for a self-deconstructive White race-consciousness evolves from examination of the prerequisite cases as a study in the elaboration of Whiteness. This examination also suggests, however, a facet of Whiteness that will certainly forestall its easy disassembly, namely, its value to Whites. The racial prerequisite cases are, in one possible reading, an extended essay on the real value of being White. They are also, by another reading, about the willingness of Whites to protect that value, even at the cost of basic justice. Seeking citizenship, petitioners from around the world challenged the courts to define the phrase "white person" in a consistent, rational manner. The courts could not meet this challenge and resorted instead to the common knowledge of those already considered White. Despite this manifest failure, only one court acknowledged the falsity of race, the rest preferring instead to formulate fictions.[73] Admittedly the courts were caught within the contemporary understandings of race, making unlikely a complete break with the prevalent ideology of racial difference. However, this does not fully explain the extraordinary lengths to which the courts went, the absurd and self-contradictory positions they assumed, or the seeming anger that colored their opinions when proclaiming that certain applicants were not White. These disturbing facets of judicial inquietude, clearly evident in *Ozawa* and *Thind,* belie mere uncertainty in judicial interpretation. Rather, the judges' words reveal the extent to which the terms they examined held deep personal significance for them. In a very real sense, they were setting the terms of their own existence. Wedded to their own sense of self, the judges proved to be loyal defenders of Whiteness, defining this identity in ways that preserved its contours even at the cost of arbitrarily excluding fully qualified persons from citizenship. Confronted by powerful challenges to the meaning of Whiteness, judges—particularly the justices of the Supreme Court—embraced this identity in full disregard of the costs of their actions to people across the country. This, perhaps, is the most important lesson to be taken from the prerequisite cases, and it is where this book concludes. When confronted with the falsity of White identity, Whites tend not to abandon Whiteness, but to embrace and protect it. The value of Whiteness to Whites almost certainly ensures the continuation of a White self-regard predicated on racial superiority.

Caveats

My ambitions in this book include setting out a general theory of the legal construction of race and elaborating through an assessment of the content of Whiteness the argument that Whites should consciously work against their racial identity. Both of these projects arise out of but are not circumscribed by the study of the typological practices of the prerequisite cases. On the other hand, there are a number of ambitions I do not pursue here. Indeed, with respect to many important facets of the prerequisite cases, and regarding Whiteness more generally, this work is quite focused. It may therefore be worthwhile to lay out what I will not attempt in this book.

The analysis I offer here with respect to the prerequisite cases is relatively limited, focusing on the processes of racial differentiation in these cases. Consequently, of the fifty-two reported decisions, I discuss only the first thirty-seven, stopping at the Supreme Court's decision in *Thind,* since subsequent lower court decisions adduce little new in terms of racial rationales. The written decisions themselves are the center of attention because they evidence the typological practices of interest. Other sources of information about the naturalization laws, such as the records of magistrates or the statistics gathered in census counts, are considered only in passing. More generally, examining the processes of racial categorization requires historicizing the cases within a particular epoch of American history, as well as periodizing them into early and late cases. These practices are aimed only at highlighting the contradictions inherent in the courts' typological practices. I do not intend to provide an exhaustive historical study of these cases, or to offer a periodization of the cases that can serve other analytical purposes. Thus, this book neither explores the prerequisite cases as social history, for example, by closely examining the lives of the applicants or the judges, nor attempts to situate the cases within the broader context of U.S. legal history. In all of these ways, the prerequisite cases remain a rich vein of information about how we became who we are as a racialized country, and deserve continued and more ambitious excavation.

The discussion of White identity is also circumscribed in a number of ways. First, this book is not a comprehensive genealogy of White identity. I do not track evolutions in White identity before, after, or outside of the prerequisite cases—for example, in terms of the emergence of a White identity in North America during the early colonial period, or with reference to contemporary challenges to White identity in urban youth culture. Second, this book is not a complete study of the legal construction of Whiteness. I do not present a full review of the legal definitions of Whiteness—for example, I neglect almost entirely those definitions that emerged from the slave codes and also the current taxonomies offered by courts interpreting antidiscrimination law. Others have undertaken these various projects.[74] Third, the view of Whiteness afforded here is limited by the dated nature of the cases. The typologies promulgated by the courts pertain to a particular time period. As one would expect, the parameters of White identity have changed since these cases. Fourth, the discussion of Whiteness here is also limited by the social status of those establishing the examined typologies, namely, the judges. The construction of race is always highly context-specific, overlapping with the development of other social identities, notably gender and class. The study of race is therefore never a study of the construction of race across the whole of society, but only among and between particular groups.[75] In this context, the prerequisite cases should perhaps be understood as providing a race-, class-, and gender-specific typology of difference. Finally, while I discuss contemporary White identity, I do so by extrapolating from the prerequisite cases and by emphasizing the methods of its construction, not by focusing on the current parameters of Whiteness. Again, much remains to be written about the nature of White identity, both past and present.

In addition to limited historical and racial pretensions, it bears mention that I am not primarily concerned here with the current disputes regarding citizenship and its attendant rights and privileges. Such debates have recently arisen both in academic discourse and in popular efforts to rewrite the laws affecting citizens and immigrants. I must say, however, that the prerequisite cases supply ample evidence for Alexander Bickel's argument that rights ought not to rest on citizenship, because citizenship, as a political status, is too easily taken away. "Citizenship is a legal construct, an abstraction, a theory. No matter what the safeguards, it is at best something given, and given to some and not to others, and it can be taken away. It has always been easier, it always will be easier, to think of someone as a noncitizen than to decide that he is a nonperson, which is the point of the *Dred Scott* decision."[76]

Citizenship, easily granted and easily withheld, is a tenuous concept on which to hang social privileges such as the right to attend school or to receive medical care. It is made even more untenable as a basis for social distinctions when one understands, as the prerequisite cases powerfully demonstrate, that citizenship easily serves as a proxy for race. Nevertheless, recent measures herald a potential return to the prerequisite cases and to *Dred Scott*. A congressional bill has recently been introduced designed to prevent children born here to undocumented immigrant parents from acquiring citizenship automatically.[77] California voters recently adopted by a two-to-one margin a proposition to deny basic social services to undocumented immigrants and their children.[78] Though I do not intend here to participate in the debates engendered by resurgent nativism in this country, perhaps this book is best read with this context firmly in mind.

2

Racial Restrictions in the Law of Citizenship

The racial composition of the U.S. citizenry reflects in part the accident of world migration patterns. More than this, however, it reflects the conscious design of U.S. immigration and naturalization laws.

Federal law restricted immigration to this country on the basis of race for nearly one hundred years, roughly from the Chinese exclusion laws of the 1880s until the end of the national origin quotas in 1965.[1] The history of this discrimination can briefly be traced. Nativist sentiment against Irish and German Catholics on the East Coast and against Chinese and Mexicans on the West Coast, which had been doused by the Civil War, reignited during the economic slump of the 1870s. Though most of the nativist efforts failed to gain congressional sanction, Congress in 1882 passed the Chinese Exclusion Act, which suspended the immigration of Chinese laborers for ten years.[2] The Act was expanded to exclude all Chinese in 1884, and was eventually implemented indefinitely.[3] In 1917, Congress created "an Asiatic barred zone," excluding all persons from Asia.[4] During this same period, the Senate passed a bill to exclude "all members of the African or black race." This effort was defeated in the House only after intensive lobbying by the NAACP.[5] Efforts to exclude the supposedly racially undesirable southern and eastern Europeans were more successful. In 1921, Congress established a temporary quota system designed "to confine immigration as much as possible to western and northern European stock," making this bar permanent three years later in the National Origin Act of 1924.[6] With the onset of the Depression, attention shifted to Mexican immigrants. Although no law explicitly targeted this group, federal immigration officials began a series of round-ups and mass deportations of people of Mexican descent under the general rubric of a "repatriation campaign." Approximately 500,000 people were forcibly returned to Mexico during the Depression, more than half of them U.S. citizens.[7] This pattern was repeated in the 1950s, when Attorney General Herbert Brownell launched a program to expel

Mexicans. This effort, dubbed "Operation Wetback," indiscriminately deported more than one million citizens and noncitizens in 1954 alone.[8]

Racial restrictions on immigration were not significantly dismantled until 1965, when Congress in a major overhaul of immigration law abolished both the national origin system and the Asiatic Barred Zone.[9] Even so, purposeful racial discrimination in immigration law by Congress remains constitutionally permissible, since the case that upheld the Chinese Exclusion Act to this day remains good law.[10] Moreover, arguably racial discrimination in immigration law continues. For example, Congress has enacted special provisions to encourage Irish immigration, while refusing to ameliorate the backlog of would-be immigrants from the Philippines, India, South Korea, China, and Hong Kong, backlogs created in part through a century of racial exclusion.[11] The history of racial discrimination in U.S. immigration law is a long and continuing one.

As discriminatory as the laws of immigration have been, the laws of citizenship betray an even more dismal record of racial exclusion. From this country's inception, the laws regulating who was or could become a citizen were tainted by racial prejudice. Birthright citizenship, the automatic acquisition of citizenship by virtue of birth, was tied to race until 1940. Naturalized citizenship, the acquisition of citizenship by any means other than through birth, was conditioned on race until 1952. Like immigration laws, the laws of birthright citizenship and naturalization shaped the racial character of the United States.

Birthright Citizenship

Most persons acquire citizenship by birth rather than through naturalization. During the 1990s, for example, naturalization will account for only 7.5 percent of the increase in the U.S. citizen population.[12] At the time of the prerequisite cases, the proportion of persons gaining citizenship through naturalization was probably somewhat higher, given the higher ratio of immigrants to total population, but still far smaller than the number of people gaining citizenship by birth. In order to situate the prerequisite laws, therefore, it is useful first to review the history of racial discrimination in the laws of birthright citizenship.

The U.S. Constitution as ratified did not define the citizenry, probably because it was assumed that the English common law rule of *jus soli* would continue.[13] Under *jus soli,* citizenship accrues to "all" born within a nation's jurisdiction. Despite the seeming breadth of this doctrine, the word "all" is qualified because for the first one hundred years and more of this country's history it did not fully encompass racial minorities. This is the import of the *Dred Scott* decision.[14] Scott, an enslaved man, sought to use the federal courts to sue for his freedom. However, access to the courts was predicated on citizenship. Dismissing his claim, the United States Supreme Court in the person of Chief Justice Roger Taney declared in 1857 that Scott and all other Blacks, free and enslaved, were not and could never be citizens because they were "a subordinate and inferior class of beings." The decision protected the slaveholding South and infuriated much of the North, further dividing a country already fractured around the issues of slavery and the power of the national government. *Dred Scott* was invalidated after the Civil War by the Civil Rights Act of 1866, which declared that "All persons born . . . in the United States and not subject to any foreign power, excluding Indians not taxed, are declared to be citizens of the United States."[15] *Jus soli* subsequently became part of the organic law of the land in the form of the Fourteenth Amendment: "All persons born or naturalized in the United States, and subject to the jurisdiction thereof, are citizens of the United States and of the state wherein they reside."[16]

Despite the broad language of the Fourteenth Amendment—though in keeping with the words of the 1866 act—some racial minorities remained outside the bounds of *jus soli* even after its constitutional enactment. In particular, questions persisted about the citizenship status of children born in the United States to noncitizen parents, and about the status of Native Americans. The Supreme Court did not decide the status of the former until 1898, when it ruled in *U.S. v. Wong Kim Ark* that native-born children of aliens, even those permanently barred by race from acquiring citizenship, were birthright citizens of the United States.[17] On the citizenship of the latter, the Supreme Court answered negatively in 1884, holding in *Elk v. Wilkins* that Native Americans owed allegiance to their tribe and so did not acquire citizenship upon birth.[18] Congress responded by granting Native Americans citizenship in piecemeal fashion, often tribe by tribe. Not until 1924 did Congress pass an act conferring citizenship on all Native Americans in the United States.[19] Even then, however, questions arose regarding the citizenship of those born in the United States after the effective date of the 1924 act. These questions were finally resolved, and *jus soli* fully applied, under the Nationality Act of 1940, which specifically bestowed citizenship on all those born in the United States "to a member of an Indian, Eskimo, Aleutian, or other aboriginal tribe."[20] Thus, the basic law of citizenship, that a person born here is a citizen here, did not include all racial minorities until 1940.

Unfortunately, the impulse to restrict birthright citizenship by race is far from dead in this country. Apparently, California Governor Pete Wilson and many others seek a return to the times when citizenship depended on racial proxies such as immigrant status. Wilson has called for a federal constitutional amendment that would prevent the American-born children of undocumented persons from receiving birthright citizenship.[21] His call has not been ignored: thirteen members of Congress recently sponsored a constitutional amendment that would repeal the existing Citizenship Clause of the Fourteenth Amendment and replace it with a provision that "All persons born in the United States . . . of mothers who are citizens or legal residents of the United States . . . are citizens of the United States."[22] Apparently, such a change is supported by 49 percent of Americans.[23] In addition to explicitly discriminating against fathers by eliminating their right to confer citizenship through parentage, this proposal implicitly discriminates along racial lines. The effort to deny citizenship to children born here to undocumented immigrants seems to be motivated not by an abstract concern over the political status of the parents, but by racial animosity against Asians and Latinos, those commonly seen as comprising the vast bulk of undocumented migrants. Bill Ong Hing writes, "The discussion of who is and who is not American, who can and cannot become American, goes beyond the technicalities of citizenship and residency requirements; it strikes at the very heart of our nation's long and troubled legacy of race relations."[24] As this troubled legacy reveals, the triumph over racial discrimination in the laws of citizenship and alienage came slowly and only recently. In the campaign for the "control of our borders," we are once again debating the citizenship of the native-born and the merits of *Dred Scott*.[25]

Naturalization

Although the Constitution did not originally define the citizenry, it explicitly gave Congress the authority to establish the criteria for granting citizenship after birth. Article I grants Congress the power "To establish a uniform Rule of Naturalization."²⁶ From the start, Congress exercised this power in a manner that burdened naturalization laws with racial restrictions that tracked those in the law of birthright citizenship. In 1790, only a few months after ratification of the Constitution, Congress limited naturalization to "any alien, being a free white person who shall have resided within the limits and under the jurisdiction of the United States for a term of two years."²⁷ This clause mirrored not only the de facto laws of birthright citizenship, but also the racially restrictive naturalization laws of several states. At least three states had previously limited citizenship to "white persons": Virginia in 1779, South Carolina in 1784, and Georgia in 1785.²⁸ Though there would be many subsequent changes in the requirements for federal naturalization, racial identity endured as a bedrock requirement for the next 162 years. In every naturalization act from 1790 until 1952, Congress included the "white person" prerequisite.²⁹

The history of racial prerequisites to naturalization can be divided into two periods of approximately eighty years each. The first period extended from 1790 to 1870, when only Whites were able to naturalize. In the wake of the Civil War, the "white person" restriction on naturalization came under serious attack as part of the effort to expunge *Dred Scott*. Some congressmen, Charles Sumner chief among them, argued that racial barriers to naturalization should be struck altogether. However, racial prejudice against Native Americans and Asians forestalled the complete elimination of the racial prerequisites. During congressional debates, one senator argued against conferring "the rank, privileges, and immunities of citizenship upon the cruel savages who destroyed [Minnesota's] peaceful settlements and massacred the people with circumstances of atrocity too horrible to relate."³⁰ Another senator wondered "whether this door [of citizenship] shall now be thrown open to the Asiatic population," warning that to do so would spell for the Pacific coast "an end to republican government there, because it is very well ascertained that those people have no appreciation of that form of government; it seems to be obnoxious to their very nature; they seem to be incapable either of understanding or carrying it out."³¹ Sentiments such as these ensured that even after the Civil War, bars against Native American and Asian naturalization would continue.³² Congress opted to maintain the "white person" prerequisite, but to extend the right to naturalize to "persons of African nativity, or African descent."³³ After 1870, Blacks as well as Whites could naturalize, but not others.

During the second period, from 1870 until the last of the prerequisite laws were abolished in 1952, the White-Black dichotomy in American race relations dominated naturalization law. During this period, Whites and Blacks were eligible for citizenship, but others, particularly those from Asia, were not. Indeed, increasing antipathy toward Asians on the West Coast resulted in an explicit disqualification of Chinese persons from naturalization in 1882.[34] The prohibition of Chinese naturalization, the only U.S. law ever to exclude by name a particular nationality from citizenship, was coupled with the ban on Chinese immigration discussed previously. The Supreme Court readily upheld the bar, writing that "Chinese persons not born in this country have never been recognized as citizens of the United States, nor authorized to become such under the naturalization laws."[35] While Blacks were permitted to naturalize beginning in 1870, the Chinese and most "other non-Whites" would have to wait until the 1940s for the right to naturalize.[36]

World War II forced a domestic reconsideration of the racism integral to U.S. naturalization law. In 1935, Hitler's Germany limited citizenship to members of the Aryan race, making Germany the only country other than the United States with a racial restriction on naturalization.[37] The fact of this bad company was not lost on those administering our naturalization laws. "When Earl G. Harrison in 1944 resigned as United States Commissioner of Immigration and Naturalization, he said that the only country in the world, outside the United States, that observes racial discrimination in matters relating to naturalization was Nazi Germany, 'and we all agree that this is not very desirable company.' "[38] Furthermore, the United States was open to charges of hypocrisy for banning from naturalization the nationals of many of its Asian allies. During the war, the United States seemed through some of its laws and social practices to embrace the same racism it was fighting. Both fronts of the war exposed profound inconsistencies between U.S. naturalization law and broader social ideals. These considerations, among others, led Congress to begin a process of piecemeal reform in the laws governing citizenship.

In 1940, Congress opened naturalization to "descendants of races indigenous to the Western Hemisphere."[39] Apparently, this "additional limitation was designed 'to more fully cement' the ties of Pan-Americanism" at a time of impending crisis.[40] In 1943, Congress replaced the prohibition on the naturalization of Chinese persons with a provision explicitly granting them this boon.[41] In 1946, it opened up naturalization to persons from the Philippines and India as well.[42] Thus, at the end of the war, our naturalization law looked like this:

The right to become a naturalized citizen under the provisions of this Act shall extend only to—

(1) white persons, persons of African nativity or descent, and persons of races indigenous to the continents of North or South America or adjacent islands and Filipino persons or persons of Filipino descent;

(2) persons who possess, either singly or in combination, a preponderance of blood of one or more of the classes specified in clause (1);

(3) Chinese persons or persons of Chinese descent; and persons of races indigenous to India; and

(4) persons who possess, either singly or in combination, a preponderance of blood of one or more of the classes specified in clause (3) or, either singly or in combination, as much as one-half blood of those classes and some additional blood of one of the classes specified in clause (1).[43]

This incremental retreat from a "Whites only" conception of citizenship made the arbitrariness of U.S. naturalization law increasingly obvious. For example, under the above statute, the right to acquire citizenship depended for some on blood-quantum distinctions based on descent from peoples indigenous to islands adjacent to the Americas. In 1952, Congress moved towards wholesale reform, overhauling the naturalization statute to read simply that "[t]he right of a person to become a naturalized citizen of the United States shall not be denied or abridged because of race or sex or because such person is married."[44] Thus, in 1952, racial bars on naturalization came to an official end.[45]

Notice the mention of gender in the statutory language ending racial restrictions in naturalization. The issue of women and citizenship can only be touched on here, but deserves significant study in its own right.[46] As the language of the 1952 Act implies, eligibility for naturalization once depended on a woman's marital status. Congress in 1855 declared that a foreign woman automatically acquired citizenship upon marriage to a U.S. citizen, or upon the naturalization of her alien husband.[47] This provision built upon the supposition that a woman's social and political status flowed from her husband. As an 1895 treatise on naturalization put it, "A woman partakes of her husband's nationality; her nationality is merged in that of her husband; her political status follows that of her husband."[48] A wife's acquisition of citizenship, however, remained subject to her individual qualification for naturalization—that is, on whether she was a "white person."[49] Thus, the Supreme Court held in 1868 that only "white women" could gain citizenship by marrying a citizen.[50] Racial restrictions further complicated matters for noncitizen women in that naturalization was denied to those married to a man racially ineligible for citizenship, irrespective of the woman's own qualifications, racial or otherwise.[51] The automatic naturalization of a woman upon her marriage to a citizen or upon the naturalization of her husband ended in 1922.[52]

The citizenship of American-born women was also affected by the interplay of gender and racial restrictions. Even though under English common law a woman's nationality was unaffected by marriage, many courts in this country stripped women who married noncitizens of their U.S. citizenship.[53] Congress recognized and mandated this practice in 1907, legislating that an American woman's marriage to an alien terminated her citizenship.[54] Under considerable pressure, Congress partially repealed this act in 1922.[55] However, the 1922 act continued to require the expatriation of any woman who married a foreigner racially barred from citizenship, flatly declaring that "any woman citizen who marries an alien ineligible to citizenship shall cease to be a citizen."[56] Until Congress repealed this provision in 1931,[57] marriage to a non-White alien by an American woman was akin to treason against this country: either of these acts justified the stripping of citizenship from someone American by birth. Indeed, a woman's marriage to a non-White foreigner was perhaps a worse crime, for while a traitor lost his citizenship only after trial, the woman lost hers automatically.[58] The laws governing the racial composition of this country's citizenry came inseverably bound up with and exacerbated by sexism. It is in this context of combined racial and gender prejudice that we should understand the absence of any women among the petitioners named in the prerequisite cases: it is not that women were unaffected by the racial bars, but that they were doubly bound by them, restricted both as individuals, and as less than individuals (that is, as wives).

3

The Prerequisite Cases

The first reported racial prerequisite decision was handed down in 1878.[1] From then until the end of racial restrictions on naturalization in 1952, courts decided fifty-one more prerequisite cases. These decisions were rendered in jurisdictions across the nation, from state courts in California to the U.S. Supreme Court in Washington, D.C., and concerned applicants from a variety of countries, including Canada, Mexico, Japan, the Philippines, India, and Syria. All but one of these cases presented claims of White racial identity.[2]

These bare facts give rise to two initial questions. First, what explains the nearly ninety-year lag between the legislative imposition of the "white person" prerequisite in 1790 and its first legal test in 1878? Second, why did all but one of the applicants petition for citizenship on the basis of a White identity, when, after 1870, naturalization was also available to Blacks? The lag between the enactment of a racial prerequisite for naturalization and its first legal test may partly reflect the relative insignificance of federal as opposed to state citizenship during this country's first century. Prior to the Civil War, state citizenship was more important than federal citizenship for securing basic rights and privileges. National citizenship gained significance only in the wake of the Civil War and the Fourteenth Amendment. After 1870, "[a]ll persons born within the dominion and allegiance of the United States were citizens and constituents of the sovereign community. Their status with respect to the states depended upon this national status and upon their own choice of residence, and it could not be impeached or violated by state action."[3] Thus, the spate of naturalization cases that began in 1878 may reflect the increased importance of national versus state citizenship after the Civil War. In addition, the initial lack of prerequisite litigation may have been a function of the early demographics of migration to this country. Those disembarking on U.S. shores through the first half of the 1800s were for the most part either clearly admissible to or obviously barred from citizenship, for example, peoples from western Europe or western Africa, respectively. "Because few non-Caucasians immigrated to the United States during the first half of the 19th century, the words 'free white alien' had not then taken on great significance."[4] Under this hypothesis, the prerequisite cases arose out of the changing nature of immigration, and more particularly, out of the increased immigration of persons not clearly White or Black. The national identities of the prerequisite litigants, who mainly hailed geographically from western Asia to Polynesia, support this explanation.

This last point, however, frames the second initial question: Why is it that all but one of the fifty-two prerequisite cases turned on whether the applicant was White, when every case was litigated after 1870, the year naturalization became equally available to Blacks? This question does not permit the tautological response that few sought naturalization as Blacks because during this period there were few "Black" immigrants. As just mentioned, many who arrived here in the second half of the nineteenth century did not fit neatly into either the White or Black category. Thus, the "race" of the immigrants does not explain the overwhelming predominance of "white person" cases. Indeed, some immigrant groups, for example the Chinese, were initially characterized as Black, suggesting that for some, attempting to naturalize as a "white person" was the more difficult route. According to Ronald Takaki, "The Chinese migrants found that racial qualities previously assigned to blacks quickly became 'Chinese' characteristics. . . . White workers referred to the Chinese as 'nagurs,' and a magazine cartoon depicted the Chinese as a bloodsucking vampire with slanted eyes, a pigtail, dark skin, and thick lips. Like blacks, the Chinese were described as heathen, morally inferior, savage, childlike, and lustful."[5] Unsurprisingly, this early social treatment of the Chinese as akin to Blacks also found legal expression. For example, in the 1854 case *People v. Hall* the California Supreme Court heard the appeal of a White defendant challenging his conviction for murder. He appealed on the grounds that he was convicted only through the testimony of a Chinese witness, and that this testimony should have been excluded under an 1850 statute providing that "no Black, or Mulatto person, or Indian shall be allowed to give evidence in favor of, or against a White man."[6] The court agreed with the defendant that the Chinese witness was barred from testifying by the 1850 statute, reasoning that Indians originally migrated from Asia, and so all Asians were conversely also Indian, and that, at any rate, "Black" was a generic term encompassing all non-Whites, and thus included Chinese persons.[7] This legal equation of Chinese and Black status was not temporally or geographically unique. Three-quarters of a century later and across the country, Mississippi's Supreme Court reached a similar decision, holding in 1925 that school segregation laws targeting the "colored race" barred children of Chinese descent from attending schools for White children.[8] Given their social and legal negroization, it may well have been easier for the Chinese and other immigrants to argue their qualification for citizenship as Blacks rather than as Whites.

That no immigrants adopted this strategy may reflect the naturalization statute's geographic emphasis in defining Blacks: the 1870 act referred to persons of "African nativity, or African descent," rather than to "black persons." By way of comparison, the naturalization statute referred to "white persons," rather than to "persons of European ancestry." The existence of more firmly established racial definitions of who was Black may also have obviated the need for new litigation. The legal definition of Blacks, unlike that of Whites, was already well established at the turn of the century.[9] In addition, however, it seems nearly certain that the social stigma and harsh discrimination imposed on those with Black status discouraged applicants for citizenship from seeking admission on that basis. Immigrants to this country quickly learn the value of being White rather than Black, and thereby learn to cast themselves as Whites.[10] No doubt this lesson influenced many an immigrant's decision to apply for citizenship as a "white person."

Whatever the reasons for the advent and character of the racial prerequisite litigation, reviewing the possible provenance of these cases is an important introduction to them. These conjectures illustrate that at issue is the complicated process by which races are fashioned, not a simple procedure by which applicants are slotted into transcendent categories. The racial definitions established in the prerequisite cases are products of their particular historical setting: they are a function of the milieu of the United States in the half-century after the Civil War, an era that included not only social turmoil and political change, but also evolving patterns of migration and the efforts of recent immigrants to define spaces and identities for themselves. The prerequisite opinions do not record the facile recognition of racial difference, but rather the convoluted processes through which race is socially and legally constructed.

Overview

Two aspects of the courts' reasoning in the prerequisite cases seem especially striking today. On the one hand, in an unexpected and disquieting way, the reasoning is amusing in its convoluted and almost quaint approach to defining the racial identity of people we now easily categorize. It is strangely entertaining to see judges struggle to use antiquated racial theories to justify what seems self-evident today. On the other hand, in a not unexpected manner, the cases are disturbing because of the judges' patent racism. The opinions are jarring in their willingness to express at the highest judicial levels derogatory views that today are almost universally condemned. The complexity of the rationalizations behind racial assignments and the racism inherent in such thinking will be more fully explored in subsequent chapters. As part of an overview of the cases, however, these two initial observations merit comment here as well, for they remind us of our position as inheritors of the racial systems created in part by the prerequisite cases, and also of the powerful role of prejudice in the elaboration of racial identities.

The first racial prerequisite case, *In re Ah Yup*, was decided in 1878 by a federal court in California.[11] It presaged the intellectual struggle and tangled reasoning that to some degree marked every subsequent prerequisite case. An excerpted version of this case appears in Appendix B. The court there in the person of Circuit Judge Sawyer described Ah Yup as "a native and citizen of the empire of China, of the Mongolian race," framing the issue this way: "Is a person of the Mongolian race a 'white person' within the meaning of the statute?"[12] Despite the seeming simplicity of the question, Judge Sawyer strained to provide an answer. Noting that the case constituted the first naturalization application by someone from China, he proceeded cautiously, even requesting that "members of the bar . . . make such suggestions as amici curiae as occurred to them upon either side of the question."[13] He also solicited the opinion of science, wrestling with the contemporary anthropological thought on racial classifications and quoting out of the "Ethnology" entry to the *New American Cyclopedia*. Not content to rely solely on the amici's arguments and scientific evidence, Judge Sawyer in addition reviewed the legislative history of the naturalization statute, carefully searching each reenactment of the prerequisite law for some clue as to its meaning. He focused particularly on the congressional debates spurred by Senator Sumner's opposition to racial restrictions, as these debates directly raised the question of

Chinese naturalization. Only after considering all of these disparate sources did Judge Sawyer brave an answer. "I am," he finally wrote, "of the opinion that a native of China, of the Mongolian race, is not a white person."[11] On this basis, the court denied Ah Yup citizenship.

The lengthy mental tussle over Ah Yup's race seems in retrospect strange. Reading the decision, some of the language and reasoning seems humorous. The extended discussions of ethnology, the solicitation of help from members of the bar, the microscopic examination of Congressional intent in repeatedly limiting naturalization to "white persons," all of Judge Sawyer's efforts seem superfluous and even laughable, in the context of a decision over whether someone Chinese is White. The answer seems so obvious. But that we now view the court's struggle as quaint or absurd should draw attention to our own historical position. Our response betrays that we are the immediate and largely unquestioning inheritors of the pronouncement that Chinese are not White. Accepting the non-Whiteness of Chinese as a commonplace truth, we are perplexed and amused by Judge Sawyer's arduous efforts to justify, or rather assert, that same conclusion. The lengthy categorical debates in the prerequisite cases seem ridiculous only because we have fully accepted the categories these cases established. Decisions about racial identity are complex; they appear obvious only in retrospect, and then only from a vantage point built upon the assumption that races are fixed, transhistorical categories. The extent to which the definitional struggles in these cases seem quaint measures on some level the extent to which we have erroneously accepted their simple conclusions. The truly curious, then, is not the typological sophistry of the courts, but our own certainty regarding the obvious validity of the recently fabricated.

In addition to its seeming quaintness, the convoluted reasoning in the prerequisite cases is also striking because of its pervasive racism. Some judges showed little reticence in expressing patently racist views. For example, a federal district court in Washington offered this rationale in 1921 to justify the racial bar to Asian naturalization:

> It is obvious that the objection on the part of Congress is not due to color, as color, but only to color as an evidence of a type of civilization which it characterizes. The yellow or bronze racial color is the hallmark of Oriental despotisms. It was deemed that the subjects of these despotisms, with their fixed and ingrained pride in the type of their civilization, which works for its welfare by subordinating the individual to the personal authority of the sovereign, as the embodiment of the state, were not fitted and suited to make for the success of a republican form of Government. Hence they were denied citizenship.[15]

In District Judge Cushman's opinion, Asians were rightfully barred from citizenship because their "yellow color" marked them as unfit for republican government. One might argue that his views turned on cultural or political, rather than racial, prejudice. However, these forms of prejudice blur together, each fading into the other. Indeed, the concept of race incorporates, and arguably partially arose out of, cultural prejudice. Audrey Smedley correctly contends that "at no time in the history of its use for human beings was the term 'race' reserved for groups based solely on their biophysical characteristics. From the start it was a cultural construct composed of social values and beliefs synergistically related in a comprehensive worldview, integral to the cognitive perceptions that the Europeans and white Americans had of themselves and the rest of the world."[16] Like Judge Cushman, some prerequisite courts expressed racial antipathies that ran this spectrum of prejudice, denigrating applicants not only in terms of color, but also of cultural and intellectual unfitness for citizenship.

In contrast to such openly racist views, some judges writing in the racial prerequisite cases proclaimed fair-mindedness on the issue of race as well as solicitude for the petitioners. For example, in 1894, Judge Danaher of the City Court of Albany, New York, barred a Burmese petitioner from naturalization in *In re Po,* but not before remarking that he "appears to be a man of education," adding, "if there is no obstacle, it would give the court great satisfaction to grant his petition, and admit him to citizenship."[17] Such solicitude, however, often seems disingenuous, or at least incapable of overcoming the strong taint of racism in these opinions. Thus, the same judge who expressed this high sentiment regarding Po manifested his subscription to the racist hierarchies of the time only a few lines further on. In sympathy for the excluded applicant, Judge Danaher complained of the 1870 revision allowing the naturalization of persons of African descent: "A Congo negro but five years removed from barbarism can become a citizen of the United States, but his more intelligent fellowmen . . . of the yellow races . . . are denied the privilege."[18] The judge in *Po* was not alone in seeing a contradiction between admitting to citizenship Blacks but not Asians. A federal district judge sitting in Oregon lamented in 1880 that Congress should have "proffer[red] the boon of American citizenship to the comparatively savage and strange inhabitants of the 'dark continent,' while withholding it from the intermediate and much-better-qualified red and yellow races."[19] A generation later and across the continent, a federal district judge in South Carolina, perhaps more pragmatic, resigned himself to the dictates of Congress thus: "It may be that a highly educated and cultivated Japanese or Chinese or Malay or Siamese is better calculated to make a useful and desirable citizen than a savage from the Guinea coast, but it is not for the courts to give effect to such reasoning."[20]

Protestations of solicitude notwithstanding, it seems safe to say, looking both at the content of the decisions and at the context of the times, that most if not every judge who heard petitions for citizenship at the turn of this century harbored profoundly prejudiced beliefs about the applicants whose fates they were charged with deciding. Thomas Ross reminds us, "Nineteenth-century Americans lived in a truly racist society. Racist talk and racial epithets were accepted forms of public discourse. Black persons were first enslaved, and later segregated and subjugated, by law. And their Supreme Court sanctioned all of this in the name of the Constitution. In matters of race, the period was shameful and tragic for the Court and the culture."[21] In reading the prerequisite decisions, one should not lose sight of the simple fact that racism played a key role in the decisions about who was White.

Although pointing out judicial racism in the midst of a discussion of cases applying laws that obviously originated out of racial prejudice might seem unnecessary, doing so serves an important purpose. Foregrounding racism counteracts the "tradition of celebration" in legal scholarship, a tradition that protects the reputations of courts and judges by systematically concealing any taint of racial prejudice.[22] This tradition of celebration is misplaced in discussions of law, for as Randall Kennedy notes, "from the point of view of racism's victims, there is little to celebrate."[23] Nevertheless, it is a prominent tradition, evident even in scholarly discussions of the prerequisite cases. Thus, one scholar, Charles Gordon, who opposed the racial restrictions on naturalization, nevertheless accepted at face value the protestations offered by the prerequisite courts that they were innocent of racism. Gordon sought to protect the reputation of the courts by noting that "many of the courts which have concluded that the racial exclusions barred the naturalization of particular petitioners have commented on the eminent qualifications of the persons before them and have deplored their inability to admit such individual applicants to American citizenship."[24] He cited several cases in support of this proposition, among them *Po*. The celebratory tradition in legal scholarship is one we must constantly guard against, for its perennial regeneration perpetuates an amnesia regarding the extent to which our judicial system, and indeed law itself, has been and remains tainted by the racism that permeates U.S. society.[25]

This taint, moreover, has consistently led to injustice. If a reminder of the ill effects of judicial racism is needed, consider the application of the "white person" restriction on the lives of two applicants, a certain Knight, whose first name does not appear in the case report, and Gee Hop. In 1909, at the age of forty-three, Knight applied for naturalization. He had served in the U.S. Navy for more than a quarter century, receiving a medal in the battle of Manila Bay.[26] Despite his long service to this country, however, as with everyone else, Knight's eligibility to naturalize turned on whether he was a "white person." To answer this question, the U.S. District Court for the Eastern District of New York recited Knight's genealogy. "It appears from the record," Judge Chatfield wrote, "that he was born on a schooner flying the British flag, in the Yellow Sea, off the coast of China; that his father was English by birth and parentage; and that his mother was one-half Chinese and one-half Japanese, having been married to the applicant's father at Shanghai, under the British flag."[27] Knight's origins demonstrate the complexity of individual ancestry as well as the absurdity of trying to categorize humanity into a small number of rigid races. Nevertheless, the court examined Knight's parentage for evidence of whether he was White, and concluded that he was not. Judge Chatfield asserted that "[a] person, one-half white and one-half of some other race, belongs to neither of those races, but is literally a half-breed," and concluded, "the application must be denied."[28] Even though Knight knew no other home and had served this country honorably for two-thirds of his life, U.S. law barred him from naturalizing because as someone not White he was racially unfit to be a citizen.

Unlike Knight, Gee Hop initially succeeded in naturalizing as an American. He secured U.S. citizenship in 1890 and in that same year applied for and received a passport from the State Department. Thus, when in 1895 he sought reentry to the country upon returning from a trip to China, he arrived armed with an official passport, a citizen of the United States.[29] Nevertheless, the port of San Francisco refused him permission to disembark from the steamship on which he had sailed, ordering the master of the ship to retain Gee Hop on board because as a Chinese person he was legally barred from entering the United States. Gee Hop sued, arguing that his naturalization and passport must mean at the least that he could enter the country of his citizenship. The U.S. District Attorney disagreed, and the federal district court for northern California ordered him permanently excluded. Noting that naturalization was open only to "white persons" and "aliens of African descent," District Judge Morrow concluded that "Mongolians, or persons belonging to the Chinese race, are not included in this act."[30] Therefore, the court reasoned, both Gee Hop's certificate of naturalization and his passport were facially void, meaningless pieces of paper because naturalization was a legal impossibility for Chinese persons. Dismissing these documents, Judge Morrow decided two days before Christmas 1895 that "Gee Hop is not a citizen of the United States, as claimed by him, and cannot be permitted to land in this country."[31] Gee Hop thought he was returning home to his country of citizenship, official passport securely in hand, only to be left expatriated at the border, stranded on a steamship within sight of San Francisco's hills.

The fates of Knight and Gee Hop were not particularly tragic or unique. Under the racial prerequisite laws, this country denied citizenship to others who had served in the military,[32] repudiated others who were long-time residents,[33] and stripped still others of the citizenship they thought secure.[34] The judges in the prerequisite cases passed judgment on the lives of individuals, and, as is always the case where law and racism combine, caused immense harm. To the extent that the judicial system still acts in racially prejudiced ways, and to the extent that we continue to accept uncritically the categorical practices evidenced in the prerequisite cases and in law generally, such harms continue today. The careful study of the prerequisite cases is thus imperative.

Rationalizing Race: The Early Cases

Between 1878 and 1909, courts heard twelve prerequisite cases, rejecting the applicants' claims in eleven of them. The courts barred the naturalization of applicants from China, Japan, Burma, and Hawaii, as well as that of two mixed-race applicants. Given the virulent anti-Asian prejudice of the times, these results are not surprising. In the one case during this period in which the petitioner did prevail, *In re Rodriguez,* a federal court in Texas in 1897 admitted to citizenship the "pure-blooded Mexican" applicant, but remarked that "[i]f the strict scientific classification of the anthropologist should be adopted, he would probably not be classed as white."[35] The court allowed the applicant to naturalize on the basis of a series of treaties conferring citizenship on Spaniards and Mexicans in the wake of U.S. expansion into Florida and the Southwest.[36] Rodriguez was thus admitted despite the court's belief that he was not White.[37] As the exception, *Rodriguez* proves the rule. In this initial period, courts virtually always opposed claims of Whiteness.

These early prerequisite cases are important, however, not in the results they reached, but because of the rationales offered by the courts in making racial assignments. The task of deciding who was White may at first glance seem a simple one. However, the evidence suggests otherwise: the favorable ruling for Rodriguez even though the court did not believe him to be White; the tentativeness of the court in *Ah Yup;* and the naturalization of some Chinese such as Gee Hop even in the face the "white person" bar. Consider also the argument John Wigmore earnestly advanced in 1894 in the pages of the *American Law Review.* The famous evidence scholar and treatise writer contended that while the Chinese were not "white persons," the Japanese certainly were.[38] Building his argument carefully, he asserted: "[I]n the scientific use of language and in the light of modern anthropology, the term 'white' may properly be applied to the ethnical composition of the Japanese race."[39] He continued:

> Having as good a claim to the color "white" as the southern European and the Semitic peoples, having to-day greater affinities with us in culture and progress and the facility of social amalgamation than they have with any Asiatic people, isolated as they are to-day from Asia in tendencies and sympathies and isolated as they have been in racial history, it would seem that a liberal interpretation should easily prevail, and that the statute should be construed in the direction indicated by American honor and sympathy [to allow the naturalization of Japanese persons].[40]

Not everyone agreed with Wigmore in his willingness to support Japanese but not Chinese naturalization. Wigmore's preference for the Japanese contrasts with the preference articulated by the editor of the *Fresno Republican,* Chester Rowell, in 1909. While against both Chinese and Japanese immigration in principle, as a businessman Rowell favored the Chinese: "Taking for the moment this [businessman's] viewpoint, we find the Chinese fitting much better than the Japanese into the status which the white American prefers them both to occupy—that of biped domestic animals in the white man's service. The Chinese coolie is the ideal industrial machine, the perfect human ox."[41] Rowell's argument demonstrates that views regarding the race of Japanese and Chinese persons and their fitness for citizenship turned on racial prejudice. Wigmore's determined advocacy, however, shows that many other factors also entered into the debates about who qualified as White. Race is often seen in fixed terms, either as a biological given or a static social category. However, as the debates about race at the turn of the century demonstrate, racial categorization is a fluid process that turns not only on prejudice, but also on factors ranging from dubious science to national honor.

An extraordinary number of rationales surfaced as criteria in the prerequisite decisions. However, in the complex task of racial definition, judges deciding prerequisite cases relied principally on four distinct rationales: (1) common knowledge, (2) scientific evidence, (3) congressional intent, and (4) legal precedent. Each of the first three rationales is present in the first prerequisite case, *Ah Yup*. "Common knowledge" rationales appeal to popular conceptions of races; for example, Judge Sawyer defined the words "white persons" in part by asserting that these words "have undoubtedly acquired a well settled meaning in common popular speech, and they are constantly used in the sense so acquired in the literature of the country, as well as in common parlance."[42] "Scientific evidence" rationales appeal to specialized, reputedly objective knowledge, as when the same court defined White by reference to the theories of Blumenbach, Buffon, Cuvier, and Linnaeus, the leading contemporary students of racial difference.[43] "Congressional intent" refers to those explanations that turned on an examination of Congress's will in passing particular pieces of legislation. For example, Judge Sawyer dedicated significant space to recapitulating the 1870 debates sparked by the efforts to strike the "white person" requirement from the naturalization laws. "It is clear," he wrote, "that Congress retained the word 'white' in the naturalization laws for the sole purpose of excluding the Chinese from the right of naturalization."[44] Finally, "legal precedent" indicates reliance on previous cases that ruled directly on the race of a particular nationality, but does not include instances where the courts cite case precedent for the appropriate legal standard, that is, common knowledge or scientific evidence. As an example of "legal precedent," the court in *In re Hong Yen Chang* relied on the holding in *Ah Yup* that Chinese are not "white" to refuse citizenship to a Chinese applicant.[45]

Table 1 in Appendix A lists in chronological order the cases considering the "white person" prerequisite to citizenship in the period from 1878 to 1909, along with annotations regarding the rationales employed. This table shows that between 1878 and 1909 common knowledge and scientific evidence pushed in the same direction, providing consistent justifications for denying naturalization. In two of the three cases in which judges relied on scientific evidence, they also appealed to common knowledge. Similarly, in two of the three cases in which courts invoked common knowledge, they also turned to scientific evidence. This simultaneous reliance on popular conceptions of racial difference and on science is evident in *Ah Yup,* which not only offered both of these rationales independent of each other, but also combined the two. "As everywhere used in the United States, one would scarcely fail to understand that the party employing the words 'white person' would intend a person of the Caucasian race."[46] During this same period, at least one legal commentator interpreting the "white person" prerequisite similarly relied simultaneously on both rationales: "Whether viewed in the light of the popular or of the scientific meaning, or of Congressional intent, therefore, the words 'white person' seem to include only individuals of the Caucasian race. Under the statute, therefore, only members of this race and of the Ethiopian race can be naturalized."[47] Common knowledge and scientific evidence worked hand in hand in the early cases. During this period these two rationales were mutually reinforcing.

Why did common knowledge and scientific evidence parallel each other? There are at least two ways in which common knowledge and scientific evidence would produce the same conclusions regarding racial difference: if they both measured the same physical fact, or, alternately, if they both were tainted by the same social preconceptions of racial difference. In the first case, if what people popularly believed about races correlated to real physical differences, and these same differences were accurately measured by science, then no contradiction between common knowledge and scientific evidence would exist. They would both be based on the same observable and measurable physical differences. Apparently, the courts in the early prerequisite cases believed this to be the case. At least during this early period, the judges who simultaneously employed both rationales seemed convinced that social preconceptions about race were grounded on real racial differences that science accurately elucidated. Consider *In re Saito,* a decision rendered by a federal court in Massachusetts in 1894 that denied naturalization to a Japanese applicant. The court in the person of Circuit Judge Colt first relied on common knowledge, stating that "[f]rom a common, popular standpoint, both in ancient and modern times, the races of mankind have been distinguished by difference in color, and they have been classified as white, black, yellow, and brown races."[48] Here, Judge Colt argues that the popular conception of race is a function of easily observed differences in skin color that mark innate racial difference. At the same time, Judge Colt relied on scientific evidence. He asserted that these differences in skin color provide the basis for the scientific division of races. "Writers on ethnology and anthropology base their division of mankind upon differences in physical rather than in intellectual and moral character. . . . [O]f all these marks, the color of the skin is considered the most important criterion for the distinction of race, and it lies at the foundation of the classification which scientists have adopted."[49] Judge Colt in effect argued that the physical features that allowed popular discernment of racial difference also served as the basis for the scientific categorization of human races. His belief that the popular conception of race followed real, accurately measured biological differences permitted concurrent reliance on common knowledge and scientific evidence to justify racial divisions. In its linking of popular beliefs and science, *Saito* seems typical of this early period. As evidence of this, it is noteworthy that the contemporary treatise on naturalization mentioned previously accepted Judge Colt's reasoning in *Saito* without question, virtually plagiarizing that holding to define who could naturalize under the "white person" bar on naturalization.[50]

There is, however, the second possibility regarding the nature of race that would also lead to a congruence between common knowledge and scientific evidence. If race were a social idea that thoroughly infected the scientific study of race, then the two principal racial rationales would square: both would measure the same thing, not physical facts but social beliefs. This possibility is far less flattering to science and to the courts, but far more plausible, especially in light of the prerequisite decisions reached after 1909. Changing patterns of migration meant that after that year the courts confronted a series of cases concerning people from western and southern Asia. Science classified these people as Caucasian in an attempt to save its simple racial taxonomies. The courts responded initially with some confusion, but ultimately followed the Supreme Court in denying these "Caucasians" naturalization in order to preserve the common knowledge about Whiteness.

Scientific Evidence versus Common Knowledge

In contrast to the early racial prerequisite cases, the prerequisite decisions from 1909 to 1923 are riven by contradictory results and rationales. For the most part, judges continued to rule that people with mixed or Asian antecedents did not qualify as White. Surprisingly, however, a court in 1909 ruled that Armenians were White, even though their origins east of the Bosporus Strait, the official geographic line between Europe and Asia, made them at least geographically Asian.[51] More perplexing still, judges qualified Syrians as "white persons" in 1909, 1910, and 1915, but not in 1913 or 1914;[52] and Asian Indians were "white persons" in 1910, 1913, 1919, and 1920, but not in 1909 or 1917, or after 1923.[53] Significantly, these contradictory results correlated with the rise of a marked antagonism between scientific evidence and common knowledge as racial meters. Table 2 in Appendix A presents the racial prerequisite cases decided between 1909 and 1923. Among the lower courts in that period, six relied on scientific evidence, while seven others embraced a common-knowledge approach. No court relied on both rationales. Moreover, in every scientific evidence case the petitioner was held to be a "white person," while in every case but one that turned on common knowledge the court barred the petitioner from naturalization. In the context of naturalization law, after 1909 scientific evidence and common knowledge were in direct and constant conflict on the issue of race—they were mutually exclusive as rationales and in terms of results. During this period, "white" was a highly unstable legal category, subject to contestation, expansion, and contraction.

The conflict over whether scientific evidence or common knowledge should serve as the arbiter of race arose in the second case of this period, *In re Najour,* which was decided in December 1909 by a federal court in Georgia. *Najour* is the first case in which an applicant for citizenship prevailed and successfully litigated his status as a "white person."[54] Significantly, District Judge Newman relied on scientific evidence to buttress his holding in *Najour.* Excerpts from *Najour* appear in Appendix B, but the first lines of this cardinal case merit quotation here:

> In admitting to naturalization the petitioner, Costa George Najour, I wish to say this: Although the term "free white person" is used in the statutes, this expression, I think, refers to race, rather than to color, and fair or dark complexion should not be allowed to control, provided the person seeking naturalization comes within the classification of the white or Caucasian race, and I consider the Syrians as belonging to what we now recognize, and what the world recognizes, as the white race. . . .
>
> Quite a recent work, which I have before me now, "The World's People," by Dr. A. H. Keane, classifies, without question or qualification in any way, Syrians as part of the Caucasian or white race, and this they are, so far as my information and knowledge go.[55]

Judge Newman's reliance on science altered the discourse of racial classification in the prerequisite cases in two important ways. First, it distinguished between skin color and race in a manner that made dark skin no bar to naturalization, and hence, to White status. Second, it transformed membership in the "Caucasian" race from one among many criteria into the sole criterion by which to judge whether someone was "white." These two steps immediately divided the prerequisite courts. Within five years of the *Najour* decision, the legal split between scientific evidence and common knowledge had fully developed. Three courts quickly followed *Najour*'s lead, naturalizing applicants as "white persons" on the basis of scientific evidence.[56] With only slightly less rapidity, four decisions rejected *Najour*, labeling the applicants non-White on the basis of common knowledge.[57] The resulting chaos was left unresolved until in 1923 the Supreme Court repudiated *Najour*'s approach.

Despite Judge Newman's assertion in *Najour* that the term "white person" "refers to race, rather than to color, and fair or dark complexion should not be allowed to control" in questions of naturalization, no judge, not even Judge Newman, was particularly comfortable with this legal point. Instead, the decisions betray judicial antipathy toward allowing dark-skinned persons to naturalize as Whites, a predictable response of the times. This antipathy can be seen in the way the various courts discussed the applicants' skin color. Consider two decisions denying petitions for citizenship issued by a federal court in South Carolina. In the first, the judge said of the petitioner, "in color, he is about that of a walnut, or somewhat darker than is the usual mulatto of one-half mixed blood between the white and the negro races."[58] In the next, the same judge described another ill-fated applicant as "darker than the usual person of white European descent, and of that tinged or sallow appearance which usually accompanies persons of descent other than purely European."[59] Though the judge did not identify skin color as a determining factor in his decisions, that the court thought it necessary to describe the applicants' complexions suggests that this factor contributed to the decisions to deny them naturalization. Concern over skin color also manifests itself, albeit in different form, in those decisions allowing applicants to naturalize. Courts ruling for naturalization either noted the applicant's light skin color or remained silent as to physical features. That no judge naturalized a person identified as having dark skin suggests an unwillingness among the courts to find such persons White. This is true even of Judge Newman. In *Najour*, he wrote of the applicant: "He is not particularly dark, and has none of the characteristics or appearance of the Mongolian race, but, so far as I can see and judge, has the appearance and characteristics of the Caucasian race."[60] Similarly, another federal court admitting several Armenian applicants remarked that they were "white persons in appearance, not darker in complexion than some persons of northern European descent traceable for generations."[61] *Najour's* holding that color was legally irrelevant to race proved highly troublesome to the courts considering prerequisite cases, both to those deciding upon the application of persons perceived as dark-skinned, and, to a lesser degree, to those finding the petitioners before them to be White.

Even more troubling for courts hearing prerequisite cases was the strict equation of "Caucasian" and White in *Najour*. This linkage eventually became the axis of division between those courts relying on common knowledge and those citing scientific evidence. The significance of a strict legal congruence between White and "Caucasian" may not be immediately apparent. This significance, however, is intimated by the broad definition of "Caucasian" quoted by *Najour* from a prominent anthropological text of the times. From A. H. Keane's *The World's People: A Popular Account of Their Bodily and Mental Characters, Beliefs, Traditions, Political and Social Institutions* (1908), Judge Newman cited the following definition: "Caucasians (white and also dark), [are indigenous to] North Africa, Europe, Irania, India, Western Asia and Polynesia."[62] This broad definition was typical of contemporary raciology. At the turn of the century, most typologies divided humans into a handful of races, although occasionally many more races were identified.[63] With some exceptions, students of race pursued a strategy similar to Keane's, attempting to fit every known population into one of four metacategories: the "Negro or Black Division," the "Mongolic or Yellow Division," the "American (Amerind) or Red Division," or the "Caucasic or White Division."[64] By the late nineteenth century, as European and American colonial expansion brought more and more people into the ambit of Western racial beliefs, this strategy had provoked a crisis in the science of race. How would these new groups fit into the extant racial paradigms? For example, the peoples of Oceania are among the many population groups of the world, including those from western and southern Asia, that did not fit neatly into the existing metatypology of race. Nevertheless, in order to preserve the underlying categories of White, Black, Yellow, and Red, Keane and other ethnologists were constrained to place them into one or another group. Consider Keane's solution with respect to Polynesians:

[T]he Maori of New Zealand, the Tongans, Tahitians, Samoans, Marquesas and Ellis Islanders, and Hawaiians . . . present a most remarkable uniformity in their physical appearance, mental qualities, customs, traditions, mythologies, folklore, and religious notions. That they are one people is obvious, and that they are an Oceanic branch of the Caucasic division is now admitted by all competent observers.[65]

As Keane's geographically diverse grouping indicates, the advent of the twentieth century saw a vast and increasing array of disparate peoples categorized as Caucasian. By labeling so many people Caucasian, however, raciologists had succeeded in expanding this category far beyond the popular boundaries of Whiteness.

The *Najour* court reasoned syllogistically from Caucasian to "white" to citizen. Doing so, it tied the "white person" restriction to a rapidly expanding anthropological classification. Herein lies the significance to the courts of the strict equation of "white" and "Caucasian." By making persons from North Africa to Oceania "white," the broad definition of "Caucasian" employed by Judge Newman arguably vitiated the restrictive impulse animating the "white person" bar, and thus undercut the prerequisite laws. If courts accepted that all those categorized as Caucasians were "white persons," many people generally seen as non-White would become White, at least for purposes of citizenship. Nevertheless, within the year, three courts followed the approach pioneered in *Najour* and relied on expansive scientific definitions of "Caucasian" to admit to citizenship Syrians, Armenians, and Asian Indians as "white persons."[66]

Other courts, however, did not follow *Najour*'s approach. Most notably, the federal district court for eastern South Carolina heard two cases in rapid succession, and in both, the court rejected science generally and the equation of "white" and "Caucasian" in particular, denying citizenship to the applicants on the basis of common knowledge. The first, *Shahid*, is excerpted in Appendix B. It was in that case, decided in June 1913, that the court described the applicant, Faras Shahid, as being in color "about that of a walnut." The court also noted that Shahid "writes his name in Arabic, cannot read or write in English, and speaks and understands English very imperfectly. . . . His answers to the questions of whether he is a polygamist or a disbeliever in organized government were in the affirmative, and he could not be made to understand in English the purport of the questions asked."[67] Momentarily setting aside the issues raised by Shahid's limited English, the judge, District Judge Smith, turned to the question of whether "a Syrian of Asiatic birth and descent is entitled under the act of Congress to be admitted a citizen of the United States."[68] Judge Smith questioned the very use of the term "white person" in the statute, protesting that, as written, "the language of the statute is about as open to many constructions as it possibly could be."[69] Nevertheless there were some constructions Judge Smith was inclined to reject, most notably the equation of White and Caucasian. After some consideration, Judge Smith propounded the following definition: "The meaning of free white persons is to be such as would have naturally been given to it when used in the first naturalization act of 1790."[70] It would not, the court stated, "mean a 'Caucasian' race; a term generally employed only after the date of the statute and in a most loose and indefinite way."[71] Nor could the term "white person" be equated with other scientific concepts, for example that of the "Aryan" race, "one still more indefinite than Caucasian," or that of an "Indo-European" race, "as sometimes ethnologically at the present day defined as including the present mixed Indo-European, Hindu, Malay, and Dravidian inhabitants of East India and Ceylon."[72] Scoffing at the notion that "a very dark brown, almost black, inhabitant of India is entitled to rank as a white person, because of a possible or hypothetical infusion of white blood 30 or 40 centuries old,"[73] Judge Smith insisted that "white persons" would mean "such persons as were in 1790 known as white Europeans."[74] In rejecting science and in referring to those known as White, the judge in *Shahid* was rejecting the Whiteness of Hindus, Malays, and, most specifically, of the Syrian applicant then before him. Nevertheless, Judge Smith declined to base the disposition of the case on Shahid's supposed racial ineligibility. Instead, the court denied Shahid citizenship because of the "personal disqualifications" noted previously, writing that "the applicant is not one the admission of whom to citizenship is likely to be for the benefit of the country."[75]

Within a year of deciding *Shahid,* Judge Smith heard and decided against naturalization in another case involving a Syrian applicant, George Dow.[76] However, in an unusual judicial move, Judge Smith granted Dow a rehearing, inviting the participation of the Syrian American Associations of the country, which had objected to the court's decision in *Shahid* as well as its first holding in *Dow.*[77] Like Shahid, George Dow argued that he was entitled to naturalize by virtue of being a Caucasian, though he also propounded the additional argument that "the history and position of the Syrians, their connection through all times with the peoples to whom the Jewish and Christian peoples owe their religion, make it inconceivable that the statute could have intended to exclude them."[78] Though Judge Smith described Dow as being in color "of that tinged or sallow appearance which usually accompanies persons of descent other than purely European," he also noted that Dow "would apparently from his intelligence and degree of information of a general character be entitled to naturalization" if racially qualified.[79] Unlike with Shahid, Dow's application could not be denied on the grounds of personal disqualification. The case would be decided squarely on the issue of Dow's racial eligibility for citizenship.

Judge Smith quickly dismissed the argument that the term "white persons" must include Syrians because they hailed geographically from the birthplace of Judaism and Christianity, suggesting without explanation that arguments of such sort should be addressed to Congress rather than the courts.[80] With respect to the more particularized version of that argument, that the denial of White status to Syrians would be tantamount to the denial of the Whiteness of Jesus Christ, Judge Smith had far more to say. Though not directly related to the question of whether Caucasians qualified as Whites, Judge Smith's response merits quotation as one of the most intriguing moments in prerequisite jurisprudence.

> Let it be claimed in the argument for the applicant that Christ appeared in the form of the Jew and spoke a Semitic language. The apostrophic argument that He cannot be supposed to have clothed His Divinity in the body of one of a race that an American Congress would not admit to citizenship is purely emotional and without logical sequence. . . . The pertinent statement rather is that a dark complexioned present inhabitant of what formerly was ancient Phoenicia is not entitled to the inference that he must be of the race commonly known as the white race in 1790, merely because 2,000 years ago Judea, a country whose inhabitants have since changed entirely, was the scene of the labor of one who proclaimed that He had come to save from spiritual destruction all mankind.[81]

Judge Smith refused via the rhetorical charge of emotivity to engage the question regarding the racial eligibility of Christ for citizenship, a very interesting question indeed given that in much White supremacist ideology Whiteness and Christianity are nearly synonymous. Instead, Judge Smith insisted that the real issue was the eligibility of the "dark complexioned present inhabitant" of Syria, thus drawing our attention once again to the importance of skin color in determining who was White enough to naturalize, and more particularly, to the problems posed by the concept of a Caucasian race not closely tied to complexion.

Moving away from the theological and historical, Judge Smith used the opportunity presented in issuing a second opinion in *Dow* to expound on his rejection of the scientific definitions of Whiteness. Though he again challenged the notion of an Aryan or Indo-European race, disparaging these concepts as, for example, "leading to the manifest absurdity of classing among whites the black Dravidian inhabitant of Ceylon or Southern India,"[82] Judge Smith devoted most of his time to criticizing the idea of a Caucasian race, focusing on the etymology of the term itself as a way of calling into question its categorical utility. Asking "What is the white race?" Judge Smith noted that "[m]ost of the courts in this country that have attempted to deal with the question have referred to the white race as the 'Caucasian' race, and said that a member of the Caucasian race was entitled to be naturalized without regard to complexion."[83] Yet, Judge Smith also correctly pointed out that few agreed as to what peoples were members of the Caucasian race, and more, that the term "Caucasian" possessed highly idiosyncratic origins. In 1781, a German professor of medicine, Johann Friedrich Blumenbach, published a racial scheme of humankind in which he denoted the European peoples as "Caucasians," a term he coined on the basis of a single skull in his possession from the Caucasus mountains of Russia. In Blumenbach's estimation, this skull strongly resembled the crania of Germans, and so he conjectured that Europeans may have originated in this mountain region.[84] Judge Smith rightly found this intellectual pedigree for the popular idea of a Caucasian race highly disconcerting. Writing in 1914, he also found that the concept of a Caucasian race was increasingly ridiculed among raciologists. His opinion thus quotes an expert on race who argued that "never has a single head done more harm to science," as well as another expert who pronounced that the notion of a Caucasian race was an "odd myth," the result of "strange, intellectual hocus pocus," and yet another who warned against crediting this racial category because, among other failings, "it brings into one race peoples such as Arabs and Swedes, although these were scarcely less different than the Americans and Malays who are set down as two distinct races."[85] These experts were no doubt correct in their criticisms, though almost certainly in ways they and Judge Smith did not fully appreciate. From all of this, however, Judge Smith concluded the following: "If there be no such race as the 'Caucasian race,' and the term Caucasian be incorrect as properly describing the white races, then the whole argument based upon the Syrian being one of a Caucasian race falls to the ground."[86]

But in the wake of the *Dow* decisions, neither the argument that Syrians were Caucasian nor the notion that "Caucasian" was synonymous with "white persons" did fall to the ground. Even as Judge Smith sought to define Whites by reference to common knowledge, insisting that the statute permitted the naturalization only of "people generally known as white,"[87] other courts continued to rely on the notion of a Caucasian race to naturalize those Judge Smith considered manifestly non-White, for example the "very dark brown, almost black, inhabitant[s] of India."[88] If Judge Smith erred regarding the immediate fate of the equation of White and Caucasian, however, he was more accurate in his characterization of the form taken by that equation: "the general inclination would be to consider the definition of Caucasian as what is supposed to be meant by white. This, however, is very loose and indefinite, for the meaning of Caucasian as at one time prevalent has been now practically exploded."[89] Judge Smith here was correct: the meaning of Caucasian *had* exploded. What this explosion would herald, however, was still unknown. Would it contribute to the demise of racial thinking in law? Or would the courts follow Judge Smith's lead and shift definitions of race entirely onto common knowledge in an effort to save the legal practice of racial categorization? These questions would be settled a decade later by the Supreme Court in *Ozawa* and *Thind*. Until then, however, the cases from *Najour* to *Dow* had set the parameters of the debate between scientific evidence and common knowledge in terms of whether "white persons" were (1) Caucasians, or (2) those generally known to be White.

4

Ozawa and *Thind*

When the Supreme Court first addressed the racial prerequisite issue, it came down squarely in the muddled middle. In *Ozawa v. United States,* the Court wrote that the term "white persons" included "only persons of what is *popularly* known as the Caucasian race."[1] It thereby ran together the rationales of common knowledge, evident in the reference to what was "popularly known," and scientific evidence, exemplified in the Court's reliance on the term "Caucasian." Within three months, however, the Court established a contrasting position in *United States v. Thind,* retreating from the term "Caucasian" and making the test of Whiteness solely one of common knowledge. Both cases are excerpted in Appendix B. Comparing the rationales put forth in *Ozawa* and *Thind* suggests that the Supreme Court abandoned scientific explanations of race in favor of those rooted in common knowledge when science failed to reinforce popular beliefs about racial differences. The Court's eventual embrace of common knowledge confirms the falsity of natural notions of race, exposing race instead as a social product measurable only in terms of what people believe.

Ozawa

Takao Ozawa was born in Japan in 1875, and moved to California as a young man in 1894. Educated at the University of California at Berkeley, he eventually settled in the territory of Hawaii and, in 1914, applied for naturalization.[2] Ozawa began the case backed only by a few close friends, but with a fervent belief in his suitability for citizenship.[3] In a legal brief he himself penned, Ozawa wrote:

> In name, General Benedict Arnold was an American, but at heart he was a traitor. In name, I am not an American, but at heart I am a true American. I set forth the following facts which will sufficiently prove this. (1) I did not

report my name, my marriage, or the names of my children to the Japanese Consulate in Honolulu; notwithstanding all Japanese subjects are requested to do so. These matters were reported to the American government. (2) I do not have any connection with any Japanese churches or schools, or any Japanese organizations here or elsewhere. (3) I am sending my children to an American church and American school in place of a Japanese one. (4) Most of the time I use the American (English) language at home, so that my children cannot speak the Japanese language. (5) I educated myself in American schools for nearly eleven years by supporting myself. (6) I have lived continuously within the United States for over twenty-eight years. (7) I chose as my wife one educated in American schools . . . instead of one educated in Japan. (8) I have steadily prepared to return the kindness which our Uncle Sam has extended me . . . so it is my honest hope to do something good to the United States before I bid a farewell to this world.[4]

As this short autobiography attests, Ozawa was, in the words of one scholar, "a paragon of an assimilated Japanese immigrant, a living refutation of the allegation of Japanese unassimilability."[5]

The U.S. District Attorney for the District of Hawaii opposed Ozawa's application on the ground that he was of the "Japanese race" and therefore not a "white person."[6] Though defeated at each successive stage, Ozawa persisted in his pursuit of citizenship for eight years, eventually reaching the Supreme Court. After Ozawa's petition for citizenship captured the attention of the country's highest court, his case quickly became an important test for the Japanese community. With the help of the Pacific Coast Japanese Association Deliberative Council, an immigrant civic association, Ozawa retained a former U.S. Attorney General, George Wickersham, to represent him before the Supreme Court.[7]

Ozawa based his case for naturalization on several arguments. The most interesting, however, was his assertion regarding skin color. Ozawa acknowledged he was of Japanese descent, but nonetheless asserted that his skin made him "white." Taking the "white person" requirement literally, Ozawa argued that to reject his petition would be "to exclude a Japanese who is 'white' in color."[8] In support of this proposition, Ozawa quoted in his brief to the Court the following from different anthropological observers: "in Japan the uncovered parts of the body are also white"; "the Japanese are of lighter color than other Eastern Asiatics, not rarely showing the transparent pink tint which whites assume as their own privilege"; and "in the typical Japanese city of Kyoto, those not exposed to the heat of summer are particularly white-skinned. They are whiter than the average Italian, Spaniard or Portuguese."[9] Perhaps Ozawa did more than simply rely on experts; he may also have relied on his own skin color. One can almost imagine Mr. Ozawa standing before the august Court, pointing with an index finger to his cheek and saying "My skin is white, I am a white person. I've lived in this country more than twenty-eight years. I deserve citizenship."

Ozawa's imaginary statement would not have impressed the Court, just as the argument he actually put forth failed. In response to Ozawa's emphasis on skin color, the Court said: "Manifestly, the test [of race] afforded by the mere color of the skin of each individual is impracticable as that differs greatly among persons of the same race, even among Anglo-Saxons, ranging by imperceptible gradations from the fair blond to the swarthy brunette, the latter being darker than many of the lighter hued persons of the brown or yellow races."[10] The Court in *Ozawa* stated a simple fact: skin color does not correlate well with racial identity. This had become quite evident to scientists by the close of the nineteenth century, prompting raciologists to downplay the importance of integument in racial classifications. This is also what led the district court in *Najour* to suggest that dark skin need not foreclose the possibility that one is White. In *Ozawa*, the Supreme Court used the imprecise relationship between race and skin color to state the converse: light skin does not foreclose the possibility that one is non-White. These statements are the flip sides of the proposition that pigmentation alone does not denote race.

By the close of the nineteenth century, scientists increasingly understood that morphological attributes, chief among them skin color, varied gradually rather than by the sharp, clearly demarcated disjunctions fundamental to the myth that races can be readily differentiated. The physical features that code as race do not change abruptly between those who are White and those who are Black or Yellow. Instead, these features permute gradually, permitting no easy divisions. As one moves up the African continent and then across the Eurasian land mass, where exactly does one find the lines between Black, White, and Yellow? Neat divisions do not exist; instead of lines one sees only clines, a numberless series of subtly different features among different population groups stemming from heredity, environment, and relative isolation. This is most dramatically true of skin color, as has long been recognized. Discussing nineteenth-century anthropology, Thomas Gossett writes:

The most obvious way in which races might be said to differ and the way in which popular opinion still tends to differentiate them is by their color. The eighteenth-century idea that there was a correlation between climate and color was challenged in Europe by Peter Simon Pallas in 1780, but students of anthropology continued to hope that some correlation between races and color might be established as a base of measurement. . . . Paul Broca, who founded the Anthropological Society in Paris in 1859, used thirty-four shades of skin color in an attempt to differentiate the races, but no scheme of classification emerged. Color as a race determinant has in the final analysis been one of the least satisfactory of the methods tried.[11]

Skin color cannot serve as a justification for the racial lines we are familiar with, for it varies without direct relation to racial identity.

The Court in *Ozawa* recognized this, writing that "to adopt the color test alone would result in a confused overlapping of races and a gradual merging of one into the other, without any practical line of separation."[12] Intent on avoiding this "confused overlapping of races," the Supreme Court rejected a racial test based solely on skin color. But the Court did not go as far as it might have in rejecting physical definitions of race.

Ozawa sought to turn skin color to his advantage, attempting to establish a White identity on the basis of his fair skin. By implication, his argument drew into question the credibility of all physical taxonomies of race, for if skin color could not be relied upon to indicate race, then perhaps no physical features could serve this purpose. This was exactly the dilemma facing the contemporary science of race. By the end of the nineteenth century anthropologists had tried and failed to fashion practical physical typologies along various axes besides skin color, including facial angle, jaw size, cranial capacity, and hair texture.[13] None of these physical indices could support the division of humankind into the races people already knew to exist. As Gossett concludes, "The nineteenth century was a period of exhaustive and—as it turned out—futile search for [physical] criteria to define and describe race differences."[14] By focusing the Court's attention on the failure of skin pigmentation to measure race, Ozawa's argument should have drawn the Court's attention to the absence of *any* physical criterion that can be used for racial classification. If even skin color, that most evident and most powerfully identified feature of racial difference, could not in practice be relied upon to determine a person's race, then what physical basis could there be to the concept? By implying such a question, Ozawa's argument undermined the basic division of humans into races, or at least into the scientific and thus supposedly physical groupings of "Caucasians," "Negroids," "Amerinds," and "Mongolians."

The Supreme Court ignored the implications of Ozawa's argument. Because Ozawa was Japanese, the justices could reject a skin color test without having to question the validity of the scientific divisions of race. Science defined Ozawa as a Mongolian, and thus the Court could continue to rely on science without considering the obvious challenge to such taxonomies posed by Ozawa's argument. As the Solicitor General of the United States argued in opposition to Ozawa's petition:

> The ethnological discussions have covered a wide range of most interesting subjects, particularly in the border-line cases, the Syrian case and the Armenian case. But the present case cannot be regarded as a doubtful case. . . . While the views of ethnologists have changed in details from time to time, it is safe to say that the classification of the Japanese as members of the yellow race is practically the unanimous view.[15]

The Solicitor's argument appealed to the Court. Regardless of the ethnological questions surrounding the status of those from western and southern Asia, the vast majority of experts consistently placed the Japanese wholly outside of the Caucasian race.[16] Relying on this, a unanimous Court held that "the words 'white person' are synonymous with the words 'a person of the Caucasian race.' "[17] The Court then held that "the appellant . . . is clearly of a race which is not Caucasian," alluding to "numerous scientific authorities, which we do not deem it necessary to review."[18] On this basis, the Court upheld the denial of Takao Ozawa's application for citizenship, establishing as the supreme law of the land first that "white" and "Caucasian" were synonyms and second that Japanese persons were not White.

The ruling in *Ozawa* allowed anti-Japanese racial animosity to continue unchecked. More, it blessed such animosity with the weight of enlightened opinion, confirming Japanese racial difference at law. In the Japanese immigrant press, one journal lauded the decision with intentional irony. "Since this newspaper did 'not believe whites are the superior race,' it was 'delighted' the high tribunal 'did not find the Japanese to be free white persons.' "[19] Most newspapers, however, took a more direct route in criticizing the Court and its decision, forthrightly "deplor[ing] the decision as an expression of 'racial prejudice' at odds with the 'original founding spirit of the nation.' "[20] These journals and the community they served recognized the Supreme Court's ruling for what it was: an unmitigated disaster for the Japanese in the United States that would substantially define their future here. Historian Yuji Ichioka argues:

> Without the right of naturalization, Japanese immigrants stood outside the American body politic . . . Japanese immigrants shared much in common with their European counterparts. Yet every European immigrant group, regardless of national origin, had the right of naturalization. And precisely because they possessed it, no matter how beleaguered they were, they were able to enter the political arena to fight for their rights . . . Excluded from the political process, Japanese immigrants were political pariahs who had no power of their own to exercise. This state of powerlessness is a central theme in Japanese immigrant history.[21]

No doubt the internment in detention camps across the western United States during World War II of persons of Japanese ancestry, citizens and noncitizens alike, is a legacy of this powerlessness and pariah status. Not until after the war, and thirty years after *Ozawa*, did Congress lift the bar on Japanese naturalization, and then it did so only as part of the general removal of racial restrictions from the naturalization statute. Even so, the attitudes entrenched by *Ozawa* undoubtedly persist today, in the form of the often-expressed suspicion that all Asians in this country are foreigners, and in the certainty that Japanese persons are not White.[22]

Thind

Three months after holding that Japanese persons were not Caucasian and therefore not White, the Supreme Court in *United States v. Thind* rejected its equation in *Ozawa* of "white" with Caucasian.[23] Bhagat Singh Thind was twenty-one years old when he arrived in the United States on the Fourth of July, 1913.[24] Born in India and a graduate of Punjab University, Thind was part of a new wave of Asian immigrants, one of approximately 6,400 Asian Indians in the United States by 1920, when he sought naturalization.[25] This latest group from Asia, however, differed in an important respect from other Asian immigrants: anthropologists classified Asian Indians not as "Mongolians," but as "Caucasians." This classification provided the springboard for Thind's naturalization petition. Drawing on the syllogism advanced in *Najour,* Thind argued he was "Caucasian," therefore "white," and therefore eligible for citizenship.

On October 18, 1920, the district court agreed with Thind and granted his petition for naturalization.²⁶ The court cited as precedent three cases that followed reasoning similar to that of *Najour*.²⁷ The federal government appealed Thind's naturalization to the Ninth Circuit Court of Appeals, which in turn requested instruction from the Supreme Court on the following question: "Is a high caste Hindu of full Indian blood, born at Amrit Sar, Punjab, India, a white person?"²⁸ The thick language of the question typifies the confusion in the courts concerning issues of racial identity. The language betrays entrenched beliefs about the racial significance of class and caste, blood and birthplace, and even religion in establishing racial identity. Consider, for example, the elision between race and religion evident in the question. The reference to Thind as a Hindu followed prevalent social nomenclature, and seems to have been more racial than religious, as few Asian Indian immigrants to the United States early in this century practiced the Hindu religion. As Ronald Takaki remarks, "Called 'Hindus' in America, only a small fraction of the Asian-Indian immigrants were actually believers of Hinduism. One third were Muslim, and the majority were Sikhs."²⁹ In the United States, "Hindu" served as a racial appellation of difference, its use of obscure but certain origin in the Western colonial discourse of race, culture, civilization, and empire. The inclusion of questions of religion, caste, nationality, descent, and geography as part of an assessment of whether Thind was "a white person" confirms the intricate sociohistorical embeddedness of racial categorization. Whatever its complexities, inaccuracies, and implications, however, the question stood: Was Bhagat Singh Thind a White person?

Oral argument before the Supreme Court was scheduled for January 11, 1923. In the winter leading up to his court date, Thind must have felt especially confident. The opinion in *Ozawa* adopting the equation of "white" and "Caucasian" came down on November 13, 1922, almost exactly two months before oral argument was to proceed in *Thind*. It must have seemed to Thind that he could not lose, for the Supreme Court itself had made Caucasian status the test for whether one was White, and every major anthropological study classified Asian Indians as Caucasians. In addition to the apparent precedential value of *Ozawa,* four lower courts had specifically ruled that Asian Indians were White, while only one had held to the contrary.³⁰ Moreover, Thind was a veteran of the U.S. Army, and though he had served only six months, he perhaps thought that his service to the country, as well as the congressional decision to make citizenship available to those who had served in the military for three years, might favorably affect his case. All of these hopes and rationalizations, however, would have been mistaken.

Addressing Thind's two-part argument, the Court did not dispute his first assertion, that, as an Asian Indian, he was a "Caucasian." The Court conceded this point, albeit tangentially and without grace, writing: "It may be true that the blond Scandinavian and the brown Hindu have a common ancestor in the dim reaches of antiquity, but the average man knows perfectly well that there are unmistakable and profound differences between them today."[31] In other words, the Court was willing to admit a technical link between Europeans and South Asians, even while insisting on their separation in the popular imagination. This insistence, encapsulated in the reference to what "the average man knows perfectly well," signaled the Court's position in the conflict over rationales that had been dividing the prerequisite courts since *Najour*. The Court made this position explicit when it turned its attention to Thind's second argument, that Caucasians were "white persons."

The Court in *Thind* repudiated its earlier equation in *Ozawa* of Caucasian with White, rejecting as well the science of race more generally. The Court began with a discussion of the philological concept of an Aryan race, an effort by scientists to use language as a proxy for lines of descent in order to study the "racial" differences that could not be confirmed by reference to only physical features. Ridiculing the claim that language could serve as an accurate proxy for race, the Court retorted that "history has witnessed the adoption of the English tongue by millions of Negroes, whose descendants can never be classified racially with the descendants of white persons notwithstanding both may speak a common root language."[32] Turning its attention to the core of Thind's argument, the Court stated that the "word 'Caucasian' is in scarcely better repute" than was the notion of an Aryan race.[33] "It is at best a conventional term," the Court asserted, "with an altogether fortuitous origin, which, under scientific manipulation, has come to include far more than the unscientific mind suspects."[34] Strikingly, the Court cited the work on races by A. H. Keane to support this proposition of fortuity and manipulation, the same authority on which Judge Newman relied in *Najour* in granting naturalization to a Syrian applicant. "According to Keane, for example," the Court noted in *Thind*, the term Caucasian "includes not only the Hindu but some of the Polynesians (that is the Maori, Tahitians, Samoans, Hawaiians and others), [and] the Hamites of Africa, upon the ground of the Caucasic cast of their features, though in color they range from brown to black."[35] Keane's writings here became not evidence that the term "white person" should be broadly interpreted, but proof that science could not be trusted to define Whiteness. "We venture to think," the Court concluded, "that the average well informed white American would learn with some degree of astonishment that the race to which he belongs is made up of such heterogenous elements."[36]

Thind ended the reign of the term "Caucasian." With this decision, the use of scientific evidence as an arbiter of race ceased in the racial prerequisite cases. In its place, the Court elevated common knowledge, ruling as follows: "What we now hold is that the words 'free white persons' are words of common speech, to be interpreted in accordance with the understanding of the common man, synonymous with the word 'Caucasian' only as that word is popularly understood."[37] The words of the statute, the Court wrote, were "written in the words of common speech, for common understanding, by unscientific men."[38] The Court adopted the "understanding of the common man" as the exclusive interpretive principle for creating legal taxonomies of race, rejecting any role for science. Applying this common man's understanding to Thind, the Court concluded: "As so understood and used, whatever may be the speculations of the ethnologist, it does not include the body of people to whom the appellee belongs. It is a matter of familiar observation and knowledge that the physical group characteristics of the Hindus render them readily distinguishable from the various groups of persons in this country commonly recognized as white."[39] The Court ignored the weight of precedent and science, reversing Thind's naturalization on the authority of "familiar observation and knowledge." On matters of race, *Thind* crowned ignorance king; as a contemporary commentator remarked, now "the most ignorant man would believe that he could infallibly say who belonged to the white race."[40]

After *Thind,* the naturalization of Asian Indians became legally impossible: Asian Indians were, by law, no longer "white persons." Even worse, many Asian Indians, like Thind himself, lost the citizenship they believed secure. In the wake of *Thind,* the federal government began a campaign to strip naturalized Asian Indians of their citizenship, denaturalizing at least sixty-five people between 1923 and 1927.[41] One former citizen committed suicide following his denaturalization. Vaisho Das Bagai arrived in the United States with his family in 1915, and subsequently naturalized. Dispossessed of his citizenship, Bagai took his own life in 1928. In his suicide note, he wrote: "But now they come to me and say, I am no longer an American citizen. . . . What have I made of myself and my children? We cannot exercise our rights, we cannot leave this country. Humility and insults, who are responsible for all of this? . . . Obstacles this way, blockades that way, and the bridges burnt behind."[42] For Bagai, his family, and Asian Indians generally, *Thind* was a tragedy. However, not all or even most Americans were disheartened by the Supreme Court's decision. In fact, many rejoiced, as the holding resonated with the antipathy toward foreigners in general, and toward those perceived as non-White in particular, which has in advancing and receding waves long swept over our country. Always outspoken on racial matters, the *San Francisco Chronicle* welcomed the decision in *Thind* on the ground that "Hindus are degraded" and unfit for citizenship. Seizing on the Court's pronouncement, the *Chronicle* demanded that the state do something to end "the menacing spread of Hindus holding our lands."[43] California obliged, vigorously enforcing its legal prohibitions on the ownership of land by those racially barred from citizenship against this newest group of permanent "aliens."[44] In *Thind*, the Supreme Court once again signed its assent to racial injustice, allowing others to use its words to perpetrate further harm.

Race and Nature

Putting aside questions about the ultimate effects of the decisions in *Ozawa* and *Thind* on immigrants then in the country, it is useful to explore the paradox these cases pose in juxtaposition. The reversal between *Ozawa* and *Thind* is dramatic: while in the earlier case the Court seemed eager to rely on science, in *Thind* it repudiated the "speculations of the ethnologist," instead resting the test of race solely on "familiar observation and knowledge." This reversal is all the more remarkable because both cases were unanimous, both were written by the same justice, George Sutherland (himself a naturalized immigrant from England), and both were handed down within a span of three months.[45] Clearly the facts of these two cases presented the Court with a highly perplexing dilemma, a question about race that went to the core of the Court's beliefs and that the Court had great trouble resolving.

The conflict marking the lower court decisions reveals the surface terms of this dilemma: should scientific evidence or common knowledge serve as the arbiter of race? However, the facts of *Ozawa* and *Thind* suggest that in fact a deeper problem loomed: whether the Court should act to preserve or to destabilize the notion of a White race. It could not have escaped the Court's attention that after 1909 every court that relied on science admitted the applicant, while all but one of those that relied on common knowledge held against the applicant. The decision of whether science or common knowledge was the appropriate meter would determine where the dividing lines of Whiteness would be drawn. Finally, from our vantage point seventy years after these decisions, we see that the real issue confronting the Court was more fundamental still than either the role of scientific evidence or the maintenance of categorical stability. Though it probably never recognized the issue in these terms, the Court faced a profound but simple question: was race natural, or merely a social construction?

The Court's answer to the surface dilemma is plain: it decided in favor of common knowledge. Why it did so is also clear from the language it used. In addition to the passages already quoted from *Thind,* the Court also wrote that the racial difference marking "Hindus" "is of such character and extent that the great body of our people recognize it and reject the thought of assimilation."[46] The Court in *Thind,* like most if not all of the courts hearing prerequisite cases, apparently relied not only on popularly conceived racial differences, but also on popularly conceived racial distastes.[47] The facts and rationales of *Ozawa* and *Thind* suggest that most likely it was this racial prejudice that pushed the Court to reject the scientific definitions of race. *Ozawa* suggests that where science and popular prejudice still worked hand in hand—for example, in the exclusion of Japanese from among those labeled "white persons"—the Court was willing to cite science. *Thind,* on the other hand, demonstrates that as the pronouncements of science increasingly problematized the basis for racial distinctions—for example, those between peoples from Europe and northern India—the Court refused to rely on science. Perhaps the Court perceived that the breadth of the term "Caucasian," while engineered by scientists like A. H. Keane to maintain racial lines, in fact served to undermine popular notions of racial difference. If so, the Court correctly questioned the curious etymology of "Caucasian," although for the wrong reason: it did so not to challenge the construction of racial beliefs, but to entrench them even further. For the Court, science fell from grace not when it erroneously confirmed racial differences, as in *Ozawa,* but when it contradicted popular prejudice, as in *Thind.* These holdings evince that the Court was committed to socially supposed races and racial hierarchies, not to a search for subtler truths.

If the justices' prejudice moved them to reject science, it also apparently determined the Court's course regarding the second dilemma, whether to preserve or destabilize Whites as a racial group. Beyond presenting the Court with two competing rationales for race, the prerequisite cases additionally called into question the integrity of Whiteness as a racial category. Science was, in the prerequisite cases, eroding the borders of Whiteness. In determining the appropriate standard for setting boundaries around "white persons," the Court had either to reverse or accelerate this erosion. Prejudice against the encroaching "heterogenous elements" seems to have decided the question. The Court stanched the collapsing parameters of Whiteness by shifting judicial determinations of race off of the crumbling parapet of physical difference and onto the relatively solid earthwork of social prejudice. The prerequisite cases confirm the words of Oliver Wendell Holmes regarding prejudice and the law. At about the time of the first prerequisite case, Holmes wrote: "The life of the law has not been logic: it has been experience. The felt necessities of the time, the prevalent moral and political theories, intuitions of public policy, avowed or unconscious, even the prejudices which the judges share with their fellow-men, have had a good deal more to do than the syllogism in determining the rules by which men should be governed."[48] How right the prerequisite cases proved Holmes, especially with respect to the law's importation of common prejudices.

The paradox evident in the contrast between *Ozawa* and *Thind* takes on its greatest significance with respect to the most fundamental question facing the Court, that concerning the nature of race. The Supreme Court in *Ozawa* manifested an abiding faith in science; but only a few months later, in *Thind,* the same Court, the same justices, even the same judicial author, became furiously apostate. Underlying both their faith and their apostasy was the deep conviction that race was natural. The Court believed that race was self-evident, a phenomenon of the natural world readily apparent to the untrained eye. The conviction that races were on the nature side of the human/nature split propelled the Court to rely on scientific evidence as the pinnacle of human knowledge concerning the physical world. However, when science not only failed to define supposed racial differences, but actually undermined them, the Court rejected science violently, as not just wrong, but as an intellectual enterprise that dangerously and suspiciously contradicted the justices' sense of themselves and the world.

Science could not do what the prerequisite courts demanded of it, or even what it thought itself capable of, because race is not part of the natural world. The scientific fixation with race did not amount to the study of nature, but rather to the study of social fabrications attributed to nature. As Audrey Smedley writes,

> The idea of race originally had no basis, no point of origin, in science or the naturalistic studies of the times. But it was subsequently embraced, beginning in the mid to late eighteenth century, by naturalists and other learned men, and given credence and legitimacy as a supposed product of scientific investigations. The scientists themselves undertook efforts to document the existence of the differences that the European cultural world view demanded and had already created.[49]

Like law, science imported into its theories and proofs the most fundamental social prejudices of the times. Science was not and is not independent of culture and society; science *is* culture and society.[50] The world out there beyond human knowledge is knowable only through social beliefs and practices, and among these number the beliefs and practices denominated science. The concept of "nature," the belief in "naturalistic studies" (science), and, indeed, the idea of a "human/nature split," are all intellectual contraptions in need of careful historicization. Thus, all taxonomies of nature—plants and animals, mice, elephants, and frogs, Black, White, Yellow, and Red races, men and women—are in important senses social constructions, labels created through social conventions to describe the world around us. Yet, the critique of race, science, and nature goes further than this. With race, unlike, for example, with gender, there is *nothing* on the nature side: there is *no* underlying reality to be interpreted in admittedly socially embedded ways; there are *no* essential differences measurable through the problematized techniques of science. Rather, there is only social belief. Race is purely a social construction, and the science of race is purely the science of social myth.

A. H. Keane's writing on the world's peoples, cited by prerequisite courts from *Najour* to *Thind,* illustrates the extent to which the scientific study of race was not an examination of nature but a defense of social prejudice. *Najour* relied on Keane for an expansive, non-color-based definition of "Caucasian," while *Thind* ridiculed Keane for the same reason. It might seem that Keane was an enlightened writer participating in the gradual dismantling of race as physical evidence increasingly called into question the existence of racial differences. Quite the contrary, however, Keane was a committed race man. His taxonomies betray a struggle to place all the peoples of the world into tight categories that would delimit not only their essential racial identity, but also (in the words of the subtitle to his book) their "Mental Characters." Keane's speculations in this area make his social embeddedness indisputably clear. Keane says of the "Negro or Black Division":

> Sensual, unintellectual, lacking a sense of personal dignity or self-respect, hence readily bending to the yoke of slavery; fitful, passing suddenly from comedy to tragedy; mind arrested at puberty owing to the early closing of the cranial sutures, hence in the adult the animal side is more developed than the mental.[51]

By comparison, Keane writes of the "Mongolic or Yellow Division":

> Generally somewhat reserved, sullen, and apathetic (Mongols proper)-; very thrifty, frugal, and industrious (Chinese and Japanese); indolent (Malays, Siamese, Koreans); nearly all reckless gamblers; science slightly, arts and letters moderately developed.[52]

Of the "American (Amerind) or Red Division" he states:

> Generally reserved, moody, taciturn, wary, with deep feelings marked by an impassive exterior towards strangers; genial and cheerful in the home; strong nervous system with great power of enduring physical pain.[53]

And finally, he says of the "Caucasic or White Division":

> Temperament of [Northern or Teutonic] slow and somewhat stolid, cool, collected, resolute, persevering ("dogged"), enterprising; of [Central or Alpine] and [Southern or Mediterranean] fiery, fickle, bright, impulsive, quick but unsteady, with more love of show than sense of duty; all three highly imaginative and intellectual; hence science, arts, poetry, and letters fully developed, to some extent from very early times; most civilisations . . . have had their roots in Caucasic soil.[54]

For Keane, everyone in the world fit into one of these four racial categories and consequently possessed not only a characteristic physique, but also a known and predictable temperament. Keane was not free of the dominant racial beliefs of the times, he was deeply convinced of them, and he contributed to their dissemination and legitimation through the ostensibly reputable medium of science. In this destructive enterprise, Keane's conduct was typical, not aberrant. Like the vast majority of his colleagues, Keane was intent on proving what he, as a member of our society, already *knew* about race. Keane, and science generally, took an impossible vow, the promise to prove right the common knowledge of race.[55]

The courts, like many scientists, firmly believed in the naturalness of race. Given this belief, the failure of science to quantify racial differences was not only frustrating, it was also suspicious. The pronouncements of science regarding dark-skinned persons from southern and western Asia must have seemed something of a betrayal to the courts that so readily perceived these peoples as non-Whites. Perhaps this sense of betrayal fueled the hostile language cases like *Shahid, Dow,* and *Thind* used in referring to science. Similarly derisive language was also often used in the opinions handed down after *Thind.* Consider the language used by a federal court in California in *In re Feroz Din:*

> This applicant for citizenship is a typical Afghan and native of Afghanistan. He is readily distinguishable from "white" persons of this country, and approximates Hindus. The conclusion is that he is not a white person. . . . What ethnologists, anthropologists, and other so-called scientists may speculate and conjecture in respect to races and origins may interest the curious and convince the credulous, but it is of no moment in arriving at the intent of Congress in the statute aforesaid.[56]

For courts that could readily distinguish between Whites and non-Whites, the inability of science to do the same must have been suspicious indeed.

Science failed to prove what was to the courts eminently obvious, the existence of natural racial differences. In the fifty-two reported prerequisite decisions, only one court concluded that the term "white person" referred not to a natural category but only to a legal one. In this anomalous 1909 case, a federal district court sitting in Boston examined and dismissed various anthropological and geographic definitions of a "white" race before adopting a textual approach to the question of whether Armenians could naturalize. Examining statutes and census documents dating back to the original colonies, the court said "it appears that the word 'white' has been used in colonial practice, in the federal statutes, and in the publications of the government to designate persons not otherwise classified."[57] Since Congress had not designated Armenians as non-Whites, the court concluded, they were still legally White and eligible for naturalization. Every other court deciding a prerequisite case, including the Supreme Court, continued to believe that races were natural and self-evident. Thus, in a 1933 case that turned on racial prerequisites, the Supreme Court in the person of the renowned Justice Benjamin Cardozo said that "[i]n the vast majority of cases the race of a Japanese or a Chinaman will be known to anyone who looks at him. . . . The triers of fact will look upon the defendant in the courtroom and will draw their own conclusions."[58] The Court, and people generally, believed that a mere glance was enough to determine a person's race, and furthermore, that they were observing race directly, rather than through a distorting lens of socially contingent ideas. It did not occur to them that their collective and continuous assignment of social meanings to certain faces and features was creating the races they so readily identified. For the courts, which saw races so easily in the physical characteristics of those who came before them, it must have been quite infuriating that science not only failed to confirm the link between features and races, but actually undermined the linkage by including persons ranging from "brown to black" as Whites.

Science today has virtually abandoned the idea that races exist in nature.[59] The empirical struggle to establish racial identities necessarily failed, and as a biological concept, race is now all but dead in the sciences—even among anthropologists, whose discipline arose largely out of the effort to confirm racial differences in humankind.[60] Obituaries for biological notions of race now appear routinely in the most mainstream of mainstream journals, such as *Newsweek*.[61] Needless to say, however, among many the fallacy lingers on. For example, some scientists concede that races have no biological basis as phenotypical divisions of humankind, but attempt to rebiologize race by arguing that as social phenomena races reflect instinctual grouping behaviors innate in humans.[62] And, of course, race as biology continues to be vigorously alive for some in the social sciences, particularly those writing "social science pornography," to use the all-too-apt phrase offered by the author of *Losing Ground* and *The Bell Curve* regarding his own work.[63]

Naturalistic understandings of race persist as well, though again not surprisingly, in law and common knowledge. Few in this society seem prepared, at the beginning of this century or now, fully to relinquish their subscription to biological notions of race. This is particularly true of Congress and the Supreme Court. Congress makes clear its anachronistic understanding of race in a recent statute that defines "the term 'racial group' [as] a set of individuals whose identity as such is distinctive in terms of physical characteristics or biological descent."[64] The Court, although purporting in its recent discussions to sever race from biology, also seems incapable of completely doing so. In a 1987 case, *Saint Francis College v. Al-Khazraji,* the Court addressed whether a U.S. citizen of Iraqi descent could recover damages for racial discrimination.[65] Answering in the affirmative for a unanimous Court, Justice Byron White seemed initially to abandon biological notions of race in favor of a sociopolitical conception. "The particular traits which have generally been chosen to characterize races have been criticized as having little biological significance," he wrote. "These observations have led some, but not all, scientists to conclude that racial classifications are for the most part sociopolitical, rather than biological, in nature."[66] Despite this initial rejection of biological race, however, Justice White continued, "The Court of Appeals was thus quite right in holding that [the law] reaches discrimination against an individual 'because he or she is genetically part of an ethnically and physiognomically distinctive subgrouping of *homo sapiens.*' "[67] Justice White's use of the lower court's talk of genetics and distinctive subgroupings demonstrates a continued reliance on biological notions of race. This understanding of race crops up repeatedly in the Court's racial jurisprudence, often in unintentionally revealing form. In 1990, for example, during oral argument in *Metrobroadcasting v. FCC,* Justice Antonin Scalia attacked the argument that granting minorities broadcasting licenses would enhance diversity by blasting "the policy as a matter of 'blood,' at one point charging that the policy reduced to a question of 'blood . . . blood, not background and environment.' "[68] As Neil Gotanda notes, " 'Blood' is a rich metaphor and includes, in this context, the suggestion of biological lines of descent. Justice Scalia's implication is that race [is] a category of biology and science."[69] For the Court, race remains natural.

The Social Construction of Race

Despite the Court's belief in the naturalness of racial categories, many of its decisions concerning race, *Ozawa* and *Thind* in particular, demonstrate that race is not a measured fact, but a preserved fiction. The celebration of common knowledge and the repudiation of scientific evidence show that race is a matter not of physical difference, but of what people believe about physical difference. To be sure, physiological differences distinguish persons from around the world. Yet, the common knowledge about race is never a naked, untainted assessment of such differences. Rather, as Barbara Fields argues, "physical impressions are always mediated by a larger context, which assigns them their meaning, whether or not the individuals concerned are aware that this is so. It follows that the notion of race, in its popular manifestation, is an ideological construct and thus, above all, a historical product."[70] Herein lies the significance of the judicial debate about skin color that *Najour* and *Ozawa* explored from opposite directions. It is not pigmentation, but rather the social understandings of integument that denote race. Thus, some dark-skinned people are identified as White, and some light-skinned individuals are denied similar status. While not entirely irrelevant to races, the role of nature is limited to providing the morphological raw materials society uses to build systems of racial meaning. Recognizing this frees us to consider the many ways in which skin color has come to connote racial difference—frees us, that is, to examine the way in which race has been constructed socially and legally.[71] Despite a natural component, race is entirely social. Race is nothing more than what society and law say it is.

In Chapter 5, I consider the manner in which law works to construct races. In Chapter 6, I turn away from legal theory to focus on White identity. Before moving to those discussions, however, we should return to the prerequisite cases to emphasize again a central point: racial categories exist *only* as a function of what people believe. The prerequisite cases make apparent the truth of this statement with respect to liminal populations, for example, Syrians and Asian Indians, who were between "white" and "yellow." These people became White or non-White according to what the courts believed about them. However, it is also true with respect to every group characterized in racial terms, no matter how securely we might currently place that population at the definitional heart of a racial category. In this respect, recall the court's struggle over the Chinese applicant's race in *Ah Yup,* Wigmore's advocacy regarding Japanese Whiteness, and the many Japanese and Chinese naturalized as "white persons."[72] We now regard Chinese and Japanese people as standing firmly within the "Asian" race and in no sense as between races. Yet, the prerequisite cases expose this placement as a matter of relatively recent social prejudice, not of transhistorical biological difference.

The same holds true for those currently categorized as White. While the prerequisite cases primarily address the racial status of immigrant groups from different parts of Asia, this should not be interpreted to mean that the racial status of Europeans has always been clear. During the nineteenth century White as a racial category underwent a rapid transformation in the United States. Many of the prerequisite cases, in striving to define the term "white persons," noted this history. For example, in *Thind,* the Court justified interpreting "white persons" as words of common speech in part by reference to the intent of the original authors. "The words of familiar speech, which were used by the original framers of the law, were intended to include only the type of man whom they knew as white," the Court wrote.[73] Yet, the Court was forced to recognize that the common knowledge about who was White had changed since the original restriction had been penned in 1790. While the Court recognized that the "immigration of that day was almost exclusively from the British Isles and Northwestern Europe, whence they and their forbearers had come," it had to concede that "[t]he succeeding years brought immigrants from Eastern, Southern and Middle Europe, among them the Slavs and dark-eyed, swarthy people of Alpine and Mediterranean stock," adding that "these were received as unquestionably akin to those already here and readily amalgamated with them."[74] The Court in effect acknowledged that many who in 1923 were considered White—for example, Italians, Greeks, Slavs, and Jews—were outside the bounds of that category as it existed in 1790 and had only later been defined as White. The common knowledge of who was White had changed remarkably from 1790 to 1923.

Although the Court acknowledged that racial categories could change over time, its reference to "ready amalgamation" shows that it continued to cling to an oversimplified view of race. The experiences of southern and eastern Europeans both at the turn of the century and today demonstrate that evolutions in racial identity occur unevenly and sometimes only partially, rather than always smoothly and fully as the language of "ready amalgamation" seems to suggest. Thus, though White for purposes of naturalization, the Italians, Slavs, and so on who arrived here in great numbers between 1880 and 1920 were nevertheless stigmatized as racially inferior to the northern and western Europeans who had immigrated to this country earlier. Such prejudice is reflected in the language the Court used in *Thind*. The Court drew upon a popular racial typology dividing Europeans into three types, the Mediterranean, the Alpine, and the Nordic. This tripartite division originated in nineteenth-century French thinking on race and is evident in Keane's description of the mental character of the White division quoted above. Popularized in the United States during the early twentieth century by Madison Grant in *The Passing of the Great Race* (1916) and by H. F. K. Gunther in *The Racial Elements of European History* (1927), this typological hierarchy of Europeans was widely accepted during the 1920s.[75] The basic terms of this racialized division of Europeans are easily outlined:

H. F. K. Gunther . . . described the characteristics of these three presumed races without equivocation as to their innateness. The Nordic, he believed, has a strong urge toward "truth and justice, prudence, reserve, and steadfastness," and exhibits calm judgment, fairness, and trustworthiness. The Mediterranean, in contrast, is "strongly swayed by sexual life." He is not as continent as are Nordics, for whom "passion has little meaning." Alpines are "petty criminals, small-time swindlers, sneak thieves and sexual perverts." Nordics are "capable of nobler crimes."[76]

Whether the Supreme Court invested the vocabulary it used with the connotations outlined above we do not know. But if it did do so, it would not have been alone. "Attitudinal surveys administered in the 1920s confirm the notion that [racial] groups were implicitly ranked on a continuum of inferiority. . . . In a variety of surveys, the American population ranked Northwestern Europeans highest, then the South-Central-Eastern Europeans, in turn the Japanese and Chinese, and finally blacks."[77] A year after the decision in *Thind,* Congress responded to this popular prejudice with immigration quotas designed severely to curtail the numbers of people who could immigrate from southern and eastern Europe.[78]

Becoming White, then, is not an either/or proposition, but rather it is an uneven process, resulting in racial identities that change across contexts and time. Thus, in the 1920s eastern and southern Europeans could be White for purposes of naturalization, but still racial inferiors in the close context of immigration and the more general milieu of social relations. Becoming White is, moreover, a continuing process. Witness today's near certainty that southern and eastern Europeans are *not* species of inferior Whites. Of course, even now, this transformation may not be complete. F. James Davis reports, "There is recent evidence that many caucasoid groups, including Turks, Iranians, Italians, and Arabs, are not perceived as white by students in Canadian schools."[79] Moreover, in an interesting twist, it seems that some Italian youths in East Coast metropolitan areas are deliberately fashioning non-White identities for themselves.[80] All of this demonstrates that Whiteness too is simply a matter of what people believe. There is no core or essential White identity or White race. There are only popular conceptions—in the language of the prerequisite cases, a "common knowledge"—of Whiteness. And this common knowledge, like all social beliefs, is unstable, highly contextual, and subject to change. Although the prerequisite cases directly address the racial identity of relatively few nationalities, they are relevant to our understanding of the racial identity of every "white person" in this country.

Recall now the question that opened this book. Judge Smith in *Shahid* asked: "Then, what is white?"[81] The above discussion suggests some answers. Whiteness is a social construct, a legal artifact, a function of what people believe, a mutable category tied to particular historical moments. Other answers are also possible. "White" is an idea, an evolving social group, an unstable identity subject to expansion and contraction, a trope for welcome immigrant groups, a mechanism for excluding those of unfamiliar origin, an artifice of social prejudice. Indeed, Whiteness can be one, all, or any combination of these, depending on the local setting in which it is deployed. On the other hand, in light of the prerequisite cases, some answers are no longer acceptable. "White" is not a biologically defined group, a static taxonomy, a neutral designation of difference, an objective description of immutable traits, a scientifically defensible division of humankind, an accident of nature unmolded by the hands of people. In the end, the prerequisite cases leave us with this: "white" is common knowledge. "White" is what we believe it is.

Postscript

A final remark is needed here regarding the role of science in law. Despite the repudiation of science in *Thind* and other prerequisite cases, courts did not abandon science altogether, but rather rejected it only in the context of naturalization. In other areas of the law, science continued to be accepted and relied upon, especially where, as in *Ozawa,* science supported popular prejudice.

The 1927 case *Buck v. Bell* probably best evidences the continued acceptance of science in law.[82] In 1924, the year that Congress relied on theories of eugenics to restrict immigration from eastern and southern Europe, the Virginia General Assembly relied on those same theories to pass a law mandating the sexual sterilization of wards of the state determined to be "insane, idiotic, feeble-minded or epileptic, and by the laws of heredity . . . the probable potential parent of socially inadequate offspring likewise afflicted."[83] Subsequent to the statute's enactment, Aubrey Strode, the principal author of the law, collaborated with Albert Priddy, the superintendent of the Virginia State Colony for Epileptics and Feeble Minded and a strong proponent of eugenics, in order to select someone for a test case which could be used to establish the constitutionality of the sterilization law.[84] They picked Carrie Buck, a young White woman of eighteen then in Doctor Priddy's care, and enlisted their friend and colleague Irving Whitehead, another eugenicist, to represent her in staged proceedings from before the Special Board of Directors of the State Colony of Epileptics all the way to the U.S. Supreme Court. In these choreographed proceedings, Priddy alleged, and Whitehead did nothing to refute, that Buck, her mother, and her daughter were all retarded, thus establishing Buck's "hereditary" defectiveness.[85] What neither Priddy nor Whitehead told any of the various tribunals was that Buck had been institutionalized at the instigation of a local family for which she had worked as a domestic in order to suppress the fact of her rape by a family member. As Mary Dudziak remarks, "the manufactured controversy over the constitutionality of eugenical sterilization was under way."[86]

The case came before the Supreme Court late in 1926, and Justice Oliver Wendell Holmes delivered the Court's opinion the following spring. By this time, eugenics had begun to collapse as a scientific discipline, its foundations revealed to be little more than class- and race-prejudice gussied up in the costume of empiricism.[87] Despite this common foundation, or rather, arguably because of it, the Court in an eight-to-one vote relied on the science of eugenics to sustain Virginia's statute. Justice Holmes used chilling language to uphold Virginia's power to end Buck's procreative ability, writing: "It is better for all the world, if instead of waiting to execute degenerate offspring for crime, or to let them starve for their imbecility, society can prevent those who are manifestly unfit from continuing their kind."[88] Clearly relying on the scientific nomenclature of IQ testing which undergirded the eugenics movement, Justice Holmes added: "Three generations of imbeciles are enough."[89] For Justice Holmes, writing late in his career and only four years after having joined in *Thind*, science continued to provide convincing evidence for preferred social policies, even where such policies sometimes amounted to nothing more than the legislation of social prejudice.

Virginia continued to sterilize people without their consent until 1972. In all, Virginia sterilized 8,300 persons under the statute Justice Holmes upheld.[90] Nationwide, some 60,000 people were forcibly sterilized under similar eugenical laws.[91] Despite its demise in the racial prerequisite cases, science did not disappear from the courtrooms and legislative houses of this country. Rather, science continues to play a powerful role in law—sometimes, as in many of the prerequisite cases and in *Buck v. Bell,* as a respectable vehicle for the importation of the common prejudice Justice Holmes himself had earlier warned about.

5

The Legal Construction of Race

Races are social products. It follows that legal institutions and practices, as essential components of our highly legalized society, have had a hand in the construction of race. The prerequisite cases support this supposition and provide an exceptionally useful vehicle for exploring the processes by which legal institutions and practices fabricate race. As a body of decisions in which the courts struggled to set the parameters of an explicit racial category in the context of changing social and scientific definitions of race, these cases constitute a relatively forthright example of the role law sometimes plays in creating, rather than simply adopting, racial definitions. Yet, this forthrightness, and in addition the changes that have taken place in the legal treatment of race between that period and today, make the prerequisite cases a less apt vehicle than we might at first suppose for understanding how laws and legal decisions currently construct races.

The prerequisite cases constitute a relatively unique body of decisions insofar as the judges there directly and self-consciously practiced racial categorization. By far the vast majority of the cases and laws implicating race relations do not involve such forthright engagement with racial categorization, but instead almost uniformly treat races as extralegal phenomena. In considering the relevance of the prerequisite cases to contemporary analyses of the legal construction of race, the uniqueness of these cases must be kept in mind. In addition, the historical context in which they were handed down must also be remembered. The single greatest difference between what we might term pre- and post-*Brown* racial jurisprudence is that, generally speaking, since *Brown v. Board of Education* declared in 1954 that separate conditions are inherently unequal,[1] our nation's laws have moved from using explicit racial categories in an oppressive manner toward using these explicit categories to ameliorate racial discrimination. Related to this is a fundamental change in the racial attitudes of judges, who are less racist today than in 1878 or 1923. The uniqueness of the prerequisite cases and their dated nature suggest that those legal processes the cases illuminate quite well—for example, the role of racially hostile courts in defining racial categories—may be less pertinent to an understanding of the current mechanisms by which law maintains racial differences. In contrast, processes that the prerequisite cases only tangentially clarify may be far more central to the legal construction of race today—for instance, the role of race-neutral laws or of non-judicial legal institutions like the police in maintaining racial divisions. Nevertheless, the prerequisite cases are relevant to an exploration of the contemporary relationship between race and law. They starkly evince many different facets of the legal construction of race; consequently, their study will be helpful in developing an understanding of the more subtle constitutive processes at play today.

The prerequisite cases demonstrate the multiple levels on which legal rules and actors construct the social systems of meaning we commonly refer to as race. Law influences what we look like, the meanings ascribed to our looks, and the material reality that confirms the meanings of our appearances.[2] That law constructs race is evident. How it does so, however, remains a more difficult question. In assessing this, inquiries along two roughly parallel axes can be pursued. First, how do legal rules fashion races? Does law operate simply to control behavior through a series of penalties and rewards, and if so, how can these devices define races? Or does law in some sense operate as an ideological system, as a source of beliefs about what society does and must look like? If the latter, how does this system influence or create ideas about race? Second, what role do legal actors play? More particularly, are judges, lawyers, and legal consumers conscious creators of racial beliefs? Or are these actors largely unaware of the legal construction of race, unwitting participants in such processes and passive victims of law's constitutive powers? To some extent, these questions simply restate in a particularized fashion the larger debates about the relationship between law and society, and may seem to require exclusive answers framed within the terms of those debates. However, these questions do not present exclusive alternatives. Law is both a system of behavioral control and an ideology, and legal actors are in some senses both conscious and unwitting participants in the legal construction of race. The purpose of these questions is to focus attention on rules and actors, and thus to invoke essential lines of inquiry that will enable the close examination of the legal construction of race.

Before beginning this examination, however, two caveats must be entered. First, though the topic is the legal construction of race, it should be clear that the "law" which underlies this inquiry and to which this book consistently refers does not exist as an abstract object. As a function of the effort to formulate a generalized theory, and also for the sake of convenience, the complex processes discussed here are often simply attributed to the operation of "law." Yet, "law" should not be conceptualized as a monolith. Rather, law encompasses a set of institutions, actors, and ideas that are interdependent and yet only infrequently, if ever, in concert with one another. Consider the various pieces of law implicated in the prerequisite cases. Institutionally, the cases involve Congress and all levels of the different state and federal court systems; among the numerous actors are judges, legislators, attorneys general, lawyers, and the petitioners themselves; and the ideas range from the specific rules governing naturalization to the conceptions of race debated in the courts. Note as well the interdependence of these various pieces: the Supreme Court, Congress, and so on do not exist apart from specific actors or absent particular ideas; the roles and powers of the judges, lawyers, and other actors are defined by their institutional affiliation and by legal norms; and the ideas regarding citizenship and so forth take on legal significance only to the extent they are given play by certain institutions and actors. There is no "law" as such. There exists instead a wealth of interdependent but ill-coordinated social practices. Despite this complicacy, however, and in part because of it, I sometimes use "law" here as a catchall phrase. As part of an initial effort to theorize the role of such disparate but interconnected practices in contributing to the construction of races, a degree of manageability is gained by referring simply to "law." Nevertheless, it is important to remember that "law" here refers to a complex, incoherent system of practices, rather than to a monolith.

A caveat regarding the term "construction" is also necessary. Referring to the legal construction of race may foster the impression that law has a unidirectional influence in the elaboration of racial ideas, or that law ought to be faulted for its role. A sophisticated conceptualization of law dispels these notions. Given the sheer number of legal actors and institutions, as well as the complexity and self-contradiction that mark legal rules and norms, it is inconceivable that law could operate within the contingent social systems of racial beliefs in any set way or in a manner susceptible to easy judgment. "Construction" here does not carry teleological or normative connotations; it refers only to complex social processes. To the extent law constructs race, it does not do so only in one direction or along a single axis. Rather, the legal construction of race pushes in many different directions on a multitude of levels, sometimes along mutually reinforcing lines but more often along divergent vectors, occasionally entrenching existing notions of race but also at other times or even simultaneously fabricating new conceptions of racial difference. Moreover, there is no indication that in and of itself the legal construction of race is normatively good or bad. It may be either; the ultimate question being not whether legal practices construct race but what role such construction plays in the attainment or frustration of social justice. Consider these two points in the context of *Thind*. There, the Supreme Court strengthened the grip of racial ideas by subscribing to a common-knowledge approach, but it did so in part by ridiculing and thus weakening the scientific notions of race, thereby adding to the social understanding of races in contradictory ways. Given this complex intervention into the social beliefs about race, the injustice of the Court's pronouncement cannot lie in its participation in the elaboration of racial ideas per se, but must be located, for example, in the Court's motivation or in the decision's effects.

In this chapter, I refer repeatedly to the legal construction of race. Yet, law should not be understood as an object, and its role in the production of the social knowledge of race should not be viewed in narrowly teleological or normative terms. The complexity of law and racial fabrication must be kept in mind even as the language of legal construction threatens their reification.

Law as Coercion

The complex processes by which law constructs races can be disaggregated along the lines of rules and actors, with each of these in turn further broken down. Beginning with rules, we should distinguish between the operation of law as a system of control or coercion and law as an ideological system, keeping in mind that such neat distinctions are not real but merely intellectually convenient. Viewing law as primarily a coercive system helps us focus on the actual rules promulgated and enforced through law and allows a rather more positivist account of how law constructs races. Here, legal rules include both legislative enactments and judicial decisions, or, respectively, statutory and case law. Even in these prosaic forms, law has contributed to the rise and persistence of races by directly participating in every level of its creation.

First, legal rules have shaped physical appearances, thus altering the basic material on which racial meaning systems are built. The prerequisite laws influenced the pool of physical features now present in this country through literal exclusion and through interference with marital choices. By shaping what we look like, the prerequisite cases, and immigration laws more generally, powerfully contributed to the racialization of the U.S. population. Such laws defined not only the racial status of the immigrant communities, but, as the prerequisite cases demonstrate, the racial identity of those already here as well. The United States is ideologically a White country not by accident, but by design at least in part affected through naturalization and immigration laws.

Naturalization and immigration laws are not, however, the only or even the most important laws that have influenced the appearance of this country's populace. More significant may be the antimiscegenation laws, which appeared in the statutes of almost every state in the union until they were struck down by the Supreme Court in 1967.[3] These laws purported merely to separate the races. In reality, they did much more than this: they acted to prevent intermixture between peoples of diverse origins so that morphological differences that code as race might be more neatly maintained.[4] Antimiscegenation laws, like lynch laws more generally, sought to maintain social dominance along specifically racial lines, and at the same time, sought to maintain racial lines through social domination. As Martha Hodes argues, "racial hierarchy could be maintained primarily through the development of a rigid color line: if blacks and whites did not have children together, then racial categories could be preserved."[5] Cross-racial procreation erodes racial differences by producing people whose faces, skin, and hair blur presumed racial boundaries. Forestalling such intermixture is an exercise in racial domination and subordination. It is also, however, an effort to forestall racial blurring. Antimiscegenation laws maintained the races they ostensibly merely separated by insuring the continuation of the "pure" physical types on which notions of race are based in the United States.

Second, positive law has created the racial meanings that attach to physical features. In a sense, this is the heart of the prerequisite cases, which at root embody the efforts of courts to inscribe on the bodies of individual applicants the term "White" or "non-White." These cases established as legal precedent the racial identities of the various faces and nationalities entering the United States at the turn of the century. Again, however, the racial prerequisites to naturalization are not the only laws that explicitly defined racial identities. Almost every state with racially discriminatory legislation also established legal definitions of race. It is no accident that the first legal ban on interracial marriage, a 1705 Virginia act, also constituted the first statutory effort to define who was Black.[6] Regulating or criminalizing behavior in racial terms required legal definitions of race.[7] Thus, in the years leading up to *Brown*, most states that made racial distinctions in their laws provided statutory racial definitions, almost always focusing on the boundaries of Black identity. Alabama and Arkansas defined anyone with one drop of "Negro" blood as Black; Florida had a one-eighth rule; Georgia referred to "ascertainable" non-White blood; Indiana used a one-eighth rule; Kentucky relied on a combination of any "appreciable admixture" of Black ancestry and a one-sixteenth rule; Louisiana did not statutorily define Blackness but did adopt via its Supreme Court an "appreciable mixture of negro blood" standard; Maryland used a "person of negro descent to the third generation" test; Mississippi combined an "appreciable amount of Negro blood" and a one-eighth rule; Missouri used a one-eighth test, as did Nebraska, North Carolina, and North Dakota; Oklahoma referred to "all persons of African descent," adding that the "term 'white race' shall include all other persons"; Oregon promulgated a one-fourth rule; South Carolina had a one-eighth standard; Tennessee defined Blacks in terms of "mulattoes, mestizos, and their descendants, having any blood of the African race in their veins"; Texas used an "all persons of mixed blood descended from negro ancestry" standard; Utah law referred to mulattos, quadroons, or octoroons; and Virginia defined Blacks as those in whom there was "ascertainable any Negro blood" with not more than one-sixteenth Native American ancestry.[8]

The very practice of legally defining Black identity demonstrates the social, rather than natural, basis of race. Moreover, these competing definitions demonstrate that the many laws that discriminated on the basis of race more often than not defined, and thus helped to create, the categories they claimed only to elucidate. In defining Black and White, statutory and case law assisted in fashioning the racial significance that by themselves drops of blood, ascertainable amounts, and fractions never could have. In the name of racially regulating behavior, laws *created* racial identities.

Third, positive law contributes to the construction of race by establishing the material conditions which often code for race. This is evident, for example, in the correlation between race and citizenship in the

Supreme Court's refusal to naturalize Bhagat Singh Thind. Ostensibly the Court refused to naturalize Thind because he was not White. Yet, it was in large part the judicial determination that Thind could not become a citizen that rendered him non-White; had the Court admitted Thind to citizenship in accord with the substantial body of precedent, the Whiteness of Thind would have been clear. Thind's exclusion from the American polity established rather than reflected his race; the condition of being a permanent alien coded Thind with a non-White racial identity. Similarly, the race of all immigrants to the United States devolved at least partly from their status here. The Irish and Italians, for example, became White only as a function of becoming United States citizens; in Ireland or Italy, whatever other social or racial identities these people might have possessed, White wasn't one of them. The "white person" prerequisite to naturalization made citizenship a condition and code for White and non-White racial identity.

This same process reveals itself in segregation laws. Segregation laws presumably separated people according to race. However, such laws also facilitated the assignment of racial identities according to separation. As a social construct, race depends on what people believe, rendering it an inherently unstable concept. Segregation laws increased the stability of racial categories by fixing mutable racial lines in terms of relatively immutable geographic boundaries. Richard Ford puts it this way: "Because race is an unstable identity, its deployment depends on a symbolic connection between the characteristics that code as race but to which race cannot be reduced (skin color, facial features, etc.) and some stable referent. . . . [T]he maintaining technologies of race [are] primarily economic and spatial."[9] While housing patterns and citizenship have depended on race, the converse is true as well: race often follows from neighborhoods and nationality. Consider the ease with which we assign racial identities knowing only that someone is from Santa Monica or South Central, Greenwich Village or Harlem. Moreover, this link between space and race functions as a matter of both external and internal identification— as a matter of what others believe of our identity, and of how we think of ourselves. One Black law professor writes, "I lost something more when I grew up and moved out of the segregated South, out of the safety of my childhood home. Because the Jim Crow laws gave me an identity and a protection I couldn't give myself."[10] The material, and in particular spatial, distinctions created by positive law have further established the racial identities now evident in the United States.

Law, then, constructs racial differences on several levels through the promulgation and enforcement of rules that determine permissible behavior. The naturalization laws governed who was and was not welcome to join the polity, antimiscegenation laws regulated sexual relations, and segregation laws told people where they could and could not live and work. Together, such laws altered the physical appearances of this country's people, attached racial identities to certain types of features and ancestry, and established material conditions of belonging and exclusion that code as race. In all of these ways, legal rules constructed race.

It is crucial to note that, in constructing race, legal rules operate through violence. The legal system enforces rules occasionally through rewards but most often through the threat or application of harm. Such potential or actual harm is often difficult to see. For example, the prerequisite cases seem at first glance to be nothing more than dry exegetical readings of ambiguous legal texts in which it is impossible to find even obscure allusions to coercive force. Nevertheless, violence is there. "A judge articulates her understanding of a text, and as a result, somebody loses his freedom, his property, his children, even his life," Robert Cover correctly insists, adding, "[w]hen [judges] have finished their work, they frequently leave behind victims whose lives have been torn apart by these organized, social practices of violence."[11] In the prerequisite cases, we may assume violence, probably literally in the corporeal forms of immigration officers and border guards, certainly figuratively in the form of constrained lives and truncated hopes, and occasionally obviously in the form of suicide. In the law of race more generally, violence is manifest in slavery, in Jim Crow segregation, in police brutality, in the discriminatory enforcement of criminal laws, in the dispossession of Native American land rights, in the internment of people of Japanese descent, in the failures of the law to provide equal justice or to protect against discrimination. In all of this violence, the law not only relied on but also constructed racial distinctions. To say that law constructs races is also to say that races are the product of, not just the excuse for, violence. James Bald[chwin remarks that "no one was white before he/she came to America. It took generations, and a vast amount of coercion, before this became a white country."[12] Courts may have been the principal institutional forum for that vast coercion, and laws its principal form of civilized expression.

Irrespective of the use of violence, however, it may seem that at this coercive level laws construct races only at the margins. Granting that races are social constructions, some may suggest that legal rules patrol only the borders between races, resolving just those rare cases not already clearly defined within the underlying social systems of racial division. Arguably, only the person not clearly White or Black has her race determined in a prerequisite case or by her neighborhood. However, a focus on the coercive aspect of law seems to explain more than just the legal construction of race at the margins. Certainly the prerequisite cases legally established the racial identity of groups we now regard as firmly at the core of racial categories, for example the Japanese, and Jim Crow laws were indispensable in maintaining and even extending the social differentiation established through the slave codes and threatened during Reconstruction. Nevertheless, the explanatory power of this model should be questioned. How does law-as-coercion explain the continuing significance of race in a postsegregation era? If races have been created through coercion, why hasn't the end to the legal enforcement of racial differences been followed by a collapse in racial systems? Or, what can such a model tell us about the prevalent belief that races are natural, and the skepticism that greets claims that races are legally fashioned? If races have been imposed, why is it that the vast majority of people embrace race so willingly? And why do these same people so vigorously deny that they have been coerced into a racial identity? Races are much more deeply embedded in our society than a theory of law-as-coercion would seem to explain. If law is a full participant in the construction of races, it must fashion races through some additional mechanism besides simple direct behavioral control.

Law as Ideology

Of course, law is not limited to direct, coercive, behavior-controlling means in the construction of race. It also operates on the level of constitutive ideology. Law does not exist as a separate phenomenon distinct from society and concerned only with policing disputes, but is an integral part of society and an essential component in the social production of knowledge.[13] It is in its capacity to shape and constrain how people think about the world they inhabit, more than in its coercive potential, that law may most powerfully affect the construction of races. "[T]he power exerted by a legal regime consists less in the force that it can bring to bear against violators of its rules than in its capacity to persuade people that the world described in its images and categories is the only attainable world in which a sane person would want to live."[14] The social relations ensconced in legal rules have been constructed out of a broad universe of possibilities, but people clothe these relations with the illusion of necessity. "Law is an essential feature in the illusion of necessity because it embodies and reinforces ideological assumptions about human relations that people accept as natural or even immutable. People act out their lives, mediate conflicts, and even perceive themselves with reference to law."[15] The images and categories embedded in law are accepted as the way things are at the same time that they limit conceptions of the way things might be. Law thus defines, while seeming only to reflect, a host of social relations, from class to gender, from race to sexual identity.[16] Understanding the role of law in the creation of races thus requires examining the cognitive significance of legal images and categories of race.

As system of ideas about the world, legal rules create racial differences in several interrelated, sometimes contradictory ways. First, law legitimates the existence of races, both in the weak sense of lending high-profile institutional support to the notion that races are biologically real, and in the strong sense that the legal recognition of races entrenches the belief that racial categorization is a necessary part of human differentiation. The courts that ruled on the race of "Mongolians," "whites," and "Hindus" validated those racial categories, giving them the prestige of law and rendering them that much more credible as categories of difference. The decision and language of *Thind* provided both the highest level of legal sanction for the existence of a "Hindu" race distinct from Whites and also confirmation of the prevailing popular image of Asian Indian inassimilability. Laws also legitimate races in the stronger sense of making it far more difficult to imagine people without reference to their race. The prerequisite statute required that each person seeking citizenship be assigned a race. The declaration that Ah Yup was a "Mongolian" made it impossible to imagine him in different racial terms, much less completely nonracial ones. This racial declaration was of vital importance in Ah Yup's life; it became his central, essential characteristic and defined a constellation of relationships between him and the rest of society. Ah Yup's fate confirms that "law is one of many cultural institutions that are constitutive of consciousness, that help delimit the world [and] make only certain thoughts sensible, thus 'legitimating' existing social relations," not least racial relationships.[17] Legal rules and decisions construct races through legitimation, affirming the categories and images of popular racial beliefs and making it nearly impossible to imagine nonracialized ways of thinking about identity, belonging, and difference.

In both the strong and weak sense, contemporary laws continue to legitimate races. This is most evident in the continued legal reliance on rigid racial categories. Racial classification remains legally permissible and in fact necessary to efforts aimed at remedying the legacy of racial discrimination in this country. Although the Supreme Court has held that laws based on racial classifications are subject to strict judicial review and will be struck down unless justified by a compelling state interest, the Court has so far stopped short of declaring all such laws invalid per se.[18] Vindicating the rights of minorities has required maintaining a legal system that distinguishes between Whites and non-Whites, even though these classifications arose from efforts to subordinate those constructed as non-White.[19] The necessary persistence of racial categories in law lends legitimacy to the notion that races exist in fact, leading people to think not only of others but of themselves in racial terms. In this context, consider the pull of antidiscrimination laws in moving people to frame their identities in terms of the racial categories recognized by law. At the level of both individuals and groups, people must conform their identities to these rigid categories if they seek legal protection from discrimination. Thus, some legal scholars have tried to frame Mexican American identity as a specifically racial, rather than ethnic or cultural, identity for the purposes of securing constitutional or statutory protection against discrimination.[20] It is not unreasonable to argue that "races may be defined in America in some significant part by their relationship to antidiscrimination law in addition to constituting an independent influence on that body of law."[21] The necessary persistence of legal classifications of race gives law a continuing role in the construction of racial identities by legitimating the practice of categorization and by limiting possible conceptions of who we are.

In addition to legitimating race, legal rules operate as an idea-system to construct races in a second way. Though race as a social concept has some autonomy, it is always bounded in its meanings by the local setting. Laws help racial categories to transcend the sociohistorical contexts in which they develop. For example, the original prerequisite statute was written in 1790, when popular conceptions of race on the eastern seaboard of North America encompassed only Whites, Native Americans, and Blacks. As a legal restriction on naturalization, however, the "white person" prerequisite of 1790 was imposed on Bhagat Singh Thind on the West Coast of the United States in 1920. It is most unlikely that those who wrote the first prerequisite law intended either to include or to exclude South Asians, for that group almost certainly existed outside the realm of their world knowledge. As one court noted, in "passing the act of 1790 Congress did not concern itself particularly with Armenians, Turks, Hindoos, or Chinese. Very few of them were in the country, or were coming to it."[22] Nevertheless, partially by its institutionalization in law, the category of "white persons" transcended the local boundaries of time, place, and imagination in which it had one meaning, persisting and expanding into remarkably different locales, where, though with a facade of continuity, it took on various new definitions.

This sociohistorical boundary crossing is normal to law. One of the defining elements of law is its universal aspiration, its will to apply equally in all cases and across all situations. However, the pursuit of universality in law can make it a profoundly conservative force in racial construction. Here, the role of precedent is particularly important. Racial lines are prevented from shifting to the extent that past racial definitions control decisions about race in the present. "Reasoning by analogy to precedent creates a *false* historicity in that it perpetually reclaims the past for the present: in theory, a dispute in 1989 can be resolved by reference to cases from 1889 or 1389."[23] Of course, the dead hand of the past does not completely control the present; precedent is often manipulated, and such manipulation is central to legal change. Nevertheless, by giving great weight to superannuated racial definitions, precedent keeps alive restrictive notions of race.

Consider the Mashpee Indian case.[24] In 1976, the Mashpee community on Cape Cod filed suit to recover alienated tribal lands using the Indian Non-Intercourse Act.[25] Designed to prevent private transactions with Native American tribes, this statute, like the naturalization laws, was originally enacted in 1790. The district court ruled that in order to proceed, the Mashpee first had to prove they were a "tribe" within the meaning of the word as defined by the Supreme Court in 1901, to wit "a body of Indians of the same or similar race, united in a community under one leadership or government, and inhabiting a particular though sometimes ill-defined territory."[26] The Mashpee, seeking in 1976 to use a 1790 law, were required to prove they existed in terms of a 1901 definition of a Native American tribe. This definition, and indeed the Non-Intercourse Act itself, contained antiquated, racist, and restrictive notions of tribal identity, not least in the establishment of racial purity as a requisite element of tribal existence and in the spirit of paternalism and domination animating the statute. For the Mashpee, recourse to the law came at the cost of resuscitating destructive ideas of an "Indian" race and identity that ultimately rendered legally incomprehensible the lived experiences of their community. The Mashpee could not prove they were a tribe under the 1901 definition, and thus their 1976 suit failed. By relying on precedent, the law often fails to grasp new forms of identity, imposing with sometimes destructive force old ideas about race. "The tragedy of power was manifest in the legally mute and invisible culture of those Mashpee Indians who stood before the court trying to prove that they existed."[27] In this way, the use of precedent in law provides a conserving, stabilizing force in racial construction by preserving the relevance of past racial definitions, thereby allowing such categories to transcend their local settings.

Law frees racial categories from their local settings in another, quite distinct sense, as well: it occasionally provides a new language with which to construct racial differences. Legal terms that do not refer explicitly to race may nevertheless come to serve as racial synonyms, thus expanding in often unpredictable ways the form and range of racial categorization. This possibility is evident in the prerequisite cases, though it is much more relevant to the legal construction of race today. The prerequisite laws spawned a new vocabulary by which to mark racial difference, the phrase "alien ineligible to citizenship." Congress and a number of states used this phrase to avoid the Fourteenth Amendment's bar against invidious race-based discrimination. In 1922 Congress proscribed the marriage of U.S. citizen women to non-White aliens by providing that "any woman citizen who marries an alien ineligible to citizenship shall cease to be a citizen of the United States."[28] Two years later Congress relied on the same phrase to ban unwanted races from the country, mandating that "[n]o alien ineligible to citizenship shall be admitted to the United States" except under restrictive circumstances.[29] Eleven states used this same phrase between 1913 and 1947 to prohibit persons of Japanese descent from owning land;[30] a twelfth, Arkansas, was not so subtle, declaring that "no Japanese or a descendant of a Japanese shall ever purchase or hold title to any lands in the State of Arkansas."[31] The Supreme Court upheld such land laws in 1923 and did not strike them down until *Oyama v. California* in 1947.[32] Concurring in *Oyama,* Justice William Murphy disposed of the pretense that "aliens ineligible to citizenship" referred to anything other than race. "The intention of those responsible for the . . . law was plain. The 'Japanese menace' was to be dealt with on a racial basis."[33] He also recognized, however, that Congress through statutory law had made this insidious racial discrimination possible. "Congress supplied a ready-made vehicle for discriminating against Japanese aliens, a vehicle which California was prompt to grasp and expand to purposes quite beyond the scope or object of the Congressional statute."[34] Legal language can allow ideas of race to transcend their historical context through precedent, and also can contribute to the construction of race by providing a new vocabulary with which to take note of, stigmatize, and penalize putative racial differences. Law thus frees racial categories not only from contextual bounds, but also from the bounds society places on the use of race. Referring to "aliens ineligible to naturalize" allowed Congress and several states to discriminate racially without running afoul of the social prohibitions against such action articulated in the Constitution. As will be emphasized later, the law's ability to provide seemingly neutral synonyms for race may be one of the most important legal mechanisms in the current processes of racial construction.

There is yet a third way in which legal rules operate as ideas to construct races. On this level, which links the cognitive and material worlds we live in, law constructs races through a process of reification. Reification here means more than simply the act of categorization, which arguably reifies the world insofar as it strips subjects of their uniqueness and supplants individuation with abstraction.[35] The term here refers to the manner in which ideas take on material forms which in turn reinforce the ideas that shape that world. To reify racial categories means to transform them into concrete things, making the categories seem natural, rather than human creations. In the context of the prerequisite cases, the disparate experiences of Armenian and Japanese immigrants demonstrate how law transforms ideas about race into differences in rights and wealth, which then confirm racial ideas.

Armenians, whose origins lay in what was geographically western Asia, were initially classified by federal authorities as "Asiatics." In 1909, however, a federal court ruled that Armenians were "white persons."[36] This changed status allowed Armenian immigrants to buy agricultural land in California, where as "Asiatics" they would have been barred from doing so by the state's alien land law. Ronald Takaki writes:

> By 1930, some 18,000 Armenians lived in the state; their access to land ownership enabled many Armenians to become farmers in Fresno county. They became wealthy farmers—owners of vast acreage and leading producers of raisins. "The Armenians, they like the Japanese," recalled a Japanese farmer of Fresno. "Lots speak only Armenian—just like Issei

[immigrant Japanese]. They came about the same time too. But I think they learned a little bit more English than the Japanese did and they looked more American and I think it helped them a lot." The experience of the Armenians illustrated the immense difference it made to be Caucasian and not "Asiatic."[37]

This difference was established, and made especially pronounced, by law.

Before their immigration here, Armenians were not part of the evolving racial schema of U.S. society. They had not yet been "raced," that is, assigned a racial identity. However, upon their arrival, and despite some initial confusion, they were pronounced legally White. This pronouncement allowed them a prosperous and privileged position in American society. This prosperity then confirmed the common knowledge of their Whiteness, which in turn served to justify the judicial treatment of Armenians as White persons. The opposite occurred with the Japanese. Again, their position in the U.S. racial schema was initially far from certain: some had been naturalized as "white persons," but others had been excluded from citizenship. Partly under court authority, however, the non-Whiteness of Japanese immigrants emerged as common knowledge. As non-Whites, the Japanese were subject to discriminatory treatment that ensured a lack of economic opportunities, and consequently poverty. These legally engineered conditions of social misery then justified the common knowledge that Japanese were not White. In California's Central Valley during the 1930s, the cooperation of law and social beliefs had created a situation in which Armenians were clearly and correctly White and entitled (literally, in being able to hold title to land), while Japanese were obviously non-White and dispossessed. Law easily precipitated the transformation of highly unstable ideas about race—are Armenians and Japanese "Asiatic" or "white"?—into entrenched differences in social status, legal rights, and wealth. The contingency of these relative positions and the role of law in creating them was lost to sight; the role of law in reifying racial distinctions was invisible.

Reification has made race a dominant feature of our social geography, one which at every turn seems to reinvigorate race with the appearance of reality. Thus, the significance of legally mandated segregation does not lie primarily in its power to police indeterminate identities through neighborhood affiliation, though this should not be discounted. It lies instead in the power of segregation to create and maintain the poverty and prosperity that society views as the results of innate racial character, rather than as predictable consequences of social and specifically legal discrimination.

Even as segregation has slipped from the nation's vocabulary, it remains a persistent reality in American society.[38] This reality seduces us with pernicious messages in the forms of ghettos and suburbs, littered streets and manicured lawns, corner liquor stores and sprawling malls, welfare recipients and white-collar professionals, school violence and college graduates, blood banks and country clubs, and on and on. These contrasting realities follow neighborhood lines—in fact, racial boundaries—and thus testify to the ultimate difference race makes. Race seems to explain, especially to Whites but also to minorities, the pathology so evident on U.S. streets. On these streets, racial differences seem fundamental, immutable, real, and self-evident, confirming not only the existence of races, but also every negative suspicion about racial characteristics.

The role of government and law in producing these differences is much less evident. How often do people remind themselves that this society is the legacy of centuries of legal slavery, years of Jim Crow laws, decades of legal hostility, and an ongoing exclusion of minorities from legislative and judicial power? How many clearly understand the continuing role of race-neutral legal doctrines in maintaining and even reinforcing, rather than dismantling, segregation?[39] The inequitable economic and social effects of segregation testify every day in a thousand ways to the existence of races and racial differences in the United States. Race is not an immanent phenomenon located only in our heads, but an injurious material reality that constantly validates the common knowledge of race. These material differences are in large part the creations of law: the segregation that confirms racial differences was and is legally fashioned and legally maintained. Through law, race becomes real becomes law becomes race in a self-perpetuating pattern altered in myriad ways but never broken.

Law does not rely solely on coercion to construct races, but fashions races on a socially constitutive level as well. Thus, we should not be surprised that little decay has occurred in racial systems since the demise of Jim Crow laws, or that few people see race as something legally imposed. Rather, we should expect this persistence of race and the relative invisibility of its origins, given its central role in the world that law requires us to inhabit and allows us to imagine. But if we are still concerned with the persistence of race, especially in its most damaging forms, then perhaps we must turn our attention to our own roles in perpetuating the legal construction of race, since at a cognitive level we are all to one degree or another implicated.

Judges and Legislators

What can be said of the role of legal actors in constructing races, particularly as to whether such actors are conscious or unwitting participants in this process? If the question is whether legal actors fully perceive the legal fabrication of race, the answer must be no. As the above discussion of law as an ideological system suggests, the legal systems of meaning that surround race largely preclude exactly this sort of an understanding. Yet if the question is whether legal actors recognize their own role in shaping racial definitions, the answer must be yes. Legislators and judges often set out explicitly to define racial boundaries, and on countless occasions people have used the courts to challenge racial definitions. On different levels, legal actors are therefore simultaneously ignorant and informed participants in the construction of races. Of course, the degree of ignorance or awareness varies from case to case and from actor to actor, with some disputes more squarely presenting questions of racial definition and some actors more clearly perceiving the implications of their arguments. Rather than attempting the impossible task of theorizing the relative levels of nescience and knowing in legal actors, it may be more fruitful to explore two more focused questions. First, how can judges and legislators frequently insist that their decisions are free of racism's taint even in concrete contexts that make such claims highly improbable? And second, to what extent are we who challenge the law, particularly those defined by the law as non-Whites, complicitous in our own oppression? While relevant to understanding the prerequisite cases, these questions have even more pertinence to an evaluation of the contemporary legal construction of race, and to the issue of how or whether race might be dismantled.

In the prerequisite cases, legislators and judges imported social prejudices into the law at every level, from the drafting of the naturalization statute to its interpretation. Nevertheless, the judges in the prerequisite cases often asserted a solicitude and fair-mindedness for the applicants that stood in marked contrast to the rest of their opinions. Recall the judge who expressed sympathy for a Burmese petitioner by remarking on the patent unfairness of a law that excluded Asians from naturalization but allowed a "Congo negro but five years removed from barbarism" to attain citizenship.[40] Or consider the Supreme Court's remark upon holding that Takao Ozawa was not White: "Of course there is not implied— either in the legislation or in our interpretation of it—any suggestion of individual unworthiness or racial inferiority."[41] Clearly, these protestations of innocence cannot be taken at face value, for they contradict the spirit and language of the decisions in which they are recorded. Sometimes this contradiction is so stark it distorts even the language of the disclaimer itself. The Supreme Court wrote in *Thind:* "It is very far from our thought to suggest the slightest question of racial superiority or inferiority. What we suggest is merely racial difference, and it is of such character and extent that the great body of our people instinctively recognize it and reject the thought of assimilation."[42] Even in proclaiming its nondiscriminatory motives, the Court revealed its racial antipathy for Asian Indians. In light of such contradictions, its assertions of fine intentions ring hollow. Yet, if these protestations cannot be taken at face value, how should they be understood?

One possibility is to regard such disclaimers as merely the statements of cynical judges, misleading utterances by men in power who recognize the importance of maintaining an unblemished image even as they pursue antisocial goals. This may accurately depict the state of mind of some judges who through their actions enforce racial subordination while through their words they extol the virtues of racial equality. For several reasons, however, such a reading becomes problematic if asserted as a means of understanding more than just a few of the many disclaimers. First, to view the repeated assertions of nonracist intent as cynical utterances requires that one believe that their authors understand the public opprobrium attached to racist actions, conceive of their actions as racist, and insist on proceeding even at the cost of deceiving the public. Such a view describes judges as immoral actors both with respect to their egregious racism and in their willingness to violate the norms of their professional positions by lying to the public. This description comports neither with the popular view of judges, which admittedly may be too rosy but nevertheless cannot be entirely baseless, nor with the way judges describe themselves. Second, picturing judges as cynical manipulators of the public requires that one attribute to judges a clear enough understanding of what constitutes racist behavior to enable them to recognize it in themselves and to conceal it in their opinions. The decisions belie this picture. That the judges failed to conceal completely their racism, for example by not bowdlerizing their remarks about savages or instinctive rejections of assimilation, contradicts the notion that the judges possessed a clear understanding of what constitutes racist thinking. Finally, such a conception of judicial self-awareness clashes with the argument that law legitimates, and so makes relatively impenetrable, certain ways of thinking about the world. Picturing the judges as pure cynics requires the assumption that judges can free themselves from the cognitive limitations of legal ideology under which the rest of us labor. It seems reasonable to suggest instead that when judges insist their reasoning is free of racist taint in opinions that strongly suggest otherwise, they do so honestly within the limits of their understanding of what constitutes racist thinking. Under this view, judges are asserting an innocence they believe in. But this says that, to some extent, judges engage in racist thinking without being aware that they are doing so.

To say that judges are unaware of their own racism is not to claim that judicial racism is fortuitous or unrelated to the decisionmaker's understanding of the world. Instead, it is to assert that social and legal conceptions of race and racism shape the judges' understandings of those phenomena, and that their resulting views, while honestly put forth as neutral perceptions of the world, are in fact heavily biased. This understanding of an embedded judicial innocence comports with the law-as-ideology view of racial construction.[43] This idea can also be expressed in terms of narrative theory. As Richard Delgado and Jean Stefancic explain, "Our identities are social constructs; we influence culture and it us. For most persons (perhaps particularly judges), society's dominant narratives will seem unexceptional and 'true'—demanding no particular improvement or expansion."[44] Perhaps most useful here, however, is to follow Charles Lawrence by expressing this idea in the language of unconscious racism:

> Americans share a common historical and cultural heritage in which racism has played and still plays a dominant role. Because of this shared experience, we inevitably share many ideas, attitudes, and beliefs that attach significance to an individual's race and induce negative feelings and opinions about nonwhites. To the extent that this cultural belief system has influenced all of us, we are all racists. At the same time, most of us are unaware of our own racism. We do not recognize the ways in which our cultural experience has influenced our beliefs about race or the occasions on which those beliefs affect our actions.[45]

To appreciate the force of this observation, one need not accept Freudian psychoanalytic theory in all its variations as the definitive description of the rise and persistence of racism in U.S. society—indeed, there are good reasons not to.[46] This statement stands on its own as a description of the prevalence of racialized and racist beliefs in U.S. society. It reminds us, in a way that talk of legal ideology or dominant narratives does not, that the common knowledge of race often takes on highly injurious forms best labeled racism.

Judges no less than the rest of us labor under unconscious racism; their actions, even if not racist in the sense of consciously seeking to harm certain groups, may still frequently be racist in the sense of drawing on unrecognized but nonetheless racially prejudiced beliefs and desires. In the prerequisite cases, unconscious racism among judges and justices alike seems to have played a prominent role in the legal construction of race. Even if we accept the Supreme Court's disclaimers, we must also accept that unconscious racism impelled the Court in *Ozawa* and *Thind* to repudiate the expanding scientific definitions of race and embrace instead the restrictive popular understanding of Whiteness.

Recognizing the presence of unconscious racism in the judiciary affords important insights into how judges and legislators continue to construct race after *Brown*. Because of the relative absence of overt legislative or judicial racism today, unconscious racism is more important in the contemporary construction of race than it was in the prerequisite cases. Unconscious racism undergirds the current legal construction of race in two interrelated ways. First, it fosters the racially discriminatory misapplication of laws that themselves do not make racial distinctions. Second, it engenders the design and promulgation of facially neutral laws likely to have racially disparate effects.

The racially discriminatory application of neutral laws is particularly pronounced in areas where the law regulates behavior often understood in racial terms—for example, in criminal law. Where unconscious racism works in the law, it perpetrates racist harms. More than this, however, it serves to reinforce unexamined racial beliefs, working as a sort of self-fulfilling prophecy that maintains races by confirming the validity of racial biases. Consider the sentencing of convicted criminals. A number of studies document large disparities in sentencing that correlate only to the race of the defendant and the race of the victim.[47] Having committed the same crime, in the same jurisdiction, with the same record of prior convictions, one is likely to receive a higher sentence if one is non-White or if one's victim is White. These disparities are particularly evident in capital cases. One study shows that in otherwise similar situations prosecutors seek the death penalty against Latinos four times more often than against Whites, and are fourteen times more likely to seek the death penalty against those who murder Whites than against those who murder

Latinos.[48] Such disparities, however, are not unique to capital sentencing. Prosecutorial discretion is exercised in racially disparate ways at every level, from the decision to seek death to the choice to offer a plea bargain. One recent study analyzed nearly 700,000 criminal cases and concluded that "as more and more cases are decided by plea bargain, whites as a group get significantly better deals than Hispanics or blacks who are accused of similar crimes and who have similar criminal backgrounds."[49]

Despite the stark statistical evidence regarding the importance of race to incarceration, prosecutors and judges rarely acknowledge the importance of racism in sentencing. In the same study of 700,000 cases, "only 11 percent of the judges and 9 percent of the prosecutors said they believe racial bias is somewhat or very evident in plea bargaining."[50] If "racial bias" is taken here to mean purposeful discrimination, perhaps these judges and prosecutors are correct. But if it means unconscious racism, they are almost certainly wrong. Unconscious racism seems to explain all too well the disparities widely evident in sentencing statistics. Judges and prosecutors are not immune to society's pervasive depiction of minorities as prone to criminality and Whites as the victims rather than the perpetrators of crime. It is almost inconceivable that they could remain uninfluenced by stereotypes of criminality and victimization, and of social worthlessness and worth, when determining the likelihood of recidivism or evaluating the extent of harm already done, two significant factors in sentencing determinations. Such stereotypes, to the extent they are accepted, would produce the existing disparities. Non-White convicted criminals would be seen as more likely to become recidivists, making longer sentences appropriate; White convicted criminals would be seen as unlikely villains, making shorter sentences reasonable. Those who victimized Whites would be seen as the greater social threat, warranting longer incarceration; those who victimized non-Whites would seem less a threat to society, thus justifying shorter terms of imprisonment.

Unconscious racism in the criminal justice system is a likely source for some of the racial disparities evident in sentencing. Nevertheless, the Supreme Court has rejected theories of unconscious racism in sentencing, and has held that sentences cannot be constitutionally challenged absent proof of purposeful discrimination. In a Georgia death penalty case, *McCleskey v. Kemp,* the Supreme Court rejected statistics similar to those mentioned above because they did not prove *intentional* discrimination.[51] This rejection seems akin to the protestations of innocence heard throughout the prerequisite cases: it is an insistence that no harm is done so long as no harm is done *purposefully.* Yet by refusing to look below the surface of intent, "the Court gave legitimacy, and a claim of inevitability . . . to the invidious racial heuristics that are as embedded in legal decisionmaking as they are in everyday life."[52] That is, this decision did more than allow an injustice in McCleskey's individual case. By refusing to recognize the role of unconscious racism in gross sentencing disparities, it legitimized the notions of race behind such disparities, and legitimized as well a pinched and parsimonious understanding of what constitutes racial discrimination. The Court's ruling in *McCleskey* ensures that under similar circumstances criminals who are Black or who victimize Whites will continue to be incarcerated more often and for greater lengths of time, thus reinforcing stereotypes of Black criminality and White victimhood. The fact of high incarceration rates for Blacks partially stems from, and subsequently is used to confirm, the mythology of Black criminality and, by implication, White innocence. The long sentences accorded those who victimize Whites in part result from, and in turn reinforce, notions of White social worth and, by implication, Black worthlessness.[53] Law makes these notions self-fulfilling prophecies that further entrench racial differences.

Criminal sentencing shows that unconscious racism among legal actors can maintain socially constructed notions of race through the misapplication of neutral laws. Unconscious racism also plays a role in the legal construction of race through the *design* and *promulgation* of statues that, while facially neutral, will inevitably result in discrimination against non-Whites. The alien land laws, which transformed the phrase "alien ineligible to citizenship" into a tool for discrimination against Japanese noncitizens, show the ease with which discriminatory statutes can be drafted without explicit reference to race. Such laws are widely evident today, and are far more crucial to the legal maintenance of race now that overt legal discrimination against non-Whites is no longer socially or constitutionally permissible. With the elimination of laws aimed expressly at imposing racial inequality, facially neutral laws with discriminatory effects arguably constitute the prime legal mechanism for the maintenance of racial hierarchy. These statutes both ideologically support the dominant narrative of racial difference and foster the material inequalities that give popular racial beliefs empirical force.

The proposed constitutional amendment to repeal the Citizenship Clause of the Fourteenth Amendment in order to deny birthright citizenship to children born in the United States to undocumented persons exemplifies current efforts to write facially neutral laws with racially discriminatory effects.[54] So does California's Proposition 187, the "Save Our State" (S.O.S.) initiative, which makes undocumented persons and their children ineligible for public social services ranging from primary education to nonemergency doctor's visits and prenatal care.[55] Approved in 1994 by a two-to-one margin but currently blocked by a series of court challenges, S.O.S. is being hailed by some national leaders as a model for the entire country. Its success dramatically confirms the role of unconscious racism in the legal construction of race.

The racial animus behind Proposition 187 is painfully evident in the imagery and language used by the proponents of the measure. Consider the questions posed in rhetorical support of S.O.S. in the official state ballot pamphlet:

> Should those ILLEGALLY here receive taxpayer subsidized education including college?
> Should our children's classrooms be over-crowded by those who are ILLEGALLY in our country?
> Should our Senior Citizens be denied full service under Medi-Cal to subsidize the cost of ILLEGAL ALIENS?[56]

Even in the context of a ballot pamphlet, where one might expect carefully considered advocacy, the structure and language of these questions betrays the stark us-versus-them distinctions that mark racial divides, creating an unbridgeable gulf between "them," the illegal aliens, and "us," the taxpayers, parents, and senior citizens. Undocumented people, whether tourists who overstayed their visas or wage laborers who crossed the border for work, are cast as a single, homogenous, undeserving, uppercase OTHER bent on victimizing the variegated but relatively defenseless and lowercase "we."

Not surprisingly, the less-restrained public campaign for Proposition 187 echoed and amplified these overtones of racial bias. In the public campaign, the issue was not immigration, it was Mexicans. In television commercials linking his bid for reelection to support for S.O.S., California Governor Pete Wilson repeatedly ran prime-time images of people running in pandemonium through a Tijuana-San Diego border checkpoint, powerfully transforming the anti-immigrant initiative into an anti-Mexican campaign.[57] As Elizabeth Martínez writes, "Wilson has almost single-handedly made the word 'immigrant' mean Mexican or other Latino (and sometimes Asian). Who thinks of all the people coming from the former Soviet Union and other countries?"[58] Wilson is not alone in race-baiting through the language of immigration reform. Evidence of racial bias also abounds in the comments of others who support restrictionist immigration policies. One grass-roots organizer argues that with immigrants, "[i]t's like animals. When there's scarcity, they don't breed. When there's plenty, they breed."[59] A founder of the prominent restrictionist lobby, the Federation for American Immigration Reform, asks: "Will the present majority peaceably hand over its political power to a group that is simply more fertile? . . . On the demographic point, perhaps this is the first instance in which those with their pants up are going to get caught by those with their pants down!"[60] A 1992 Republican presidential hopeful stated "that immigrants 'mongrelize' our culture and dilute our values."[61] The divisive rhetoric of us and them, the repeated depiction of Mexicans rushing across the border, and the invective about breeding and mongrelization all slander the reality of immigration to this country in the hostile terms of racial inferiority. This language completely disregards the reality Gerald López seeks to remind us of, that when it comes to immigration, "They are we."[62]

In light of these xenophobic comments and the long history of nativism in the United States, it is difficult to conclude that anything but racism provides the primary force behind anti-immigrant measures such as Proposition 187. Nevertheless, it must be noted that the vast majority of those supporting such legislation insist they are not driven by racism. Thus, the proponents of the S.O.S. initiative stress that race is irrelevant to their concerns, and that they are solely interested in curtailing the flow of undocumented migration. They insist that supporters of the measure include "all races, colors and creeds with the same common denominator. We are American."[63] Again, we might understand such comments as rank cynicism, and for some, it doubtless is. More worrisome, however, is that in all likelihood such comments, while sincere, are products of unconscious racism. Consider Charles Lawrence's explanation for what drives racism into the unconscious mind:

> Freudian theory states that the human mind defends itself against the discomfort of guilt by denying or refusing to recognize those ideas, wishes, and beliefs that conflict with what the individual has learned is good and right. While our historical experience has made racism an integral part of our culture, our society has more recently embraced an ideal that rejects racism as immoral. When an individual experiences conflict between racist ideas and the societal ethic that condemns those ideas, the mind excludes his racism from consciousness.[64]

It may be that those who draft or support such laws are unconscious racists in the sense that they operate under the influence of prevalent social prejudices but cannot admit even to themselves the racial antipathies that rule their fears and desires. Racial prejudice against immigrants is a long tradition in the United States, evident certainly in the prerequisite cases. In the western states, racial discrimination against Mexicans shares an almost equally long history, appearing for example in California's 1855 "Greaser Act," an antiloitering law that applied to "all persons who are commonly known as 'Greasers' or the issue of Spanish and Indian blood . . . and who go armed and are not peaceable and quiet persons."[65] Prejudice forms an established part of the contemporary social fabric, even as it stands in contradiction to society's expressed disapproval of racial discrimination. Racial prejudice, though not consciously recognized as such, exists at a level that motivates and directs social hostility, giving it rhetorical and, more importantly, legal form.

The relative lack of intentional racial animus behind Proposition 187 and similar anti-immigrant legislation does not reduce the effect such laws have in maintaining and deepening racial hierarchies. Like racial prerequisites, antimiscegenation laws, and de jure segregation, anti-immigrant laws construct races coercively and ideologically. These laws force people apart, using state violence to assign meanings of belonging or exclusion, racial worth or worthlessness, to people possessing certain features, ancestries, and nationalities. At the same time, the prejudices evident in the discourse of immigration and race translate into material disadvantages that affect all immigrants. Handicaps such as exclusion from schools and health care or vulnerability to employer exploitation exacerbate the inequalities of wealth and status which in part form the basis for assertions of innate racial difference, and more, of racial inferiority. Anti-immigrant laws, drawing on deep social beliefs in racial hierarchy, give effect to and entrench those same social beliefs.

The prevalence and daily material reinforcement of racist beliefs in our society ensure the continued legal construction of race in the form of ostensibly neutral but actually discriminatory laws put forward by those who assure us, and are genuinely convinced of, their own good intentions. Unconscious racists will continue to perpetuate through law the most injurious forms of racial difference. Yet, we should not focus on the unconscious racism of others without examining ourselves for this same fault. Herein lies a further reason for refusing to reject assertions of good intent as mere cynical utterances, whether from the judges of the prerequisite cases or from our contemporaries. To the extent we describe their assertions as cynical, we who imagine ourselves to be sincere too easily reject our own potential for racism. "We thus conclude that those [racists] from the past must have been acting against conscience, that is, had vicious wills and realized that what they were doing was wrong (as we realize it today), but went ahead and did it anyway. Yet, we think, '*I* do not act against conscience and neither do my friends.' "[66] We do not hold a monopoly on sincerity, just as others do not monopolize racism. If the prerequisite judges could sincerely disavow racism, then perhaps our own felt innocence is similarly self-deluding. We cannot rely on faith in our own goodness as a substitute for the careful examination of our beliefs and actions. This is particularly true for those constructed as White in this society, since, as I argue in the next chapter, Whiteness is virtually defined by a host of largely unexamined assumptions of superiority and inferiority, worth and worthlessness. It is also true, however, for people socially defined as non-White. Even those of us who challenge and are most directly harmed by the legal construction of race participate to an extent in its perpetuation.

Non-Whites

Judges and legislators continue to participate in the legal construction of race, if for some only through the internalization of socially prevalent racist beliefs. But what of nonlegal actors? The role of nonlegal actors in the legal construction of race can be understood as a question about whether people obey or acquiesce to the law. To obey suggests a rational, considered relation to law in which the law coerces through threats and rewards that are evaluated and form the basis for decisions about how to act. Acquiescence suggests a more complex relationship with law, one in which the actor accepts the norms and assumptions underlying law as legitimate or at least binding, leading to behavior conditioned, not just through a rational calculus of risks and rewards, but through subscription to the normative world of the legal regime.[67] This question of obedience or acquiescence among nonlegal actors is central to assessing the intractability of existing racial categories. If people merely obey the law, then altering laws might promise quick changes in racial construction; however, change might be more difficult if through a lifetime of acquiescence people have fully embraced the assumptions about races embedded in current laws. Questioning whether people obey or acquiesce to law takes on a significantly different character, however, when posed in a discussion about the role of people of color in the legal construction of race. In this context, the question becomes one of complicity: If rather than simply obeying the law we have acquiesced to it, are we complicitous in our own oppression?

One legal scholar addressing this question arguably answers no. Critical legal scholars have argued that the dual effect of legal legitimation and reification constrains the imagination of individuals and leads them, even in the absence of coercion, to embrace the world contained in law, implicating them in the perpetuation of that world. Kimberlé Crenshaw rejects these arguments, insisting that coercion more than ideology constitutes the most important force in shaping the lives of African Americans. "The Critics' principal error is that their version of domination by consent does not present a realistic picture of racial domination. Coercion explains much more about racial domination than does ideologically induced consent. Black people do not create their oppressive worlds moment to moment but rather are coerced into living in worlds created and maintained by others."[68] Crenshaw's argument is strong. The liberal legal ideology that critical scholars deconstruct to explain the acquiescence of the polity to the existing regime is more relevant to Whites than to non-Whites, who have long been excluded from the liberal promises of inalienable rights, equal justice, and so forth. Even so, however, coercion is not the whole story. The prerequisite cases suggest that to some extent non-Whites are in fact complicitous in creating moment to moment the oppressive worlds we inhabit.

Bhagat Singh Thind's argument before the Supreme Court is instructive on the question of obedience, acquiescence, and complicity. Thind did more than claim, as required by law, that he was White; he asserted his Whiteness in a manner that relied on and enhanced notions of White superiority and non-White inferiority. After first listing a number of anthropological texts categorizing South Asians as Caucasian, Thind's argument proceeded as follows:

> The foregoing authorities show that the people residing in many of the states of India, particularly in the north and northwest, including the Punjab, belong to the Aryan race. . . . The Aryan language is indigenous to the Aryan of India as well as the Aryan of Europe.
>
> The high-class Hindu regards the aboriginal Indian Mongoloid in the same manner as the American regards the negro, speaking from a matri-

monial standpoint. The caste system prevails in India to a degree unsurpassed elsewhere.

With this caste system prevailing, there was comparatively a small mixture of blood between the different castes. Besides ethnological and philological aspects, it is a historical fact that the Aryans came to India, probably about the year 2000 B.C., and conquered the aborigines.[69]

Thind characterized himself as White, first in terms of Caucasian ancestry, and second in terms of Aryan language. He further characterized himself as White, however, by reference to the purity of his blood, by the fact that his were a conquering people, and by his disdain for non-Whites (the "aboriginal Indian Mongoloid"). Even in challenging the parameters of White identity, Thind affirmed some of the fundamental aspects of Whiteness. He reinforced the notion that Whiteness was defined by purity, superiority, and a disdain for inferiors when he claimed these characteristics for himself as proof he was a "white person."

Thind's argument should not, of course, be taken at face value. Like others who directly challenged the legal construction of race, Thind had no choice but to pursue his challenge within the institution, pursuant to the rules, and according to the language that would be used to judge him. We should keep in mind that, as is often the case, for Thind the law encompassed contradictory roles in the legal construction of race, on the one hand imposing racial boundaries, and on the other mediating challenges to those same lines.[70] It is conceivable, even likely, that Thind understood these contradictory roles and couched his arguments in terms calculated to receive the most favorable hearing. Martha Minow cautions, "Signs of assimilation by a group treated as less powerful than the majority deserve a second look because they may indicate subtle acts of resistance and accommodation by people seeking to retain an independent identity without risking conflict or further suppression."[71] Perhaps Thind's apparent assimilation of even the most harmful aspects of Whiteness reflected his recognition that racial dialogue must be framed in ways that pander to the mindset of those with power over one's life. However, although we cannot know for sure, it still seems that Thind's argument reveals a partially real, rather than wholly calculated, subscription to the purity and superiority of Whites and the corruption and inferiority of non-Whites. It would seem impossible to completely corral such views of the self and world within the confines of the calculating mind. Repeating in many different ways on every new day the worth of Whites and the worthlessness of non-Whites cannot but affect the self-regard and world view of those who utter or hear the incessant mantra of White superiority. Thind to some extent may well have believed his own words about Whiteness.

This internalization of racialized beliefs harms not only the individual but society as well. Acquiescing to a world view predicated on White superiority directly implicates people of color in the construction of the patterns of domination and subordination that mark race relations in the United States. Even supposing Thind's brief went publicly unnoted, an unlikely proposition given the importance of his case to the Asian Indian community in this country, his arguments at the very least confirmed rather than challenged the Supreme Court's racial prejudice, the same prejudice that allowed the Court to exclude him and all Asian Indians from citizenship. More likely, however, Thind's arguments were widely reported, and were consequently more widely injurious.

In this regard, consider the advocacy of Kiyoshi Karl Kawakami on the issue of Japanese naturalization. Born in Yamagata Prefecture, Japan, Kawakami came to the United States in 1901 as a student, eventually receiving an M.A. from the University of Iowa and becoming a bilingual journalist who published widely in English on the question of Japanese in the United States.[72] Kawakami focused a substantial amount of his writing on the effect of the prerequisite laws on Japanese immigrants. In an article entitled "The Naturalization of the Japanese," published in the *North American Review,* Kawakami argued in favor of naturalization in a manner that, like Thind's legal argument, denigrated non-Whites.[73] Kawakami put his strongest argument for naturalization simply: few Japanese, only the elite, would actually naturalize. "I have stated," he wrote, "that only a small number of Japanese will swear allegiance to the Republic; that such Japanese will be recruited from among the best classes of the Mikado's subjects; [and] that ignorant and undesirable laborers care to remain in this country no longer than is necessary to save a modest sum of money."[74] Assuring his readers that "there will be no danger of the United States becoming infested by the undesirable classes of Japanese immigrants," he added that they need not fear "clannish" Japanese behavior either, since in "no city have they established their 'Chinatown' or their 'Ghetto.' "[75]

Kawakami's argument that Japanese immigrants should be allowed to naturalize because most of them would not do so is at best curious. At worst, it was quite harmful to the Japanese community and other non-Whites, particularly Chinese and Blacks, in its repetition and validation of the tired stereotypes of ignorance, infestation, undesirability, and clan-nishness. Contrast this depiction of non-Whites with Kawakami's view of Whites, expressed a few years later in a veneration of America "Here is a country . . . where social caste has never been established; where all the blessings of modern civilization—schools, libraries, museums, and what not—are placed at the disposal of everyone."[76] In Kawakami's writings, (White) Americans held out the promise of civilization for all, while the Japanese posed a threat of infestation. Such beliefs did not go unheeded. Noting the spread of what he ironically termed the "Yankee spirit," Kawakami wrote that the children of Japanese immigrants "disdainfully call the newcomers from Japan 'Japs.' "[77] Though Kawakami perhaps ex-aggerates the degree and form of assimilation among Japanese immi-grants, such assimilation doubtless existed to some extent. It is clear, moreover, that such assimilation sometimes came at the very high price of self-hatred, and more, that this self-loathing took a specifically racial form. Kawakami is partially responsible for this. Though he argued for reform in the prerequisite laws, he did so in terms that made those racial bars on citizenship seem reasonable, even prudent. And he did so in ways which spread and deepened the destructive messages of racial superiority and inferiority.

Kawakami's writings, Thind's legal arguments, even Takao Ozawa's testament of full assimilation, all lead to a single conclusion: Those people constructed as non-Whites in this country have been complicitous in this construction. The extent to which we are complicitous, of course, remains an important and highly charged question. Kawakami, for ex-ample, is notable not because he was typical—he was not—but because he was such an outspoken apologist for America. Almost certainly, Thind and Ozawa were atypical as well in the sense that their unstinting pursuit of naturalization suggests that they more than most were deeply wedded to the idea of assimilation. The question of complicity becomes even more charged when asked today. Certainly we are *all* implicated in the legal construction of race to the extent we uncritically accept the racial cate-gories employed by law. However, the complicity of some is much more profound than this. Kawakami is not a phenomenon solely of yesterday; moreover, his counterparts today have access to positions not only as journalists, but also as jurists in the highest courts of the land. Further-more, the modern versions of Thind and Ozawa, those who purposefully seek to use the law to end discrimination or gain advantages for minority communities, may also substantially though unwittingly contribute to the legal legitimation of racial domination and subordination. Derrick Bell's argument that civil rights litigation is a delaying tactic that serves White and not Black interests, for example, suggests that this is true.[78]

Nevertheless, whatever the extent of this complicity, Crenshaw is almost certainly correct to identify coercion and not cognitive collaboration as the key force in the imposition of inequality on people of color in the United States. Racial equality cannot be achieved unless minorities free their minds of the injurious mythologies of racial hierarchy. But even freed of these mythologies, minorities will not be equals in this society until the material oppression that circumscribes the lives of the vast majority of people of color in this country has ended. Here it is important to note a separate point Crenshaw makes about the relationship of coercion and consent. "Black people are boxed in," she argues, "largely because there is a consensus among many whites that the oppression of Blacks is legitimate. This is where consensus and coercion can be understood together: ideology convinces one group that the coercive domination of another is legitimate."[79] It is White race-consciousness, a consciousness guilty of abiding the continuing destruction of minority communities and minority lives, that requires immediate and sustained attention, not the race-consciousness of non-Whites. As Crenshaw writes, "efforts to address racial domination . . . must consider the continuing ideology of white race consciousness . . . chipping away at its premises. Central to this task is revealing the contingency of race and exploring the connection between white race consciousness and the other myths that legitimate both class and race hierarchies."[80] The next chapter begins this task by examining White race-consciousness as it exists today.

6

White Race-Consciousness

The prerequisite cases show that race is a social construction fabricated in part by law. More than this, these cases specifically illuminate the construction of Whiteness, constituting that rare instance when White racial identity is unexpectedly drawn out of the background and placed abruptly in question. Moving away from legal theory, it is useful to ask what the prerequisite cases tell us about Whiteness. It may seem that these cases say relatively little, both because the courts failed to offer a developed definition of White identity, and also because they seemed to concern themselves much more with who was not White. In the end, however, it is exactly these practices that tell us the most about the nature of White identity today, drawing into view both the maintaining technologies of transparency and the relational construction of White and non-White identity. Exploring these two facets of White identity, in this chapter I work toward the argument that Whiteness as it is currently constituted perpetuates injurious racial identities and should be abandoned. Whites need to develop a race-consciousness that places their racial identity squarely in view in order better to disassemble the meaning systems of racial superiority and inferiority. A self-deconstructive White race-consciousness is key to racial justice.

Transparency and the Naturalization of Whiteness

The judges in the prerequisite cases encountered real difficulty in giving content to the ostensibly unambiguous term "white person." Despite the centrality of White identity in U.S. history, evidenced for instance by its use as a condition for national citizenship, the judges in the prerequisite cases were unable to develop a freestanding definition of Whiteness. Instead, the courts delved into the confusing morass of scientific evidence on race, speculated about the legislative intent behind the prerequisite statute, cited each other for precedential but no less poorly reasoned support, and offered only tautological comments concerning the common knowledge about Whiteness. None of these approaches proved particularly consistent or helpful; the final result was that the courts reached a series of startlingly contradictory decisions that were incoherent in terms of both holdings and rationales. This confusion is especially evident with respect to South Asians, who were White for purposes of naturalization according to scientific evidence but subsequently non-White in denaturalization proceedings as a matter of familiar observation, and with respect to Armenians, who were initially non-Whites by geography but who successfully challenged and changed their status on the grounds of skin color, culture, and anthropology. As courts continued to hear and struggle with prerequisite challenges, the ambiguities in the term "white person" became ever more apparent, prompting some judges to give written release to their frustrations. As Judge Smith lamented in *Shahid*, "the language of the statute is about as open to many constructions as it possibly could be."[1] It may be that some of the confusion over the meaning of the phrase "white person" stemmed from the lack of meaning marking all racial categories. However, a particular lacuna apparently existed concerning the nature of Whiteness. For the most part, it seems, Whiteness was so obvious to the judges it was transparent. Though the judges themselves were White, the self-evident quality of their racial identity inhibited their ability to articulate what defined a "white person."

Transparency, the tendency of Whites to remain blind to the racialized aspects of that identity, is omnipresent. A story about a recent legal feminist conference captures one manifestation of this phenomenon. At the conference, the participants were asked to pick two or three words to describe themselves. All of the women of color selected at least one racial term, but none of the White women selected a word referring to their race, prompting Angela Harris to comment that "[i]n this society, it is only white people who have the luxury of 'having no color.' "[2] This anecdotal impression is borne out in an informal study recently conducted among students at Harvard Law School. A student interviewer asked ten African Americans and ten Whites: "How do you identify yourself?" Eight African Americans referred to race in their answers, but only two Whites did so.[3] Interestingly, the two Whites who referred to their race were women. Perhaps among Whites, women—more often attuned to thinking in terms of subordinated identities—are more likely to be mindful of the significance of racial identity. Some recent legal writing by

White women lends support to this hypothesis.[4] This point serves as a reminder that aspects of White identity such as transparency vary among individuals as well as along all the social axes that run through the White community. Nevertheless, the tendency not to see oneself in racial terms is widespread among Whites. Transparency "may be a defining characteristic of whiteness: to be white is not to think about it."[5]

Transparency is due in part to positional privilege. "White supremacy makes whiteness the normative model. Being the norm allows whites to ignore race, except when they perceive race (usually someone else's) as intruding on their lives."[6] Existing at the center of racial relations, Whites very rarely find themselves burdened by race in a manner that draws this aspect of identity into view; their Whiteness therefore remains unexamined, shrouded in background shadows. Indeed, for many Whites their racial identity becomes uppermost in their mind only when they find themselves in the company of large numbers of non-Whites, and then it does so in the form of a supposed vulnerability to non-White violence, rendering Whiteness in the eyes of many Whites not a privileged status but a victimized one. Nevertheless, the infrequency with which Whites have to think about race is a direct result of how infrequently Whites in fact are racially victimized. Most often the beneficiaries of racial privilege rather than the subjects of racist offense, Whites rarely have cause to consider their own racial identity.

It should be noted, moreover, that at the same time that transparency results from positional privilege, it also adds to that privilege. The infrequency with which society forces Whites to think about their race confers upon Whites a great psychological benefit. "Many whites think that people of color are obsessed with race and find it hard to understand the emotional and intellectual energy that people of color devote to the subject. But whites are privileged in that they do not have to think about race, even though they have one."[7] Never forced to experience or reflect upon the petty indignities and intentional slights of racism, most Whites are free to act in the world with energies undiminished by the anger and self-doubt engendered among racism's victims.[8] A result of privilege, transparency also confers privilege.

Privilege, however, does not fully explain transparency. That Whites often do not see themselves in racial terms because they are constructed as the racial norm is at best only a partial explanation for transparency. Indeed, it might be equally plausible to suggest the contrary, that privilege should magnify White racial self-consciousness. The centrality of race in White lives would seem to make a consciousness of Whiteness unavoidable. Living at the center, experiencing the benefits of ideological superiority, and enjoying the advantages of material comfort arguably should make Whites acutely aware of their own Whiteness, rather than unconscious of it. Moreover, at a different level than transparency, Whites do possess an acute consciousness of their own racial identity. A concrete certainty among Whites regarding their own Whiteness both lies behind transparency and belies it. Whites may rarely think of themselves in racial terms, but when pushed, few experience even the slightest doubt about their own fundamental Whiteness. Thus, as Ruth Frankenberg argues, "by themselves, the material, daily relations of race cannot adequately explain whether, when, and in what terms white[s] . . . perceive race as structuring either their own or anyone else's experience."[9] Privilege in daily race relations cannot serve as the sole explanation for the rise and maintenance of transparency. Instead, there must exist complementary maintaining technologies to White myopia regarding race. The prerequisite cases suggest the naturalization of Whiteness.

In a literal sense, the prerequisite cases naturalized Whites by granting citizenship to those found to be "white persons." However, these cases implicate the naturalization of Whites in other senses as well. First, the cases physically naturalized Whites, in that they treated Whiteness as a biological aspect of nature rather than as a constructed part of human society. In this context, recall the startling language used in *Knight,* discussed in the introduction to the prerequisite cases in Chapter 3.[10] In *Knight,* the court denied citizenship to an individual because he was of mixed English, Japanese, and Chinese descent. The court rested its denial on the ground that a "person, one-half white and one-half of some other race, belongs to neither of those races, but is literally a half-breed," and therefore cannot be considered a "white person."[11] The court's language suggests at least four intertwined but analytically distinguishable ways in which the prerequisite cases treated races as physical groupings: races were (1) hereditary, a matter of birth; (2) innate, an essential characteristic unalterable by human agency; (3) universal, insofar as everyone belonged to a race; and (4) exclusive, because no one belonged to more than one race. By using the zootechnical language of breeds, the court intimated the innate and hereditary nature of race, treating it as an inescapable, essentially biological identity acquired through birth. In its insistence on assigning Knight a racial identity, even if that of "half-breed," rather than simply concluding that the question of race was irrelevant, the

court conformed to the assumption that race is universal. And by labeling Knight a "half-breed," the court also conformed to the requirement
of exclusivity, which prohibited Knight from belonging simultaneously to
more than one race. *Knight* is typical of the other prerequisite cases in
reasoning as if race were physical—meaning innate, heritable, universal,
and exclusive.[12]

The constituent assumptions of physicality present in the prerequisite
cases continue to hold considerable sway today. For instance, each of
these assumptions underlies the way the U.S. census treats nonstandard
responses to questions about racial identity. One commentator summa-
rizes Census Bureau classificatory techniques this way: "[C]ensus data on
race continue to present data as if people were classifiable with a single
race. For example, before 1980, a mixed-race person was assigned to the
father's race but since 1980, this person is now assigned to the mother's
race. In cases where the written-in response was, for example, 'Italian,'
the person would be reassigned to the White race."[13] The census treats
race as a matter of heredity (one's race follows the race of one's parents),
as innate (individuals cannot define their own racial identity, for example
as Italians), as exclusive (only one racial identity is assigned), and as universal (all persons are assigned races).

These assumptions of physicality are only now being questioned. In the
summer of 1994, the Office of Management and Budget held a round of
hearings to reexamine the use of exclusive racial categories in the census.
However, these hearings were not prompted by calls for the recognition
that race is entirely social, a point quite evident in the history of racial categorization in the census. Rather, the hearings were prompted by calls for
the establishment of a new racial category, that of "multiracial."[14] Ostensibly designed to encompass all those not of a pure racial identity—a category that would include everyone in this country, or no one, because
"pure" races do not exist—this category is in fact meant to include those
whose parents are socially recognized as belonging to different races.[15]
Far from challenging the idea of races, proponents of multiracialism seek
a new category that assumes and further solidifies the basic validity of the
extant racial schema, not least with respect to the racial identity of parents. Advocates of this new grouping vociferously point out the absurdity of exclusivity in racial identity, but seem quite content to leave the
other assumptions of physicality intact. The prerequisite cases reasoned
in a way that physically naturalized race, and such reasoning remains
compelling and commonplace today.

The prerequisite cases also naturalized Whiteness by linking cognitive and cultural traits to physical difference. The prerequisite courts tied temperament, culture, intellect, political sophistication, and so on to physical features, treating questions of behavior as innate elements of human biology rather than as aspects of acquired identity.[16] Reconsider the justification offered by one court for the racial bar on Asian naturalization: "The yellow or bronze racial color is the hallmark of Oriental despotisms."[17] This language draws a direct link between race and political temperament, thereby making culture a function of racial rather than social variability. This view of race seems to undergird the prerequisite laws, rendering fitness for citizenship not a question of learned behavior but of innate predispositions. To see this, contrast the remark about "despotisms" with the view commonly held at the turn of the century that the White race was, as a leading scholar put it, "peculiarly fitted for self-government. It submits its action habitually to the guidance of reason, and has the judicial faculty of seeing both sides of a question."[18] Whites qualified for citizenship because they were fit by nature for republican government; non-Whites remained perpetual aliens because they were inherently unfit for self-rule. Putative differences in temperament and culture were naturalized as "racial" differences.

In turn, these differences were further naturalized by their arrangement into supposedly inherent hierarchies. Fundamental to the cultural depiction of races was "the imposition of an inegalitarian ethos that required the ranking of these groups vis-à-vis one another. Ranking was an intrinsic, and explicit, aspect of the classifying process."[19] The prerequisite courts frequently cited this hierarchy in protesting the admission of Blacks but not Asians to citizenship—for example, in the lament that Congress had "proffer[red] the boon of American citizenship to the comparatively savage and strange inhabitants of the 'dark continent,' while withholding it from the intermediate and much-better-qualified red and yellow races."[20] The courts treated behavior as a function of race, and race as a matter of fundamental physical difference and inherent inequality, thereby naturalizing cultural identity as a question of innate biotic difference along a spectrum of superiority to inferiority. At the turn of the century, and arguably still today, a racial hierarchy existed that behaviorally placed Whites at the top and Blacks at the bottom, with Asians and other racial others in between, naturally.

Finally, the prerequisite cases naturalized Whiteness by locating the definitions of racial difference in common knowledge. These cases treated questions of race as matters of common sense, an approach that naturalizes race by insisting it is part of the reality in which we find ourselves, something observed and easily known to all, and not constructed and dependent on the human knower. Herein lies the significance of *Thind*'s repeated rhetorical references to what "the average man knows perfectly well,"[21] to the "understandings of the common man,"[22] and to "matter[s] of familiar observation and knowledge."[23] The Court located race in the familiar and readily observed realm of nature. Despite this language, however, the Court relied not on the common knowledge of just anyone, but on the common sense of "the average well informed white American."[24] In doing so, the Court seemed to recognize that common knowledge varies across society. "Common sense is an eclectic phenomenon. Its constituent symbols, images, and meanings are loosely assembled from diverse sources of political and popular culture. Partly for this reason it is not monolithic across a society or culture—it would be a mistake to think about socially constructed common sense in terms of some absolute ideological hegemony."[25] The Court avoided this mistake by specifying White common knowledge as the relevant tool of racial categorization, thereby drawing upon more restrictive notions of who counted as White. It also incidentally highlighted the fact that it is among Whites that the contrived truths about Whiteness seem most like common sense.

These various forms of naturalization combine in many ways to hide from Whites a consciousness of their own racial identity. Locating Whiteness in the physical world obscures the contingency of this construction, assuring Whites that their racial identity is as inherent and unalterable as their facial features and skin color, something so essential to their being as to require no cultivation and little if any reflection. The linkage of cognitive traits to race transforms questions of individual temperament and cultural practices into manifestations of innate differences, terms that subsequently allow the rationalization of social inequality in ways that protect White privilege from close scrutiny. The insistence that Whiteness is common knowledge, even against considerable evidence that it is a complex and ill-defined category, obviates and deflects inquiries about race. Race need not and cannot be interrogated because its essence is immediately and already known, particularly among Whites, who possess the repository of common knowledge about Whiteness. Through these various forms of naturalization, Whiteness becomes transparent, a protected status that one either has or does not have, but about which one need not think.

The Content of White Identity

The prerequisite cases not only naturalized Whiteness, but also elaborated its substance. Fathoming the content of White identity requires a shift from thinking about races as categories toward conceptualizing races in terms of relationships. Race provides one among many ways to describe human variation, where such "descriptions" are always subjective and comparative rather than objective or meaningful in the abstract. Race works like other terms of relational difference—for example, gender, class, and nation—to accentuate particular aspects of physical, social, cultural, or political variability, investing such differences with a transcendent categorical significance that oversimplifies and dwarfs the actual scale of heterogeneity. The resulting categories are relational and hierarchical, in the sense that the definition of one category is also the definition of other categories as well as of their respective normative positions. This conception of social categorization suggests, and the prerequisite cases confirm, that the construction of race is the construction of relationships. It is in the elaboration of these relationships—invariably relationships of domination and subordination, normativity and marginality, privilege and disadvantage—that White identity is given content.[26]

Conceptualizing races in terms of relationships brings with it the advantage and risk of emphasizing the dualistic nature of racial construction. As the prerequisite cases show, the principle terms in racial construction are in binary opposition: applicants were either White or non-White. This dualism constitutes a central facet of the elaboration of racial paradigms; it allows races to be defined against one another, by reference to what other races are and are not. The construction of race becomes diacritical, to use Janet Halley's term: The identity of Whites is dependent on and at the same time helps to define the identity of non-Whites.[27] However, this dualistic structure makes race completely unstable. There can be no stability in racial meanings where those meanings are dependent on diacritical oppositions in a multiform world. Richard Ford writes:

> [B]ecause the symbolic structure of race is grounded in a dualism which does not conform to its object, racial meanings cannot be fixed either by

reference to some essence or even in an arbitrary or non-essential manner. In short, they do not refer to their professed object, but only (through a false paradigmatic opposition) to other meanings within the structure, and even this self-referentiality is unstable because the opposition on which it is based is a false one: there are not only two terms within the racial paradigm but a large, perhaps infinite, number.[28]

The risk, then, to conceptualizing races in terms of relationships is that it creates the illusion that racial identities possess an internal stability that does not actually exist. The categories White and non-White do not function as shifting counterbalances on a steady scale; instead, racial construction is complex and volatile precisely because society in all its heterogeneity is forced into a myriad of false binary forms. Consider, for example, the insertion of Asians into the White/Black system of racial meanings in the wake of the recent Los Angeles riots. There, Asians-as-victims-of-Black-violence came to stand in for Whites in the racial semiotics of Los Angeles, but Asians-as-victims-of-crimes were Black for the purposes of police protection in that same semiotics.[29] More than simply contradicting itself, this binary construction forecloses an examination of the ways in which Asians and Blacks have been racialized against each other, rather than simply each in contrast to Whites, and impedes as well the conceptualization of Asians as members of diverse communities with particular histories. The binary form of racial construction produces an inherently incoherent system of racial meanings that distorts and hides the underlying heterogenous reality of life in U.S. society. Nevertheless, it is within this diacritical meaning system that White identity has been defined.

The prerequisite cases defined Whites by exclusion, by who was not White, rather than by adducing an independent definition of "white persons." More pertinent to our exploration of the content of Whiteness, these cases established relational differences not simply or even most importantly in physical terms, but rather in terms of supposed cultural and behavioral differences. As Jayne Lee argues, "racial classifications do their most important work not as objective arrangements of physical differences, but as loci for a series of beliefs and judgements about the nature of the people within those categories. The notion of heritable physical traits becomes an abbreviation for heritable moral and cultural qualities."[30] The significance of the prerequisite cases thus lies not so much in the morphological distinctions they proffered as in their normative claims regarding racial difference. In the terms used in the prerequisite cases, Whites are civilized, capable of republican government, and deserving of citizenship; non-Whites are savage, fit subjects of despotism, and perpetual aliens. In this relational construction, Whites fashioned themselves as the superior opposite to those constructed as others. White identity implicitly existed as the positive mirror image to the explicit negative identities imposed on non-Whites. In our day, these contrasting dualities remain. Whites continue to be defined, and to define themselves, as the positive opposite to minorities, even with respect to citizenship and alienage.[31]

The content of White identity, we might conclude, is largely a compilation of positive myths that celebrate imagined virtues and conceal real failings. Whiteness is a chimera. Caution, however, must be exercised here. This self-fashioned quality of Whiteness has spurred some commentators to suggest that Whiteness is nothing more than mythical, nothing other than chimerical, that there is *no* content to Whiteness. In his book *Towards the Abolition of Whiteness,* historian David Roediger puts this point forcefully: "It is not merely that whiteness is oppressive and false; it is that whiteness is *nothing but* oppressive and false. . . . Whiteness describes, from Little Big Horn to Simi Valley, not a culture, but the absence of culture. It is the empty and therefore terrifying attempt to build an identity based on what one isn't and on whom one can hold back."[32] Under this conception, Whiteness is utterly empty of content, existing only in its exclusion of others. In *White Women, Race Matters: The Social Construction of Whiteness,* Ruth Frankenberg echoes this reasoning: "Within the dualistic discourse on culture, whiteness can by definition have no meaning: as a normative space, it is constructed precisely by the way in which it positions others at the borders."[33] Contrast these views of Whiteness with Roediger's assertion that Blacks exist as a constructed race, and that Blackness exists as a culture forged out of the bitter experience of life in America. "We speak of African American culture and community, and rightly so. Indeed, the making of disparate African ethnic groups into an African American people . . . is a genuine story of an American melting pot."[34] For Roediger, Blackness retains some actual content even after the myth of race has been stripped away, but Whiteness does not.

Races clearly exist in terms of fabricated attributes and failings. These aspects of identity, whether positive or negative, are ontologically empty. In this sense Roediger correctly describes Whiteness as utterly false. Like racial divisions themselves, characterizations of races are only ideologically meaningful. Yet in another sense, these characterizations are real, exactly because they exist as a powerful ideology about the world that has profoundly sculpted social geography. In peoples' subjective conceptions of themselves and others, insubstantial racial stereotypes take on concrete form. Many Whites believe themselves inherently civilized, capable of republican government, and deserving of citizenship; many also believe in the perpetual foreignness of non-Whites. Moreover, these beliefs lead to action, thereby giving them material form in the distribution of wealth and legal rights, not least in the enactment of racially restrictive naturalization laws. Race is only an idea, but it is an implacable one whose material effects pervade and predominate all social relationships. Roediger is correct that Whiteness has been constructed as a series of myths about Whites and non-Whites. He is wrong, however, in thinking that White identity is therefore empty: These myths form part of the content of White identity because people believe and act as if they are, and because our social landscape looks as if they are.

Whiteness has content in another sense as well, one often stressed by Whites themselves. White identity is constructed not just as the antonym to the identity of non-Whites, but also as an Americanized amalgamation of European ethnic cultures. American culture is thoroughly mestizo, an indivisible, uneven mixture of the cultures brought by each of the groups now in this country, European and non-European. Yet within this mixture, the remnants of European cultures, however influenced by the non-White customs of the United States, remain not only discernible, but central to the self-conception of many Whites. Richard Alba notes in *Ethnic Identity: The Transformation of White America* that "two-thirds of whites present themselves in terms of an ethnic identity, and about half view their ethnic backgrounds as of moderate importance."[35] This is not to say that Whites live according to specific European cultures or within certain ethnic communities. Compelling evidence suggests that European ethnic group boundaries do not constitute important lines of social division among Whites. Using marriage as a barometer of social integration, it is noteworthy that in 1980 "three of every four marriages of whites involved some degree of ethnic boundary crossing," but in that same year "only 0.1 percent of non-Hispanic whites had married blacks."[36] The dividing lines in our society continue to be drawn between races, not ethnic groups. Nevertheless, European ethnic identity remains important to many Whites. There has emerged among Whites, in Alba's estimation, "a new ethnic group . . . one based on ancestry from *anywhere* on the European continent."[37] Alba argues that these "European Americans" come together through a shared subjective "presumption of some commonality in the experiences of the descendants of immigrants from widely varying European societies."[38]

The existence of a community predicated on European heritage provides a separate source for White identity, one apparently not dependent on the construction of Whiteness as the opposite to non-Whiteness. However, the recent construction of a European-American identity in fact functions as part of the elaboration of an identity based on the double negative of not being non-White. During the first third of this century social status in the United States turned strongly on particular European ethnic identities, but the importance of inter-European ethnic differences declined precipitously during and after the Depression. The resurgent emphasis on White ethnic identities now evident coincided with and came in response to the civil rights movement. It was an effort by Whites to articulate some basis for solidarity not explicitly racial, but still racially determined.[39] As even Alba notes, "the European-American identity provides a way for whites to mobilize themselves, bridging what were once their own ethnic divisions, in opposition to the challenges of non-European groups."[40] It is here, as a means of opposing non-Whites, that we must locate the rise of the new White ethnics. Most Whites entertain a subjective belief in their commonality based on descent from European immigrants; however, this pan-European heritage is significant only insofar as it contrasts with that of non-Europeans, that is, non-Whites. It is difficult to discern any difference between the new European-American solidarity and old-fashioned White solidarity. The differences between the two seem even more minimal if "whites" are defined, as Alba suggests they should be, as "the descendants of European immigrants."[41] The construction of a European ethnic identity gives Whiteness a content still largely bound to notions of superiority. Whiteness continues to exist primarily as an identity constructed in opposition to that imposed on racial minorities, even when it is fashioned in terms of European identity.

Positive White Identity and Race Blindness

Having examined the transparency of Whiteness and the content of White identity, it remains to explore the implications of these observations for White race-consciousness. How can the dynamics of self-blindness and superiority be overcome? One suggestion is to develop a race-consciousness centered on the elaboration of a positive White racial identity. Another alternative, one which has intuitive appeal as well as some current popularity in the form of color-blindness, is to eschew any race-consciousness whatsoever on the grounds that races are harmful fictions. Though there is something to be said for these suggestions, in this section I examine and ultimately reject both of them. In the next section I advocate a third approach, the development of a White race-consciousness predicated on rejecting Whiteness.

Barbara Flagg argues for making a conscious attempt to develop a "positive White racial identity," where "positive" is apparently used in the sense of "laudatory." She writes that "reconceptualizing white race consciousness means doing the hard work of developing a positive white racial identity,"[42] and refers to "the development of a healthy white racial identity"[43] as well as to "the development of a positive white racial identity that does not posit whites as superior to blacks."[44] However, fashioning a laudatory White identity seems both a redundant and a dangerous proposition in the current social context. The dominant racial discourse already fashions Whites as the superior opposite to non-Whites; an uncritical celebration of positive White attributes might well reinforce these established stereotypes. At the same time, because races are constructed diacritically, celebrating Whiteness arguably *requires* the denigration of Blackness. Celebrating Whiteness, even with the best of antiracist intentions, seems likely only to entrench the status quo of racial beliefs.

It may be, however, that Flagg does not mean to use "positive" in a laudatory manner, but only in the more limited sense of "real" or "explicit." In this way, a "positive" White identity would contrast with a "transparent" one; it would denote a self-conscious rather than a subconscious racial identity. Flagg's usage of "positive" allows either interpretation. She seems to use "positive" as a synonym for "explicit," for example, when she calls for "the development of a positive white racial identity, one that comprehends whiteness not as *the* (unspoken) racial norm, but as just one racial identity among many."[45] In this more limited sense, there is much to be said for developing a positive White identity. A self-conscious recognition by Whites of the relevance to their lives of racial identity and racial privilege is an important, even an essential, first step in any effort to alter the racial meaning systems tying White and Black identity together. Nevertheless, even when used in this more limited sense, the call for Whites to develop a positive/self-conscious White identity remains problematic in the light of current racial dynamics, and still threatens to entrench the status quo.

Perhaps with great care a self-conscious White identity could be elaborated in a manner that did not unduly laud Whites or denigrate minorities. For example, an ever-present awareness of the way in which Whiteness has been constructed and a keen concern for the dangers implicit in celebrating Whiteness might permit one to avoid these pitfalls. A positive White identity that, while race-based, nevertheless carefully emphasized characteristics not usually associated with racial superiority might not be harmful to minorities, and might even lead to a "happily cacophonous universe" where, in the words of Patricia Williams, "white is white and white is good, and black is good and black is really black."[46] Yet, as Williams warns, even with great care we may not be able to construct this happy universe without a debilitating racialized struggle over what is good.[47] Moreover, in the course of such a struggle, we might only come to recognize that, given the inextricable relationships of meaning binding White and Black, it is impossible to separate an assertion of White goodness from the implication of Black badness. Frantz Fanon gives some indication of how deeply Blackness is tied to badness and Whiteness to goodness:

> In Europe, the black man is the symbol of Evil. . . . The torturer is the black man, Satan is black, one talks of shadows, when one is dirty one is black— whether one is thinking of physical dirtiness or of moral dirtiness. It would be astonishing, if the trouble were taken to bring them all together, to see the vast number of expressions that make the black man the equivalent of sin. In Europe, whether concretely or symbolically, the black man stands for the bad side of the character. . . . Blackness, darkness, shadow, shades, night, the labyrinths of the earth, abysmal depths, blacken someone's reputation; and, on the other side, the bright look of innocence, the white dove of peace, magical, heavenly light.[48]

Tied into a double helix of good and bad, it may prove impossible to retain White and Black as racial terms absent their destructive normative meanings. No matter how carefully elaborated, White race-consciousness runs the high risk of furthering the ugly racial patterns of superiority and inferiority so painstakingly fashioned throughout our country's history.

Consider Flagg's proposal that every White decision-maker combat transparency by "labeling herself and her community's existing standards as white whenever possible."[49] This modest proposal does not call for the creation of a laudatory White identity, but aims only at overcoming the tendency of Whites not to see themselves in racial terms. Even so, the risks of contributing to existing racial stereotypes are manifold. For example, how would a judge's constant proclamation of her own Whiteness be understood? Would it be heard as a neutral, nonderogatory statement of fact, or as an acknowledgement of an important socially constituted identity? Perhaps some would hear it in one of these ways; however, it seems likely that others would infer from this a jarring racial pride on the part of the judge, one that implicitly tied her abilities and social position to her Whiteness. Or, suppose the judge said instead that her goal was fairness for criminal defendants, and she identified this goal as somehow a White "community standard." Would her remark be understood as a thoughtful qualification highlighting the extent to which notions like "fairness" may be culturally relative? Again, it seems more likely that such a discordant comment would suggest to many listeners that the judge harbors suspicions about the commitment of non-Whites to fairness, judicial or otherwise. For Whites even to mention their racial identity puts notions of racial supremacy into play, even when they merely attempt to foreground their Whiteness. Such notions would be inescapable if Whites identified not only their race, but also its supposed positive attributes. As a result of the hierarchical relationship between Whiteness and non-Whiteness, articulating a positive White identity would inevitably support notions of White superiority and buttress rumors of minority inferiority, whether positive is used to mean "laudatory" or only "explicit."

This suggests, perhaps, that all talk of racial categories should be abandoned. If the words "White" and "Black" cannot be spoken without conjuring up destructive racial stereotypes, perhaps these terms should not be used at all. There are, in addition, other reasons for abandoning talk of race. For example, racial terms bolster the false belief in the existence of races. Not surprisingly, scholars on both the left and the right have argued that because racial terms rely on the false idea of race and are tied to injurious conceptions of human worth, rejecting the entire concept provides the best mechanism for eradicating racism. To use "left" and "right" loosely, Anthony Appiah argues from the left that "to maintain the terminology of difference is to make possible the continuance of . . . racism, which has usually been the basis for treating people worse than we otherwise might, for giving them less than their humanity entitles them to."[50] From the right, Lewis Killian insists that the word "race" should be struck from our lexicon because it reflects "bad thinking," and that since races do not exist, neither should legal schemes of racial remediation such as affirmative action or employer set-asides.[51] The prerequisite cases might be seen as supporting these sorts of arguments. These cases demonstrate the arbitrariness of racial divisions, as well as the injustices that are perpetrated in reliance on them. Many readers may see the prerequisite cases as the paradigmatic example of why all talk of racial differences, good or bad, should be rejected.

The argument that all talk of race should end, labeled here an argument for "race-blindness," can be understood as an amplification of the argument for color-blind constitutionalism, the insistence that government should never take race into account. In its most extreme form, race-blindness amplifies color-blindness by forbidding not just race-based decisions, but all reference to race, and by extending its prohibitions not just to government, but to all members of society. As ideals, both race-blindness and color-blindness have intuitive appeal. Given the falsity of racial categories, the injustices such categorization has facilitated, and the social divisiveness engendered by racial politics, perhaps our society would be a better place without races, even if this came at the expense of the social diversity the belief in racial differences has fostered. As an ideal, a society without racial divisions is appealing. However, as *methods* for achieving that ideal, race-blindness and color-blindness must be resoundingly rejected. To understand this, consider the basic flaws and perversities that lie at the heart of color-blindness as applied.

Color-blind constitutionalism has been widely criticized on a number of grounds. Justice Harry Blackmun, however, posed perhaps the simplest and most telling critique: "In order to get beyond racism, we must first take account of race. There is no other way."[52] Just so here: In order to get beyond racial beliefs, we must first be race-conscious. This is the basic flaw of color-blindness as a method of racial remediation. Race will not be eliminated through the simple expedient of refusing to talk about it. Race permeates our society on both ideological and material levels. It is irrelevant that there is no transhistorical reality underlying races. The absence of an objective basis for racial distinctions, so readily apparent in the prerequisite cases, does not mean that ignoring race or refusing to discuss it will make racial divisions go away. Socially constructed racial divisions dominate the conceptual and socioeconomic landscape of the United States and constitute an essential element of American world view and social structure. Race is part of the fabric of American life. Refusing to speak of race would not dislodge the racial beliefs with which we each have been socialized; neither would it alter the material status quo, which is the direct product of those beliefs.

Rather—and here is the perversity of color-blindness—to banish race-words redoubles the hegemony of race by targeting efforts to combat racism while leaving race and its effects unchallenged and embedded in society, seemingly natural rather than the product of social choices. If all mention of race, whether White or Black, remedial or discriminatory, is equally suspect, the reality of racial subordination is obscured and immunized from intervention.[53] This is the unfortunate reality of color-blindness as applied. Under this approach, the Supreme Court strikes down principally those government actions aimed at racial remediation, because only such laws refer to race explicitly. In *Richmond v. J. A. Croson Co.* (1989), for example, the Court relied on color-blind constitutionalism to dismantle an ameliorative employer set-aside scheme in the old capital of the Confederacy because this remedy specifically referred to race.[54] At the same time, the Court allows to stand state action taken with clearly racist intent, so long as such action is couched in race-free language. In *Presley v. Etowah County Commission* (1992), for instance, the Court found no Voting Rights Act violation where White commissioners in two Alabama counties greatly diminished the decision-making authority of each individual county commissioner immediately after the election of the first Black, because they did so without ever directly mentioning race.[55] In one county, the commissioners shifted the newly integrated commission's duties to an appointed administrator. In the other, the power of the individual commissioners was transferred to the commission as a whole voting by majority rule.[56] As in these counties, White power is easily and now perhaps principally maintained without any overt reference to race. And as in these cases, color-blindness renders such power maintenance unassailable. Rejecting all talk of race would produce comparable effects across society. Under race-blindness, the language necessary to remake racial ideology could not be used, since such language would necessarily refer to race. Meanwhile, race-blindness would not challenge the continuation, extension, and innovation of new patterns of discrimination, so long as these patterns did not explicitly make distinctions on racially impermissible bases.

Race-blindness ironically targets not the harmful effects of racism, but the efforts to ameliorate such harms. In this way, race-blindness threatens the gains racial minority groups have recently made not only in law, where color-blindness has already significantly weakened the force of re-medial legislation, but in popular culture as well. People of color in the United States have long affirmed their own worth in racial terms, re-sponding to their racial marginalization by fighting for a better life along lines of racial exclusion. This is the story of the Japanese community in the United States organizing to support Takao Ozawa's petition for nat-uralization; it is the story of every minority civic group or church. Race-blindness threatens these organizations and accomplishments by disal-lowing race-based action or pride. Race-blindness is perverse: Although it purports to combat racial stereotypes, it actually leaves racist beliefs in-tact and attacks instead the efforts to challenge and remake those beliefs.

The struggle against the pernicious effects of race must take place within the context, and using the language, of racial beliefs as currently constructed. To refuse to discuss this already-constituted reality is not to escape it. Indeed, even the refusal to discuss race carries powerful racial meanings. In our race-conscious society, the act of enforcing racelessness is itself a racial act, one in which, as Neil Gotanda argues, race must first be recognized in order to be ignored.[57] Further, race-blindness is a racial act to the extent that it maintains the status quo, thus serving certain racial group interests and not others. Finally, race-blindness is racialized insofar as its appeal turns on transparency. Race-blindness suits best those who are already accustomed to never thinking about themselves and their social position in racial terms. For people whose self-identity is closely linked with a racial label, on the other hand, race-blindness entails a much more significant psychic dislocation.[58] Race constitutes a funda-mental, inescapable element of our society and imagination. Any new racial theory or praxis cannot ignore the extant racialization of all social relations, both material and conceptual.[59] Of course, because the extant language of race carries within it the very structures of oppression we hope to dismantle, using this language threatens to enmesh us in its reifi-cation.[60] Thus, the fight for equality must rely on and at the same time re-make the discourse of inequality; it must "necessarily be caught up in the very metaphysical categories it hopes finally to abolish."[61] To challenge the current deployment of racial ideas, we must be race-conscious in the sense of grappling with those ideas, for only by explicitly contesting racial meanings can the pervasive social beliefs in races and their attendant characteristics be altered. There is no other way.

The development of a positive or merely self-conscious White racial identity unavoidably reinforces the existing myths of White supremacy.

Paradoxically, abandoning all talk of race achieves virtually the same result, leaving the myths of supremacy intact while targeting minority efforts to rehabilitate their identities. Neither strategy will lead to the amelioration of racial injustice, and both should be eschewed.

At this point, however, some readers may feel that at some level I want it both ways, that I criticize as destructive the articulation of a positive White identity, and at the same time fault race-blindness for preventing the development of positive minority identities. If recognizing Whiteness is problematic because it entrenches the idea that races exist, the critique might go, then celebrating minority identities must pose the same danger. Moreover, if all racial identities are constructed relative to one another, then the elaboration of *any* laudatory racial identity, White or Black, necessarily threatens to denigrate the racial identity of others, at least by implication.

There exists some truth to the first objection: Black pride, like White identity, can rely uncritically on the notion of natural races, and thereby reify racial categories. As one example of this reification in action, many African Americans, in order to maintain a race-based pride in being "Black," refuse to acknowledge the magnitude of intermixture between persons of European and African descent in the United States. In her article *Passing for White, Passing for Black,* Adrian Piper notes the reluctance among many Blacks to "explore their white ancestry—approximately 25 percent on average for the majority of blacks," though she is sympathetic to this reaction.

> For some, of course, acknowledgment of this fact evokes only bitter reminders of rape, disinheritance, enslavement, and exploitation, and their distaste is understandable. But for others, it is the mere idea of blackness as an essentialized source of self-worth and self-affirmation that forecloses the acknowledgment of mixed ancestry. This, too, is understandable: Having struggled so long and hard to carve a sense of wholeness and value for ourselves out of our ancient connection with Africa after having been actively denied any in America, many of us are extremely resistant to once again casting ourselves into the same chaos of ethnic and psychological ambiguity that our diaspora to this country originally inflicted on us.[62]

Piper powerfully suggests that important differences exist in the sources and functions of Black and White racial identity, even as she confirms that racial pride, whatever the race involved, cannot help entrenching the notion that races exist. In this, White and Black pride are equally suspect.

However, because races are relationally constructed not in a vacuum but, as Piper's comments emphasize, in the social context of domination and subordination, the objection that minority pride may denigrate Whites in the same way White pride harms minorities is wrong. The development of laudatory minority identities need not result in a derogation of Whites. Indeed, the development of positive race-based minority identities may be a necessary first step in deconstructing races, particularly Whiteness.

To see this, compare the slogans "Black is Beautiful" and "White is Beautiful." Asserting that "White is Beautiful" restates the accepted truth about races, confirming standards of attractiveness and worth that already place Whites at the top and non-Whites at the bottom. In extolling Whiteness, this phrase resonates with the current construction of race, confirming the stereotypes of White superiority and minority inferiority. In contrast, the conscious celebration of racial identity by people of color works against the dominant construction of race. Proclaiming that "Black is Beautiful" destabilizes racial myths by drawing into question the stereotypes regarding minorities *and* Whites. The pejorative connotations of the various descriptors assigned to supposedly Black physical features—thick lips, kinky hair, dark skin—are all challenged by the assertion that these features are beautiful rather than ugly. Simultaneously, the positive connotations associated with purportedly White features—blue eyes, blond hair, fair skin—are destabilized by the assertion of Black attractiveness inasmuch as such assertions force the recognition that physical beauty is not exclusively embodied by White features. Like so much else in U.S. society, standards of attractiveness are not neutral in terms of race, but instead have been racialized in a hierarchical fashion which places Whites and White attributes at the top. In this context, positive minority identities differ remarkably in their political implications from a positive White identity. Positive minority identities call into question the core notions of racial identity.

This is true not only in terms of physical (really social) beauty, but along the entire spectrum of racial semiotics. Thus, in the prerequisite cases, the common knowledge of race was shaken when dark-skinned people were portrayed as citizens rather than as aliens. This portrayal upset the dominant rhetoric of difference by challenging the fundamental notions of insider and outsider routinely applied to dark- and light-skinned people. This is also true in more contemporary terms, for example in the dynamics of supposed Black criminality and White innocence. Consider here Richard Ford's explanation for the animus of the race-mob in Howard Beach:

> [The] three unarmed Black men [who became lost in Howard Beach] threatened to undo the very concept of white that so occupies the imagination of Europe and America that it blots out everything else. The threat that the Black Other brings to white space is not that more houses will be robbed but that the crime rate will *not* rise in their presence—that they will actually come and go peacefully and without incident. This would be the greatest catastrophe because then it would be inescapably revealed that whites rob the homes of other whites, that white men rape white women, that the evils of white society are attributable to whites, and ultimately that whites do not exist because the defining characteristic of whiteness—innocence and purity—is a phantasm.[63]

Characterizing Blacks as innocent challenges the dominant stereotype of Black criminality and, as importantly, concomitantly forces a more honest appraisal of White innocence.[64] Given the powerfully negative characterizations of minorities and the equally powerful positive depictions of Whites, asserting that Black is beautiful may be, for however mundane, one of the most fruitful strategies available for combatting the current construction of race. This potential for challenging the racial status quo distinguishes the development of celebratory non-White as opposed to White identities and justifies the development of positive minority identities even where these further entrench the deeply buried notion of race. Though the reification of race is always deleterious, the harms of a continuing racial hierarchy are much greater.

Dismantling Whiteness

Current systems of racial meaning define Whites and non-Whites in hierarchical relationship to each other, giving Whiteness a content directly tied to the identities imputed to minorities. Elaborating a laudatory or merely self-conscious White identity without further entrenching these systems of meaning seems impossible, while simply ignoring race similarly leaves the racialized structures of our society intact and in fact immunized from disturbance. A third alternative is to dismantle the meaning systems surrounding Whiteness. For those constructed as White, dismantling Whiteness would allow them to know themselves and others directly, or at least without having to look through the distorting lens of White superiority. For society as a whole, dismantling the ideology of Whiteness would be a key step towards racial justice.

An unquestioning acceptance of one's own Whiteness is supremely alienating. Whiteness exists as a pole around which revolve imaginary racial meanings. As a category, it depends on a demonization of non-Whites so that by comparison Whites are deified. The self-conception of individual Whites, then, often depends upon these revolving meanings, this other-demonization and self-deification. Whiteness becomes in this way not something transparent, but something opaque that occludes what lies behind one's own racial identity and the racial identities of others.[65] Never questioning one's White identity precludes knowing those categorized as non-White because the mythology of inferior non-White identities cannot fully be comprehended or transcended without interrogating the superior characteristics attributed to Whites. Accepting one's White identity without examination makes it impossible fully to know non-Whites outside the terms of superiority and inferiority dictated by racial categorization. This is so, and perhaps even more true, even if one does not know one's self in explicitly racial terms—that is, as a White person—but rather only in terms of specific attributes, for example, as fair, honest, hard-working, concerned, and so on. These attributes, while superficially unrelated to race, are in fact strongly associated with racial identity. Knowing one's self only in these terms without recognizing the central role of race in constructing positive and negative identities further entrenches the meaning systems of racial categorization and thus makes it even more difficult to transcend those systems in one's conception of non-Whites. Through the same process, but conversely, internalizing a White identity distorts the identity of others perceived as White. Again, the dominant narratives of race will supply the terms in which others are known, terms that automatically shroud other Whites with positive identities. Finally, uncritically accepting a White identity requires the burial of one's own identity. Whiteness requires constructing oneself not in terms of the failings and virtues that all people share, but in the mythical terms decreed by Whiteness. The unquestioned embrace of Whiteness alienates one from others, non-Whites and Whites alike, and from oneself. Claiming a White identity creates an uncrossable divide within the self and an unbridgeable gulf between the self and others.[66]

Claiming a White identity additionally opens a deep chasm between the self and society. For Whiteness to remain a positive identity, it must remain free from taint. Thus, Whiteness can only retain its positive meanings through the denial at every turn of the social injustices associated with the rise and persistence of this racial category. The lines between races exist as axes of power and privilege that, while not the only such axes in our society, have nevertheless been key fault-lines for violence. Put more concretely, the diacritical construction of Whiteness and non-Whiteness took place first in the context of the dispossession of Native Americans and the enslavement of Africans, and subsequently in a long history of continued exploitation and oppression justified in racial terms. Arguably, racial systems persist today only to the extent races remain violent fault-lines in the distribution of social goods. Maintaining Whiteness as a source of identity requires that one deny the costs associated with Whiteness; it requires a refusal, that is, fully to engage with the history and condition of our society and of all those living in it without the safety of White identity. It requires complacency, and more, the continued participation in social inequity. James Baldwin emphasizes the moral disengagement required by Whiteness. Whites "have brought humanity to the edge of oblivion: because they think they are white. Because they think they are white, they do not dare confront the ravage and the lie of their history. Because they think they are white, they cannot allow themselves to be tormented by the knowledge that all men are brothers."[67] Baldwin's words have a fire to them that may sear too deeply and broadly. Nevertheless, there is an important truth to what he says. An unexamined acceptance of White identity requires the uncritical, perhaps unconscious, protection of that identity. It requires disengagement from society by forbidding consideration of the social ills Whiteness created and creates. Accepting without question and, more so, seeking to protect one's White identity requires a social engagement either aimed at entrenching the status quo or dedicated to tepid reform unlikely to affect racial differences. In either case, Whiteness is maintained by avoiding full involvement with society.

Reflecting critically on one's own Whiteness, on one's construction as a person at the center, as the privileged source of society's injustices, is the only way to span the racial divides created in the name of Whiteness. This is not to argue that Whites should deconstruct Whiteness out of some sense of guilt or responsibility. White complicity in the construction and maintenance of racial subordination is indisputable. At the same time, White anxiety about such complicity provides an important force in the formation of contemporary racial practices, in particular the practices of denial which assert that race is no longer a social scourge and that, whatever the sad history of past racism, contemporary society and in particular Whites today are not to be held responsible. Nevertheless, the goal in impugning White supremacy for the gross injustices it has perpetrated is not to induce or argue about White guilt.[68] Rather, it is to insist that those constructed as White stand to benefit from abandoning Whiteness. Self-consciously abandoning Whiteness is the only means by which Whites can know themselves, their place in society, and others. This knowledge, of course, must come at the high price of relinquishing the privileges of Whiteness and of acknowledging one's role in maintaining such privileges. These costs, however, are inseverably a part of self-knowledge, more an argument for than against abandoning Whiteness. "Whites must come to terms with their whiteness by recognizing, not their guilt and blameworthiness for racism past and present, but that which is much more difficult to face: their own idealized, self-fashioned identity as a narcissistic fantasy and nothing more."[69] Only by abandoning this fantastic identity can those currently constructed as White hope to understand themselves and others as people.

Beyond its existential importance, however, there is a far more pressing reason for the deconstruction of Whiteness. Whiteness exists as the linchpin for the systems of racial meaning in the United States. Whiteness is the norm around which other races are constructed; its existence depends upon the mythologies and material inequalities that sustain the current racial system. The maintenance of Whiteness necessitates the conceptual existence of Blacks, Latinos, Native Americans, and other races as tropes of inferiority against which Whiteness can be measured and valued. Its continuation also requires the preservation of the social inequalities that every day testify to White superiority. David Roediger asserts that "the questions of why people think they are white and of whether they might quit thinking so" are the "most neglected aspects of race in America."[70] These questions are also the most pressing aspects of race today. Racial equality may well be impossible until Whiteness is disarmed. Only the complete disassembly of Whiteness will allow the dismantlement of the racial systems of meaning that have grown up in our society over the past centuries and thus permit the end of racism and the emergence of a society in which race does not serve as a proxy for human worth. All who are interested in racial justice must concern themselves with remaking the bounds and nature of Whiteness, for this category stands at the vortex of race in America. However, Whites' assistance in this endeavor is particularly crucial, because they exercise the great bulk of the tremendous power necessary to construct and maintain Whiteness. The goal of White race-consciousness should be the disassembly of Whiteness.

How the meaning systems that constitute Whiteness might be altered, and what effect this would ultimately have on society, remain open questions. Whiteness is so deeply a part of our society it is impossible to know even whether Whiteness can be dismantled. Nevertheless, efforts to challenge Whiteness are already underway. Some such efforts are in the form of scholarship designed to force Whites to recognize their own racial identity. Thus, legal scholars have directly called upon Whites to overcome transparency, arguing that "Whites need to reject this privilege and to recognize and speak about their role in the racial hierarchy."[71] In this vein, Barbara Flagg offers White readers a set of questions calibrated to expose Whiteness.

> In what situations do you describe yourself as white? Would you be likely to include *white* on a list of three adjectives that describe you? Do you think about your race as a factor in the way other whites treat you? For example, think about the last time some white clerk or salesperson treated you deferentially, or the last time the first taxi to come along stopped for you. Did you think, "That wouldn't have happened if I weren't white"? Are you conscious of yourself as white when you find yourself in a room occupied only by white people? What if there are people of color present? What if the room is mostly nonwhite?[72]

For Whites, posing and honestly answering such ready-made questionnaires begins the process of dismantling Whiteness by bringing this identity into conscious view.

More direct efforts to challenge Whiteness have been undertaken outside of academia. One of the most intriguing is a periodical entitled *Race Traitor: A Journal of the New Abolitionism,* published under the slogan "Treason to Whiteness is Loyalty to Humanity." Dedicated to achieving racial justice through dismantling Whiteness, this journal offers specific pointers on how to be a "race traitor," defined as "someone who is nominally classified as white, but who defies the rules of whiteness so flagrantly as to jeopardize his or her ability to draw upon the privileges of white skin."[73] Among the suggestions:

> Answer an anti-black slur with, "Oh, you probably said that because you think I'm white. That's a mistake people often make because I look white."

And:

> The color line is not the work of the relatively small number of hard-core "racists"; target not them but the mainstream institutions that reproduce it.[74]

These suggestions, though somewhat wry, are also potentially racially revolutionary. Whiteness demands that all Whites denigrate, at least passively, those constructed as non-White. It is only through this iterated denigration, this constant reinforcement by Whites of the lines between "us" and "them," that the boundaries of Whiteness can be maintained. If enough seemingly White people were to reject such differentiation by claiming to be among the "them," the "us" at the base of White identity would collapse. By actively pursuing this agenda, *Race Traitor* represents the potential for deconstructing Whiteness. Perhaps more importantly, the advice proffered in *Race Traitor* also highlights the power of Whites to exercise choice with respect to their racial identity.

Choosing the Future

To many, it may seem that race is fate, in the sense that one is born into a race, and that there is little if anything to be done about it. Yet, taking seriously the notion that race is a social construction means accepting the idea that race in the United States, and one's own racial identity in particular, are partially products of the choices we make as a society and as individuals. "If race lives on today," Barbara Fields points out, "it does not live on because we have inherited it from our forbearers of the seventeenth century or eighteenth or nineteenth, but because we continue to create it today."[75] A race, once established in popular thought, does not take on a life of its own, independent from the surge of social forces. Instead, we continue to revitalize race at every moment, as a society, and, more pertinent to this discussion, as individuals. "Simone de Beauvoir wrote that one is not born a woman," Henry Louis Gates, Jr., has noted, adding "no, and one is not born a Negro."[76] Neither is one born White. Rather, one becomes White by virtue of the social context in which one finds oneself, to be sure, but also by virtue of the choices one makes. It is in this ability to choose, an admittedly constrained ability but one nonetheless always present, that Whites as individuals and as a community possess the power to dismantle Whiteness.

In order to see this, it may be helpful to use the terms chance, context, and choice to disaggregate the functioning of race in our daily lives.[77] Chance refers to features and ancestry, context to the contemporary social setting, and choice to quotidian decisions. In the workings of race, chance, context, and choice overlap and are inseverable. Nevertheless, these terms allow an analysis of race that focuses on the extent to which race is, and is not, a matter of volition.

Chance and context together largely define races. Chance encompasses features and ancestry in that we have no control over who our parents are or what we look like. Because of the importance of morphology and ancestry, chance may seem to occupy almost the entire geography of race. Certainly, for those who subscribe to biological notions of race, chance seems to account for virtually everything: One is born some race and not another, and therefore fated to a particular racial identity, with no human intervention possible. However, because race is socially constructed, the role of chance is actually minimal. In largest part, racial identity is not directly a function of features and ancestry, but rather of the context-specific meanings that attach to these elements of identity. Context is the social setting in which races are recognized, constructed, and contested; it is here that race gains its life. Within a social context, racial systems of meaning, although inconstant and unstable, are paramount in establishing the social significance of certain features, such as skin color, and of particular ancestries, for instance European. Context superimposed on chance largely defines racial identity in the United States.

Chance and context, however, are not racially determinative. Choice composes a crucial third ingredient in the construction of racial identities. Features and ancestry gain their racial significance through the manner in which they are read by social actors. Yet people exercise conscious choices with regard to their features and ancestry in order to alter the readability of their identity. In this respect, consider the popularity of hair straightening, blue contact lenses, and even facial surgery.[78] Or note that in 1990 alone $44 million was spent on chemical treatments to literally lighten and whiten skin through the painful and dangerous application of bleach.[79] In our highly racialized society, few people leave their looks to chance; we instead constantly seek to remake them in obeisance to the power of racial aesthetics. So too with ancestry. Ancestry seems to be a biological concept, yet it is instead largely a social one. If an individual drew a family tree back over a few hundred years, assuming that he or she was descended from each ancestor in only one way, it would have nearly a million branches at the top.[80] Identifying one's ancestry, then, involves a large degree of choice, where this choice turns at least partially on the social significance of one line of descent versus another. At the same time, decisions regarding mates, which can be understood as the prospective creation of lines of descent, are also heavily influenced by the racial status of the respective persons involved. Because the significance of ancestry and the status of prospective mates vary in racial terms, decisions in these areas become decisions about racial identity. Features and ancestry may seem to be securely in the province of chance, and their significance a function simply of context, but in fact race is also partially a matter of the choices people make.

Racial choices occur both on mundane and on epic levels. Perhaps the most graphic illustration of choice in the construction of racial identities comes in the context of "passing." The ability of some individuals to change race at will powerfully indicates the chosen nature of race. The majority of racial decisions, however, are of a much more mundane nature. Because race in our society infuses almost all aspects of life, many daily decisions take on racial meanings. For example, seemingly inconsequential acts like listening to country and western music or moving to the suburbs constitute means of racial (dis-)affiliation. So too do a myriad of other actions taken every day by every person, almost always without conscious regard for the racial significance of their choices. It is here, in deciding what to eat, how to dress, whom to befriend, and where to vacation, rather than in the dramatic decision to leap races, that most racial choices are rendered. These common acts are not racial choices in the sense that they are taken with a conscious awareness of their racial implications, or in the sense that these quotidian decisions by themselves can establish or change a person's racial identity. Racial choices must always be made from within specific contexts, where the context materially and ideologically circumscribes the range of available choices and also delimits the significance of the act. Nevertheless, these are racial choices, if sometimes only in their overtone or subtext, because they resonate in the complex of meanings associated with race. Given the thorough suffusion of race throughout society, in the daily dance of life we constantly make racially meaningful decisions.[81]

Drawing upon this conception of choice, the challenge for Whites committed to dismantling Whiteness can be broken down into three steps. First, Whites must overcome the omnipresent effects of transparency and of the naturalization of race in order to recognize the many racial aspects of their identity, paying particular attention to the daily acts that draw upon and in turn confirm their Whiteness. Second, they must recognize and accept the personal and social consequences of breaking out of a White identity. Third, they must embark on a daily process of choosing against Whiteness. For those who decide to dismantle Whiteness, these steps pose considerable difficulties. They must ask themselves to what extent their identity is a function of their race, how this racial self is constituted in daily life, and what choices they might make to escape the circular definition of the self implied in the unconscious acceptance of a racialized identity. Then they must make those choices. All of this will be supremely difficult and, unless many Whites undertake similar efforts, will probably also do little to dismantle Whiteness. Yet there is at least the promise of personal reconstruction, and there is also the optimism that springs not from the likelihood of eventual success but from the decision to resist.[82] Moreover, the possibility exists that ultimately Whiteness as now constituted might be ended. If the racial systems of meaning that tie Whites and non-Whites together into hierarchies of social worth are to be brought down, it will only be through choice and struggle.

Of course, it is not clear what sort of racial future would emerge if Whiteness is eventually dismantled. Perhaps the deconstruction of Whiteness would lead to a truly color-blind society by resulting in the collapse of all notions of race, thereby producing a future in which personal identities are no longer constructed in racial terms and the term "race" has no meaning. In such a universe, human variability would no longer be measured by reference to races, and every current manner of distinguishing people—for example, gender and class—would be radically transformed by the absence of a racial referent. Indeed, perhaps the complete elimination of Whiteness and races generally would work an even more profound change on our society. Howard Winant, a leading proponent of the social constructionist theory of race, offers an extreme evaluation of the implications of a totally raceless future:

> The five-hundred year domination of the globe by Europe and its inheritors is the historical context in which racial concepts of difference have attained their present status as fundamental concepts of human identity and inequality. To imagine the end of race is thus to contemplate the liquidation of Western civilization.[83]

However, it might be that deconstructing Whiteness does not portend the liquidation of civilization, or even the end of racial ideas. Perhaps without White supremacy race would continue to be socially relevant as a popular synonym for ethnicity or culture, simply another word in a vocabulary that recognizes and respects human diversity, with no one supposing that race constitutes a transhistorical identity. Winant, in a less apocalyptic moment, pictures a bright future in which race does not stand in for inequality:

> [W]e may have to give up our familiar ways of thinking about race once more. If so, there may also be some occasion for delight. For it may be possible to glimpse yet another view of race, in which the concept operates neither as signifier of comprehensive identity nor of fundamental difference, both of which are patently absurd, but rather as a marker of the infinity of variations we humans hold as a common heritage and hope for the future.[84]

Whatever the racial future, one thing is certain. The tightly wrought nature of Whiteness and non-Whiteness insures that such scenarios are very far off. In the meantime, we must begin the difficult process of fathoming the construction of Whiteness, in order better to choose against it.

7

The Value to Whites of Whiteness

The prerequisite cases provide an invaluable study in the construction of the White race and offer important insights into the structuring and content of Whiteness as a legal and social idea. These insights have prompted the argument that in the interest of racial justice Whites must adopt a race-consciousness that renounces the privileged construction of Whiteness. However, the prerequisite cases afford a variety of different readings. One interpretation in particular draws into question the likelihood of a self-deconstructive White race-consciousness. The cases can be read as an extended discourse on the tremendous value of Whiteness to Whites, suggesting that Whites are much more likely to embrace than dismantle their identity.

The prerequisite cases demonstrate that when confronted with the falsity of racial lines, many Whites—even those in the highest positions of public trust and under the greatest charge to do justice—will choose to entrench White identity and privilege rather than allow its destabilization. *Ozawa* and *Thind* confronted the Supreme Court with compelling evidence that the racial boundaries that defined Whites lacked objective meaning. In these cases the Court had the opportunity to call into question the very notion of a White race upon which the racial prerequisite to naturalization depended. Second-guessing historical actors, always fraught with danger, remains a scholarly necessity.[1] While it would be an obvious error to criticize the Court for failing to live by ideas and ideals unknown at the time, there is no such risk in suggesting that the Court could have followed the weight of precedent and refused to overturn Bhagat Singh Thind's naturalization. By so doing, the Court would have broadened and softened the parameters of Whiteness, rather than narrowing and rigidifying Whiteness as it did. But the Court preferred instead to shore up the fractured definition of Whiteness by embracing popular prejudice. While the Court's decision is intelligible on a number of levels, it is perhaps best understood as an expression of the value of

Whiteness to Whites. White identity provides material and spiritual as-
surances of superiority in a crowded society. We should thus not be too
surprised that the prerequisite courts clung to the notion of a fixed White
race, even when confronted by its falsity.

Contemporary evidence suggests that among Whites, White identity
continues to be highly valued. Despite its superficial transparency, Whites
widely continue to recognize the value of their own Whiteness. In *Two
Nations: Black and White, Separate, Hostile, Unequal*, Andrew Hacker
recounts the following: When White college students were asked what
sort of compensation they would expect should they have to endure the
remainder of their lives as someone suddenly made physically "Black"
but not otherwise changed, the majority "seemed to feel that it would not
be out of place to ask for $50 million, $1 million for each coming black
year."[2] Although this figure seems more metaphorical than accurate in its
roundness, it is a metaphor that testifies to the immense value Whites attach to White identity. But perhaps these students were far more accurate
than they could imagine in estimating the value of White identity. After
all, what would one pay to be accorded the differing treatment meted to
Whites as opposed to Blacks?

Adrian Piper has known both sides as a light-skinned Black woman. She
remarks of the difference looking White makes in the way one is treated:

> A benefit and disadvantage of looking white is that most people treat you
> as though you were white. And so, because of how you've been treated, you
> come to expect this kind of treatment, not, perhaps, realizing that you are
> being treated this way because people think you are white, but rather falsely
> supposing that you're being treated this way because people think you are
> a valuable person. So, for example, you come to expect a certain level of re-
> spect, a certain degree of attention to your voice and opinions, certain lib-
> erties of action and self-expression to which you falsely suppose yourself to
> be entitled because your voice, your opinion, and your conduct are valuable
> in themselves.[3]

Presumptions of worth accompany Whiteness. In her position between
Black and White, Piper is conscious of these presumptions in a way that
few Whites are. Having been both granted and stripped of personal worth
through changing evaluations of her race, Piper now perceives their operation clearly. In contrast, never experiencing their loss, most Whites
continue to falsely suppose presumptions of worth are accorded them because they are valuable in themselves, rather than because they are White.

There is at least one young White college student, however, who knows intimately the worth of Whiteness. Joshua Solomon, a student at the University of Maryland, recently took a semester off to relive the experiences of John Griffin, the White journalist who in 1959 darkened his skin and subsequently wrote *Black Like Me*.[4] Solomon too used drugs to change his skin pigmentation; then, when he thought himself suitably dark, he set off from Baltimore for Forsyth County, Georgia. His racial odyssey was short-lived. By the time he checked into a hotel in Gainesville, just short of Forsyth County and only two days after starting his trip, Solomon had given up his plan.

> When I got to the room, it hit me. I was sick of being black. I couldn't take it anymore. I wanted to throw up. . . . Now people acted like they hated me. Nothing had changed but the color of my skin. I went to the closet, pulled out my suitcase. After all of two days, the experiment was over. Maybe I was weak, maybe I couldn't hack it. I didn't care. The anger was making me sick and the only antidote I knew was a dose of white skin.[5]

Perhaps Solomon's experiences, like Piper's, are unique. But if they are exceptional, they are so only in the sense that few people come to know first-hand both the benefits of being White and the burdens of being Black.[6] What makes their experiences extraordinary is not that they have lived through the presumptions of worth and worthlessness that attach to racial identity per se, but that they have experienced both sets of presumptions.

Much later in his book, Hacker acknowledges the implausibility of the hypothetical posed to the White college students, a question impossible to answer since few Whites can truly imagine themselves Black. Even this implausibility, however, confirms the importance of Whiteness to Whites.

> No matter how degraded their lives, white people are still allowed to believe that they possess the blood, the genes, the patrimony of superiority. No matter what happens, they can never become "black." White Americans of all classes have found it comforting to preserve blacks as a subordinate caste: a presence, which despite all its pain and problems, still provides whites with some solace in a stressful world.[7]

Others echo this sense that Whiteness possesses a fundamental, inestimable value for Whites. In *Faces at the Bottom of the Well,* Derrick Bell writes:

> Black people are the magical faces at the bottom of society's well. Even the poorest whites, those who must live their lives only a few levels above, gain

their self-esteem by gazing down on us. Surely, they must know that their
deliverance depends on letting down the ropes. Only by working together
is escape possible. Over time, many reach out, but most simply watch, mes-
merized into maintaining their unspoken commitment to keeping us where
we are, at whatever cost to them or to us.[8]

Francis Lee Ansley similarly observes:

White supremacy is concretely in the interests of all white people. It assures
them greater resources, a wider range of personal choice, more power, and
more self-esteem than they would have if they were (1) forced to share the
above with people of color, and (2) deprived of the subjective sensation of
superiority they enjoy as a result of the societal presence of subordinate
non-white others.[9]

These excerpted assertions of the value of Whiteness to Whites are to
some extent oversimplified. They elide such important questions as how
racial ideology both benefits and disadvantages Whites, about how and
why race is experienced differently among Whites, and about how and
why some Whites actively oppose racial privilege.[10] Nevertheless, it seems
incontestable that, on the whole, Whites greatly value their racially superior identity.

The racial prerequisite cases make clear that Whiteness is a social artifact by highlighting both the failure of science to find any physical basis
for racial differentiation and also the ultimate importance of common
prejudice in the creation and maintenance of racial lines. The central role
law plays as both a coercive and ideological force in the construction of
race is also evident. The cases demonstrate as well that races are relational constructions, and that Whites have fashioned themselves as the
superior opposite to those denigrated others designated non-Whites.
They suggest too that Whites cannot know themselves, and that society
cannot overcome racism, until Whiteness is dismantled. But perhaps most
sadly of all, these cases may tell us that the tremendous value of Whiteness to Whites, a value still evident today, makes those constructed as
White unwilling to relinquish the privileges of Whiteness.

8

Colorblind White Dominance

The U.S. public and indeed many scholars are increasingly certain that the country is leaving race and racism behind. This reflects more than the modest belief that, at least if measured since 1954, race relations have improved. It is instead a claim that race and racism will soon disappear altogether—that they have little power in the lives of average Americans, and soon will have none. Some give credit to *Brown v. Board of Education* and the civil rights era, when activists, lawyers, and laws helped a broad social movement turn the nation away from segregation and toward equality. Others point to changing demographics, emphasizing the rising number of mixed-race marriages and the increasing Asian and Hispanic populations that are eroding the historic Black-White divide. My sense of our racial future differs. Not only do I fear that race will continue fundamentally to skew U.S. society over the coming decades, I worry that the belief in the diminished salience of race makes this more rather than less likely; relatedly, I suspect that law no longer contributes to racial justice but instead legitimates continued inequality.

Race as it is understood and practiced in the United States will change rapidly over the next few decades. Partly, this reflects the simple historical fact that racial ideas constantly mutate. Settler colonialism in North America gave rise to racial beliefs that justified the expropriation of land and the exploitation of humans, but while race since then has served consistently to rationalize hierarchy, racial beliefs themselves have been grounded variously in religion, color, nation, physical biology, eugenics, ethnicity, and, most recently, culture.[1] Only those who still understand race as primarily a natural phenomenon continue to suppose that notions of race remain relatively fixed. We should expect, however, particularly rapid change in today's regnant racial ideas. The United States is once again in the midst of a period of dramatic racial ferment. The current dynamism is sparked primarily by two racial dislocations directly rooted in the civil rights era: (1) the substantial decrease in the public acceptability of supremacist ideologies, and (2) the new demographics produced by altered immigration as well as intermarriage patterns.

Broad social support for explicit claims of racial superiority has all but ended, with large swaths of U.S. society now espousing a commitment to racial equality. This shift in the racial zeitgeist since the civil rights movement marks an important step toward a racially egalitarian society—but not its actual achievement, as racial hierarchy has continued. The persistence of racial subordination partly stems from the inertia of past patterns of systematic harm. But to avoid breaking down, racial hierarchy must also be newly produced and reproduced.[2] For those committed to preserving the racial status quo, the new spirit of widespread antiracism raises practical and ideological problems. On the former level, new methods of maintaining racial hierarchy that are not patently designed to foster subordination must be devised. The greater task, however, is ideational: new justifications must be elaborated to explain the otherwise striking contrast between our public commitments and our lived realities. The elaboration of practices and rationales that at once comport with the ideals of non-racialism but preserve and deepen racial inequality, I suggest, form one of the hallmarks of our current racial era.

Simultaneously, a demographic revolution is underway. The racial ethos of the civil rights era chipped away at the social prejudices regarding inter-group marriage, while civil rights reforms reopened immigration to groups previously excluded on racial grounds. Today, a mixed-race population that accounts for one out of every forty Americans has given rise to a multiracial movement that strongly—indeed, disproportionately, given its size—influences the U.S. racial imagination.[3] Meanwhile, Asian Americans represent the fastest growing immigrant group today, with a population that increased by over seventy percent during the 1990s.[4] The greatest source of demographic change, however, comes in the burgeoning Hispanic population. Latin Americans for several decades have composed the largest immigrant group in the United States, and this trend will continue, if not accelerate. The U.S. Latino population increased 58 percent between 1990 and 2000, and this group, the largest minority in the country, now accounts for more than one of every eight Americans.[5] A recent Newsweek estimate predicts that by 2100, one in three Americans will be Latino.[6]

Racial Futures

Given these ideological and demographic changes, how will race evolve? Four options are commonly put forth: White exceptionalism, which foretells whites remaining a racial overclass even as they become a numerical minority; Black exceptionalism, wherein Blacks continue as the primordial racial minority while other groups increasingly integrate; multiracialism, projecting that race will lose all salience as a form of hierarchy and will come to stand only for cultural differences; and Latin Americanization, which envisions continued but softened racial hierarchy engendered by a move away from the Black-White dichotomy and strict bioracial notions of difference and towards a racial continuum policed along socio-racial lines.[7]

White exceptionalism sees Whiteness continuing as the most powerful racial fault line. Under this vision of our racial future, racial hierarchy continues unabated and perhaps intensifies. Some attribute continued racial conflict to efforts by dominant groups to maintain racial privilege. Michael Lind, for instance, sees the emergence of a dominant White class that maintains its privileged position vis-à-vis non-Whites (and less well-off Whites) through its "near-monopoly of the private-sector and political branches of the American institutional elite" as well as by the creation and cooptation, through racial preferences, of minority elites.[8] Others see racial conflict continuing not because of efforts to retain privilege but because Whites will respond to perceived assaults by culturally inassimilable groups, mainly Hispanics. Samuel Huntington's most recent book decrying the threat posed by Latino immigrants to our supposed "core Anglo-Protestant culture" fits this mold, as do many others, such as Victor Hanson's *Mexifornia*.[9] Setting aside the important differences in these various strains, White exceptionalism has been the norm as a historical matter: since the seventeenth century, a "White" identity has been the linchpin to racial dominance in what would become the United States.

Black exceptionalism has two component claims: that Blacks are fundamentally different from other racial minorities, and that non-Black groups will gradually integrate. Put another way, this model posits that there will soon be effectively only two races, Blacks and non-Blacks. Nathan Glazer's recent scholarship typifies this sentiment: "The two nations of our America are the black and the white, and increasingly, as Hispanics and Asians become less different from whites from the point of view of residence, income, occupation, and political attitudes, the two nations become the black and the others."[10] Rather than locating the distinctive position of African Americans in retrograde notions of biological difference, proponents of Black exceptionalism often strike a tone of racially progressive concern, typically ruing the historic forces that so deeply subordinated Blacks. This analysis sometimes leads proponents of Black exceptionalism to support affirmative action and other remedies for past and on-going discrimination, at least for African Americans.[11] But it often seems that an equally—or sometimes more—central point for proponents of Black exceptionalism is that Latinos and Asians should be excluded from civil rights benefits because these groups allegedly have not suffered mistreatment as non-Whites on par with the subordination imposed on Blacks.[12] In this way, Black exceptionalism as often marks not concern for Blacks but hostility toward claims of racial discrimination by Asians and Hispanics.

Multiracialism sees us rapidly evolving toward a postracial society in which race is unmoored from status and demarcates not so much innate groups as loosely defined communities bound together primarily by cultural affinities. The "racial" in multiracialism parallels the "cultural" in multiculturalism: both posit an ideal world in which race is supplanted by culture and in which racial hierarchy, racism, prejudice, xenophobia, bigotry, and bias have ceased to operate, at least insofar as these rely on notions of innate biological differences of the sort currently understood as racial. Race-mixing—the intermarriage of persons from ostensibly different races and the resultant blending that occurs—holds out great promise, according to proponents of multiracialism. David Hollinger, for instance, extols the virtues of amalgamation (a word he prefers over miscegenation), while Roberto Suro enthuses over what he terms mixed doubles.[13] Many multiracialists also see favorable portents in Hispanic immigration, in the belief that in their racial heterogeneity Latinos already embody the postracial ideal, and will only push the United States in this direction more rapidly. Writing from Southern California and focusing on by far the largest Latino group, Gregory Rodriguez, for instance, claims that "[h]aving spent so long trying to fit into one side or the other of the binary system, Mexican Americans have become more numerous and confident enough to simply claim their brownness—their mixture. This is a harbinger of America's future."[14] Race as hierarchy, according to the basic claim advanced by multiracialists, will dissipate as the lines between putative racial groups are blurred.[15]

The *Latin Americanization* of race in the United States is a more likely short-term development, according to others. Race in Latin America purportedly differs from the U.S. version in two crucial respects: (1) rather than operating in terms of a sharp divide between White and Black, race functions along a continuum with gradations of racial difference, often coded in terms of skin color; and (2) race depends not solely on ancestry or morphology (bio-race), but also often reflects socioeconomic factors such as wealth, professional attainment, educational level, and so forth (socio-race). Like those who foresee multiracialism, those who predict an increased Latin Americanization of race see the United States being pushed in this direction by Latino immigrants, who theoretically not only bring with them a supposedly enlightened Latin American racial sensibility but also—along with mixed-race persons and the growing Asian population—increasingly destabilize the White-Black divide.[16]

Unlike the multiracialists, however, those who predict that the United States is moving toward a Latin American racial model do not anticipate the complete dissipation of race in the short to medium term. Race as hierarchy will continue, though along increasingly socio-racial lines, and with some softening. Even as they acknowledge continued inequality, Latin Americanists see a gradual amelioration in which socio-racial understandings operate to moderate the harsh stratification historically grounded in the United States along bio-racial lines. This easing, they expect, will extend as well to African Americans, facilitating their increased integration. Indeed, the racial status of many prominent Blacks often emerges as supposed evidence that the United States is already moving from a bio-racial to a socio-racial system, one in which ever more minorities function in society as if they were effectively White. Some expect this trend to herald the strong emergence of color as a basis for social ordering: the coding of skin tone and physical features as racially light or dark may increasingly replace membership in ordinal races such as African American or Asian as the primary basis for discriminatory treatment.[17] The Latin Americanization of race is not a phenomenon that pertains to Hispanics alone, but arguably will alter the categorical boundaries of all races, thereby gradually weakening racial subordination in the United States.

Colorblind White Dominance

In contrast to these four visions of future racial dynamics, I believe instead that we are headed toward a hierarchy of *colorblind White dominance.* This looming racial paradigm has three central elements, which I discuss in turn: (1) continued racial dominance by Whites; (2) an expansion of who counts as White along socio-racial rather than bio-racial lines; and (3) a colorblind ideology that simultaneously proclaims a robust commitment to antiracism yet works assiduously to prevent effective racial remediation. To be sure, there will be significant regional differences in the evolution of race in the United States, but racial politics is now sufficiently national that I expect colorblind White dominance to provide the basic framework for race relations throughout the country.[18]

White racial dominance. I use the term "dominance" in contradistinction to "supremacy." "White supremacy," if understood to mean racial domination explicitly grounded in a theory of racial superiority, is largely over, though of course there remain pockets of White supremacist agitation as well as the possibility of recrudescence.[19] The rejection of White supremacy as rhetoric, however, has not been accompanied by an end to the dominant social, political, and financial position of Whites. The materiality of continued White privilege can be measured across many indices. In 2003, the real median income for non-Hispanic Whites was $48,000, but only $30,000 for African Americans.[20] The total poverty rate among African Americans was 24 percent and it was 22 percent for Hispanics, compared to 8 percent for Whites.[21] That same year, 20 percent of African Americans and 33 percent of Hispanics had no health insurance, while 11 percent of Whites were uninsured.[22] Discrepancies in incarceration rates are particularly staggering. There is currently a 28.5 percent chance an African-American man will spend some time in a state or federal prison during his lifetime, while the comparable figure for Whites is 2.5 percent. There are twelve states in which between 10 percent and 15 percent of African American adult men are incarcerated, while in ten states Latino men are thrown behind bars at rates five to nine times greater than White men.[23]

In presenting these statistics, I do not claim that all Whites are equally privileged by racism and racial hierarchy. While Whites as a group have long arrogated the resources of this country to themselves, from land to jobs to control over the government, industry, and military, deep class schisms divide White society.[24] Rather than belying the power of race, however, these internal rifts more likely reflect race's utility in palliating intra-group conflict among Whites. Racial ideology does not guarantee equality among Whites; it serves rather to mask and distract from gross inequalities that divide that group. That said, it remains the case that

Whites as a race (though not all Whites individually) have maintained their position at the social and material apogee for centuries—and the numbers above demonstrate the profound role race and White dominance continue to play in the organization of U.S. society. Despite predictions of race's demise, the great weight of social statistics point to continued White dominance.

The claim that White dominance is evaporating in the face of shifting demographics and the public espousal of civil rights platitudes ignores not only contemporary statistics but historical patterns as well. It's true that our population looks far different today than it did in 1965, let alone 1865. But demographic change has historically led only to shifts in where, not whether, racial lines are drawn. Today we may use "White" as shorthand for "racially dominant," but this requires that we recognize the inclusion of Germans as White in the 1840s through 1860s, the Irish in the 1850s through 1880s, and eastern and southern Europeans in the 1900s to 1920s.[25] It's also true that a leading rationale for racial inequality, the self-evident nature of White superiority, weakened dramatically over the twentieth century, especially during the civil rights era. But defeating a justification for hierarchy is not the same as toppling that hierarchy. Again, ideologies rationalizing White dominance have often undergone dramatic mutations, from religious doctrines contrasting Christians and heathens to Manifest Destiny to eugenics to, most recently, notions of cultural difference. The justificatory rhetoric of race, like the composition of the population, constantly changes, even as racial inequality consistently endures.

White dominance continues partly as a vestige of the past, but also because race and racism remain useful to powerful segments of U.S. society. The nation did not embrace the civil rights movement until the mid-1960s, and then grudgingly, only to see the country's mood turn firmly against substantive racial equality with President Richard Nixon's election in 1968. As a country, we enjoyed a very few years of civil rights reforms but continue to stagger under three decades and more of backlash aimed at preserving the basic parameters of a racial status quo itself built on the edifice of three centuries of White supremacy.[26] This backlash is testament to the fact that racial hierarchy remains profoundly in the material and status interests of those who can claim the mantle of Whiteness (whether as previously understood or as reconfigured). In access to country clubs and gated communities, in preferences for jobs and housing, in the moral certainty regarding one's civic belonging and fundamental goodness, in all of these ways and many more, being White affords advantages across the range of material and status divisions that mar our society. In seeking to disestablish race and racism, Fredrick Douglass's words are no less true today than when uttered against slavery: "Power concedes nothing without a demand. It never did and it never will."[27] Be assured: racial hierarchy continues as a measure of White power in our society. To change racial dynamics for the better will require, as it has in the past, concerted efforts between broad social movements and national elites, and probably in addition propitious historical circumstances conducive to change, such as war or economic boom times.[28] Neither demographics nor antiracist bromides by themselves will defeat the power race wields in our society.

White redefined. Though White dominance will continue, what will likely change is how Whiteness—or, better, membership in the racially dominant group—is defined. The term "White" has a far more complicated history in the United States than people commonly recognize. For most of this country's history, Whiteness stood in contradistinction to the non-White identities imposed upon Africans, Native Americans, the Mexican peoples of the Southwest, and Asian immigrants. On this level, from the earliest years of this country Whiteness marked one pole in the racial hierarchy. Simultaneously, however, White served more as a marker of a shared color than as an indicia of a shared race among European groups, where until recently putatively "racial" divisions among Europeans were supremely important in marking social positions in U.S. society. Only in the first half of the twentieth century was "White" transformed into a relatively monolithic and undifferentiated group encompassing all persons of European descent in the United States.[29] As with justifications for racial hierarchy, the ideas surrounding racial categories—and the boundaries of Whiteness in particular—have shown a remarkable fluidity that seems likely to continue in the immediate future.

It seems increasingly that some Hispanics, Asians, Native Americans, and African Americans are migrating into the White category. This trend may mark a radical disjuncture in racial logic. While the melding of various European groups into the racially dominant category "White" effectuated tremendous changes in prevailing racial ideologies, these shifts nevertheless comported with the underlying belief that the most basic racial divisions exist between continental populations. For however unsupportable, the continental theory of races—Whites from Europe, Blacks from Africa, and Asians from Asia—has long served as one of the most enduring and popular understandings of race. This conception, however, cannot accommodate the incorporation of Reds, Yellows, and Blacks identified with America, Asia, and Africa into the White category linked to Europe. In this sense, the expansion of a White identity to include members of these groups may portend not just a broadening of Whiteness, but a change in its basic conceptualization. Whether this change is more fundamental than previous ones is not clear, though. The social certainty regarding the racial distinctiveness of southern and eastern European immigrants at the turn of the twentieth century, "beaten men from beaten races, representing the worst failures in the struggle for existence" in the words of the times, may have been no less great than the current (eroding) conviction that, for instance, Asians aren't White.[30] In any event, who counts as racially dominant has long been an evolving construct—and seems poised to shift anew.

Perhaps we should distinguish here between three sorts of White identity. Consider first those "passing as White." There have always been persons who racially pass—persons who, because their physical appearance allows them to, hold themselves out as members of a group to which by social custom they would not be assigned on the basis of their ancestry.[31] In contrast to this liminal group, we might think of some persons as "fully White," in the sense that, with all of the racially relevant facts about them widely known, they would generally be considered White by the community at large (consistent with a social constructionist understanding, racial identity turns not on particular criteria per se, but on the establishment of and the significance given such elements by community norms). Of persons of Irish and Jewish descent in the United States, for example, one might say that while initially some were able to pass as White, now they are fully White.[32]

Unlike both those passing as White and those fully White, however, a new group is emerging, persons perhaps best described as "honorary Whites." Apartheid South Africa first formally crafted this identity: seeking to engage in trade and commerce with nations cast as inferior by apartheid logic, particularly Japan, South Africa extended to individuals from such countries the status of honorary Whites, allowing them to travel, reside, relax, and conduct business in South African venues otherwise strictly "Whites only."[33] Persons who pass as White hide racially relevant parts of their identity; honorary Whites are extended the status of Whiteness despite the public recognition that, from a bio-racial perspective, they are not fully White.

In the United States, an honorary White status seems increasingly to exist for certain persons and groups whose minority identity seems un-equivocal under current racial schemas, but who are nevertheless extended a functional presumption of Whiteness.[34] The quintessential example would be certain Asian American individuals and communities, particularly East Asians. Asians have long been racialized as non-White in the United States as a matter of law and social practice; given high levels of immigration, this negative racialization, tied as ever to xenophobia, continues. Moreover, the continental theory places Asians securely among non-Whites. But despite these clear indicia of non-Whiteness, the model minority myth and professional success have combined to free some Asian Americans from the most pernicious negative beliefs regarding their racial character. This trend reveals in part a shift toward a more socio-racial system. Individuals and communities with the highest levels of acculturation, achievement, and wealth increasingly find themselves functioning as White, at least as measured by professional integration, residential patterns, and intermarriage rates. Focusing on this near-White status, George Yancey argues that "if Asian Americans overcome the perceptions that they are biologically different from the majority group members, then it can be argued that Asians Americans will eventually assimilate into the dominant group in society in the same way that southern/eastern European ethnic groups have become 'White.' "[35] I posit instead that they need not overcome a biological presumption of difference: today, some Asians can function as honorary Whites, an identity that contemplates both White status and a biologically non-White identity.[36]

Latinos also have access to honorary White identity, though their situation differs from that of Asians. Unlike the latter, and also unlike African Americans, Hispanics have long been on the cusp between White and non-White in the United States. Despite pervasive and often violent racial prejudice against Mexicans in the Southwest and against Puerto Ricans and other Latino groups in the Caribbean during the nineteenth century and enduring until today, the most elite Latin Americans in the United States have historically been accepted as fully White. This pattern reflects the relatively greater influence of socio-racial rather than strictly bio-racial parameters in Hispanic racialization. With no clear identity under the continental theory of race, and with a tremendous range of somatic features marking this heterogeneous population, there has long been relatively more room for the use of social rather than strictly bio-racial factors in the imputation of race to particular Latino individuals and groups. Seeking to take advantage of their liminal position, elite Hispanics have traditionally claimed for themselves and their communities White identities. From the 1930s through the 1950s, for instance, Mexican community leaders in the United States challenged segregation not on the grounds that it was wrong per se, but by arguing that they were White, thereby initiating a persistent trend in which certain Latinos seek assimilation through claims of Whiteness.[37] The racial pride movements of the late 1960s saw segments of the Mexican and Puerto Rican communities reject this racial politics in favor of pride in a non-White identity—indeed, the Chicano and Young Lord movements deserve extended study as among the few historical episodes during which large groups rejected a White identity and instead embraced non-Whiteness.[38]

The racial divide among Latinos continues: by the census count, almost half consider themselves White (though this number has declined over the last three censuses and by another major survey the number is closer to one in five; in addition, a steady three percent of Hispanics consider themselves Black).[39] It seems likely that an increasing number of Hispanics—those who have fair features, material wealth, and high social status, aided also by Anglo surnames—will both claim and be accorded a position in society as fully White. Simultaneously, many more Latinos—similarly situated in terms of material and status position, but perhaps with slightly darker features or a surname or accent suggesting Latin American origins—will become honorary Whites.[40] Meanwhile, the preponderance of Latinos as well as most others traditionally constructed as racial minorities will continue to be relegated to non-White categories. The advent of an honorary White identity for some does not portend the elimination of race for all, a point to which I return below.

Even so, the future of race in the United States will be profoundly shaped in the coming decades by how Asians and to an even greater extent Latinos come to see themselves and in turn come to be seen racially. While the population as whole grew by 13 percent in the last decade of the twentieth century, the Asian population jumped by 72 percent and the Latino population boomed by almost 60 percent.[41] Beyond the sheer rates of increase, the absolute numbers are striking. According to the census bureau, people counted as other than Black or White increased from less than 1 percent of the population in 1970 to over 12.5 percent in 2000.[42] This last figure is conservative, for it does not include the nearly half of Latinos the census bureau counts as White. And consider another striking fact: births to Latina mothers now outnumber all other deliveries combined in bellwether California.⁴³ The racial future of the United States is inexorably bound up with Latino and Asian racial identity.

In the context of U.S. race relations, why so many should seek the privileges and positive presumptions of Whiteness is obvious (though also politically and morally troubling, insofar as seeking to be White inevitably contributes to the perpetuation and legitimation of White dominance). But why do many Whites appear willing to extend—or, at least, not actively to resist the extension of—Whiteness? For some, the answer surely lies in the positive accomplishments of the civil rights era, including not only the defeat of notions of White supremacy but also the partial integration of many social institutions, including labor environments, higher learning, athletics, and entertainment. We must be careful not to discount the willingness of significant sectors within the White community to extend a presumption of full human worth to racial minorities—nor should we be surprised that this presumption of full humanity often translates into treating ostensibly non-White persons as if they were White.

But for other Whites, the willingness to extend a presumption of Whiteness reflects strategic thinking about the numbers. The census bureau predicts, for instance, that Whites will comprise 78 percent of the nation's population in 2020—but only if its projections regarding the number of Hispanics who will identify as White bear out. If no Latinos are included, the White population will amount to only 61 of every 100 Americans and by 2050, if not sooner, Whites will comprise a numerical minority in this country.⁴⁴ There are many—I have in mind here the corporations that supported affirmative action in the Michigan cases, the military brass who did the same, and the Republican Party with its cynical version of right-wing affirmative action that promotes a few minorities into highly visible positions—who see these numbers and understand that future power depends on at least the symbolic inclusion of some minorities today.⁴⁵

So Whiteness is expanding, and changing. This is not a particularly dramatic nor felicitous development (except, to some extent, for the newly White). First, the move in the socio-racial direction, in which racial significance attaches to wealth, professional attainment, and so forth, is a much less profound change than is often suggested, because race in the United States has always had a socio-racial dimension. A developing scholarship now impressively demonstrates that even during and immediately after slavery, at a time when racial identity in the United States was presumably most rigidly fixed in terms of biological difference and descent, and even in the formal legal setting of the courtroom, determinations of racial identity often took place on the basis of social indicia such as the nature of one's employment or one's choice of sexual partners.[46] This "performance" of race, as some scholars term it, has a long pedigree in the United States.[47]

Second, despite the increased salience of social indicia to the achievement of a privileged racial identity, physical features will remain foundational in racial categorization. To be sure, individuals and groups who would have been clearly non-White under the racial regime in place just a few decades ago now function more and more as White. But rather than fully supplanting the role of physical features in racial determinations, socio-racial factors more accurately mainly supplement them. It is not just any community or individual who can become honorary Whites; instead, it is those whose physical characteristics most closely resemble the morphology associated with Whites. In this context, color—meaning those somatic details such as skin tone, facial features, hair shade and texture, and so on, upon which racial classifications were erected in the United States—will continue to have tremendous significance, as those minorities with the lightest features will have the greatest access to White identity. Those who are darker, be they Latinos or South Asians or African Americans, will rarely be accorded White status despite their individual or group achievements precisely because their phenotype positions them too far toward the putatively inferior end of the color spectrum.[48] Race will remain, as it long has been, supremely color-coded. Under antebellum racial logic those Blacks with the fairest features were sometimes described as "light, bright, and damn near White."[49] If today we switch out "damn near" for "honorary," how much has really changed?

Race will not cease to have a major physical component, nor will ordinal categories like Black, Brown, White, Yellow, and Red soon disappear. The basic belief in continental racial divisions will persist, ensuring a sense that those with almost exclusively European ancestry are fully White while others remain honorary Whites—White as a form of social courtesy, but not unquestionably White. Indeed, most likely one attribute of Whiteness as social courtesy is the extent to which it can be easily withdrawn. The belief in continental races will likely also ensure a continued special stigma for those with African ancestry, where this ostensible stain has been so central to the elaboration of race in the United States. A few African Americans have achieved a functional White identity, but it will remain significantly more difficult for Blacks than for many Asians and

Latinos to function as Whites. Honorary White status will be available to the most exceptional—and the most light-skinned—Blacks, but to few other African Americans, and on terms far more restrictive than those on which Whiteness will be extended to many Latinos and Asians.[50]

Finally, in contrast to the expectations of those who herald the Latin Americanization of race in the United States, the redefinition of Whiteness does not portend a positive movement toward racial democracy. Under a redefined White category, racial hierarchy will continue unabated. The strongest evidence in this regard is Latin America itself. Most Latin American countries are marked by extreme racial hierarchies that distinguish between Whites, mixed-race persons, Blacks, and indigenous populations. Those who predict a felicitous Latin American racial future in the United States do so only by ignoring the history of race in the very region they extol as a model. To give even cursory attention to the reality of racial stratification in Latin America (as opposed to simply accepting the rhetoric of racial egalitarianism that dominates much of elite Latin American discourse about domestic race relations) is to recognize that the shift toward a socio-racial system is not in any way tantamount to the end of racial hierarchy.[51]

But on another account, perhaps the United States is moving in a Latin American direction. Latin American societies often proclaim that they have transcended race even as they remain riven by racial subordination, and boast of robust civil rights laws that in fact do nothing to ameliorate inequality.[53] These celebratory claims have long served in many Latin American countries as a form of propaganda that masks the much bleaker reality of not just persistent racial subordination but of steadfast resistance by racial elites to any reform programs likely to succeed. In this sense, we *are* becoming like Latin America: we are developing a public discourse that assures us that we have indeed transcended race and need take no further efforts, as well as a legal regime that at once presents itself as aggressively committed to rooting out racism but that in fact excels only at forestalling state and private efforts to disestablish racial hierarchy. In the United States, these new elements take the name of colorblindness.

Colorblindness. Continued White dominance will be rationalized and protected through the ascendant racial ideology of colorblindness. The specific command of colorblindness—that the state should not take race into account—is not new, nor particularly contentious in its own right. Indeed, after bearing witness to several centuries of racial hierarchy, there is an intuitive appeal to the admonition that as a society we eschew race once and for all. But the colorblindness proselytized by the racial right today (and widely accepted by most Whites) is altogether different from a considered response to racial inequality. It propounds, even as it occludes, a powerful set of understandings about the dynamics of racial subordination as well as about the nature of racial groups. Colorblindness is in this sense not a prescription but an ideology, a set of understandings that delimits how people comprehend, rationalize, and act in the world.[54] Though colorblindness now dominates the country's racial imagination its origins lie in race law, making a genealogy of legal colorblindness indispensable to fathoming its constituent claims.

Colorblindness is frequently traced back to the Supreme Court's decision in *Plessy v. Ferguson,* which upheld Jim Crow segregation in the South and prompted Justice John Marshall Harlan's famous dissent that "our constitution is colorblind, and neither knows nor tolerates classes among citizens."[55] Harlan's dissent is today widely invoked for the proposition that the state should never take race into account; his felicitous turn of phrase has now entered the legal and cultural canon. But, of course, colorblindness did not take hold during Jim Crow's reign, and, indeed, Harlan was hardly committed to the proposition attributed to him, for in *Plessy* itself he extolled the superiority of the White race and denigrated the Chinese, and just a few years later he wrote an opinion upholding segregated schools.[56]

For the first half of the twentieth century, colorblindness represented a radical and wholly unrealized aspiration, the hope that de jure racial subordination might be suddenly and thoroughly dismantled. It was in this vein that, as counsel for the NAACP in the late 1940s and early 1950s, Thurgood Marshall encouraged his colleagues to cite to Harlan's invocation of colorblindness to make the argument that, as Marshall put it in a 1947 brief to the Supreme Court, "classifications and distinctions based on race or color have no moral or legal validity in our society. They are contrary to our constitution and laws."[57] But neither society nor the courts embraced colorblindness when doing so might have sped the demise of White supremacy. Even during the civil rights era, colorblindness as a strategy for racial emancipation did not take hold. Instead, the courts and Congress dismantled Jim Crow segregation and proscribed egregious forms of private discrimination in a piece-meal manner that banned only the most noxious misuses of race, not any reference to race whatsoever.

In the wake of the civil rights movement's limited but significant triumphs, the relationship between colorblindness and racial reform changed remarkably. Whereas colorblindness in the context of Jim Crow was heavy with emancipatory promise, in the civil rights era and since, its greatest potency instead lies in preserving the racial status quo. As explicitly race-based subordination came to an end but racial inequality stubbornly persisted, racial progressives increasingly recognized the need for state and private actors to intervene aggressively along racial lines to dismantle entrenched inequality. Rather than call for colorblindness, they began to insist on the need for affirmative, race-conscious remedies. In this new context, colorblindness appealed instead to those *opposing* racial integration. Enshrouded with the moral raiment of the civil rights movement, this rhetoric provided cover for reactionary opposition to racial reform. Within a year of *Brown,* southern school districts and courts had recognized that they could forestall integration by insisting that the Constitution allowed them to use only "race-neutral" means to end segregation—for instance, school choice plans, which predictably produced virtually no integration whatsoever.[58] By the late 1970s and early 1980s, defenders of de facto segregation had adopted colorblindness as their strongest rhetorical weapon in the battle against race-conscious remedies. When the Supreme Court split on affirmative action in 1978, Thurgood Marshall, now as a justice, spoke out against the colorblind rhetoric newly adopted by conservatives: "It is because of a legacy of unequal treatment," he inveighed, "that we now must permit the institutions of this society to give consideration to race in making decisions about who will hold the positions of influence, affluence, and prestige in America."[59] With the change in racial context from Jim Crow to civil rights, colorblindness as an approach to race jumped political valence, from radical to reactionary.

Wielding the ideal of colorblindness as a sword, racial conservatives on the Supreme Court have refought the battles they lost during the civil rights era, cutting back on protections from racial discrimination as well as severely limiting race-conscious remedies. *McCleskey v. Kemp* insists that, even accepting as uncontroverted the fact that Georgia sentences to death Blacks who murder Whites at *twenty-two times* the rate it orders death for Blacks who kill Blacks, the Constitution perceives no discrimination in Georgia's death penalty machinery.[60] Meanwhile, *City of Richmond v. Croson* tells us that when the former capital of the Confederacy adopts an affirmative action program to steer some of its construction dollars to minority owned firms it impermissibly discriminates—even

when, without the program, less than one percent of construction con-
tracts went to minorities in a city over 50 percent African American.[61] The
embrace of colorblindness by the conservative Court has converted our
vaunted constitutional commitment to racial equality into a tool for preserving a racial status quo of continued White dominance.

But perhaps the greatest power of reactionary colorblindness lies not
in its immediate judicial impact but in the story it tells about race and
racism. Justice Clarence Thomas has emphatically stated:

> [T]here is a "moral and constitutional equivalence" between laws designed
> to subjugate a race and those that distribute benefits on the basis of race in
> order to foster some current notion of equality. . . . In each instance, it is
> racial discrimination pure and simple.[62]

What understanding of racism, and of race itself, could justify this strict
moral and constitutional equation of Jim Crow and affirmative action?

Colorblind partisans have supplied answers widely appealing to
Whites. To begin with racism, they define it as any direct invocation or
use of race. Under this conception, most racism (and in particular the virulent racism of White supremacy) was defeated by the early, pre-
affirmative action civil rights movement, which drove racist discourse out
of the public arena. As a result, colorblind advocates present the contemporary United States as free from deep racial division. We are, instead,
now "a nation of minorities," comprised no longer of dominant and subordinate races, but instead of a shifting mosaic of ethnic groups in equal
competition with each other. As Justice Lewis Powell averred in 1978,
"the United States had become a Nation of minorities. Each had to struggle—and to some extent struggles still—to overcome the prejudices not of
a monolithic majority, but of a 'majority' composed of various minority
groups."[63] This view insists that racial domination belongs to the increasingly distant past and claims that Whites no longer operate in society as
a dominant race, but now exist only as a welter of European ethnicities.[64]
"The white 'majority' itself," Powell insisted, "is composed of various minority groups, most of which can lay claim to a history of prior discrimination at the hands of the State and private individuals."[65] Under this theory, preferences for "minorities" threaten to extend to almost every
group. As Powell explained, "Not all of these groups can receive prefer-
ential treatment and corresponding judicial tolerance of distinctions
drawn in terms of race and nationality, for then the only 'majority' left
would be a new minority of white Anglo-Saxon Protestants."[66] With its

triumphal claims about overcoming racism and its fragmentation of the White overclass into myriad ethnic minorities, colorblindness has erased Whites as a dominant group and instead conjures them as the true victims of racism in the brave new world of civil rights and racial remediation.

Regarding race, colorblind partisans justify equating affirmative action and Jim Crow racism by depicting race as unmoored from social practices. In the most common version of this claim, race is equated to skin color or ancestry, nothing more. In more sophisticated conceptions, race lacks meaning because it is a fiction, an incoherent social construction. Whether it is physical or fictional matters little; the essential claim is that race has nothing to do with social practices of status competition and subordination. Consider the reasoning in *Hernandez v. New York,* a case involving a Hispanic defendant and the use of a Spanish-language translator, in which the prosecutor peremptorily struck from the jury every Latino. He did so, he said, because he did not believe that these potential jurors "could" set aside their familiarity with Spanish. The phrase "could," rather than "would," is telling, for while the latter term suggests concern about individual temperament, the former invokes a sense of group disability.[67] Also raising concern, the prosecutor questioned only Hispanic potential jurors but no others about their ability to speak Spanish. Nevertheless, the Court upheld the exclusion, finding no bias on the part of the prosecutor. Justice O'Connor's rationale, offered in a concurring opinion, is especially revealing. She thought it irrelevant that the basis for exclusion correlated closely to Hispanic identity and operated to exclude all and only Latinos. Because the strikes were not explicitly justified in racial terms, O'Connor reasoned, no basis existed for constitutional intervention. The strikes "may have acted like strikes based on race," O'Connor conceded, "but they were not based on race. *No matter how closely tied or significantly correlated to race* the explanation for a peremptory strike may be, the strike does not implicate the Equal Protection Clause unless it is based on race."[68] Ostensibly, social practices not tied directly and explicitly to skin color or ancestry by the use of some specifically racial term do not involve race. Race is empty—either purely physical, a matter of skin color or ancestry, or purely abstract, an erroneous fiction. It is not, as O'Connor and colorblindness partisans in general insist, a function of how one is perceived and treated.

The colorblind conceptions of race and racism function similarly: both exist only when mentioned. Race and racism operate under this conception almost as magic words: speak them, and they suddenly spring into being, but not otherwise. This magic-word formalism strips race and racism of all social meaning and of any connection to social practices of group conflict and subordination. *Hernandez* and *McCleskey,* the Georgia death penalty case, are of a piece here: no matter how extreme the discrimination, nor how closely correlated to race, the Court insisted in both cases that race and racism were not involved because no one could be shown to have uttered a racial word. In *Croson,* in contrast, racism obtained because Richmond said explicitly that some contracting dollars should go to "minorities." Under this understanding, White racism is a thing of the past because few White racists today tie their views or actions explicitly to race. In contrast, race exists and racism operates primarily among racial progressives, who constantly invoke race and demand race-conscious remedies. Colorblindness equates Jim Crow segregation and affirmative action by redefining racism as any mention of race, and race as something utterly empty of social content or history.

The claim that race and racism exist only when specifically mentioned, and not otherwise, also allows colorblindness to insulate from critique a new White racial politics in which racial proxies become politically and socially acceptable substitutes for explicit racism. The civil rights movement worked a major change in U.S. society in making open expressions of White supremacy culturally unacceptable. This was a far cry, however, from actually ending White racial mobilization. Instead, this mobilization, often orchestrated by White politicians, has continued over the last several decades in the form of interlinked panics about criminals, welfare cheats, illegal immigrants, and, most recently, terrorists.[69] More generally, culture and behavior have become the targets of racial reactionaries: one can understand Samuel Huntington's recent attack on Latino immigration in this way, as he at once rejects the old ideas of White racial superiority and at the same time aggressively promotes the notion of a superior Anglo Protestant culture.[70] Lawrence Bobo labels theories that lay minority failure at the feet of culture "laissez-faire racism" to highlight the way in which Whites attribute their superior social position to a supposed special affinity for the values, orientations, and work ethic needed by the liberal individual in a capitalist society.[71] I agree with Bobo, but emphasize a different point: it's not just that culture and behavior provide coded language for old prejudices, but that colorblindness excuses and insulates this new White racism.

Consider how colorblindness protects current attacks on "illegal immigrants." This is not racism, we're told, because it is not about race at all, but simply about those who violate our laws. The animus is not racial, we're assured, because the targeted group is racially under- and over-inclusive: "illegals" doesn't sweep in all Latinos, but does supposedly include Whites who cross the border without documents. Yet obviously current efforts to enflame passions about securing the border with guards, walls, and guns share deep similarities with the racial hysterias that accompanied the mass deportation of Mexican Americans during Operation Wetback in the 1950s, the internment of Japanese Americans during World War II, and the initiation of the Asiatic Barred Zone that prohibited all Asian immigration through the first half of the twentieth century. Race and racism have long been used to patrol the nation's literal and figurative borders; racial politics are just as much at work today, notwithstanding the public foregrounding of seemingly non-racial concerns or the general absence of crude racial slurs. By insisting that race operates only if someone uses one among a narrowly drawn band of racial terms, reactionary colorblindness protects the new racism's efforts to locate minority inferiority in cultural deficiencies and pathological behaviors. It cannot be racial, colorblind partisans tell us, for race has nothing to do with social practices, and White racism is a thing of the past.

Conclusion

Our faces and our racial ideology maybe changing, but the fundamental racial dynamic of White dominance in our country will not end anytime soon. Instead, it will continue, even as the definition of who counts as White expands, in large part because the material interests of so many demand it, but also because the ideology of contemporary colorblindness protects and perpetuates White dominance. Proponents of reactionary colorblindness wear their antiracist pretensions boldly, professing their deep commitment to ending racial inequality. But this is a sham, for colorblindness promises to curtail race-conscious efforts to promote racial justice, even as it refuses to acknowledge ongoing racial subordination. Worse, colorblindness redefines race and racism in a manner that excuses contemporary manifestations of racial scapegoating as legitimate concerns over inferior cultures and behavioral delinquency. For the next several decades, at least, we will suffer this racial future of colorblind White dominance.

Appendix A
The Racial Prerequisite Cases

The following tables list the prerequisite cases. The tables are chronologically divided to coincide with the periodization offered in the text, namely, early, late, and post-*United States v. Thind* cases. They include annotations regarding the principle rationales employed by the courts. The annotations are listed in an order that roughly correlates to the apparent degree of reliance on each rationale. Thus, if a court seemed to base its decision primarily on legal precedent but also used congressional intent and, to a lesser extent, common knowledge, the annotations would appear in that order.

TABLE I
Racial Prerequisite Cases, 1878–1909

Case	Holding	Rationales
In re Ah Yup 1 F. Cas. 223 (C.C.D.Cal. 1878)	Chinese are not White.	Scientific evidence Common knowledge Congressional intent
In re Camille 6 F. 256 (C.C.D.Or. 1880)	Persons half White and half Native American are not White.	Legal precedent
In re Kanaka Nian 6 Utah 259 21 Pac. 993 (1889)	Hawaiians are not White.	Scientific evidence
In re Hong Yen Chang 84 Cal. 163 24 Pac. 156 (1890)	Chinese are not White.	Legal precedent
In re Po 7 Misc. 471 28 N.Y. Supp. 838 (City Ct. 1894)	Burmese are not White.	Common knowledge Legal precedent
In re Saito 62 F. 126 (C.C.D.Mass. 1894)	Japanese are not White.	Congressional intent Common knowledge Scientific evidence Legal precedent

TABLE 1 *Continued*

Case	Holding	Rationales
In re Gee Hop 71 F. 274 (N.D.Cal. 1895)	Chinese are not White.	Legal precedent Congressional intent
In re Rodriguez 81 F. 337 (W.D.Tex. 1897)	Mexicans are White.	Legal precedent[a]
In re Burton 1 Ala. 111 (1900)	Native Americans are not White.	No explanation
In re Yamashita 30 Wash. 234 70 Pac. 482 (1902)	Japanese are not White.	Legal precedent
In re Buntaro Kumagai 163 F. 922 (W.D.Wash. 1908)	Japanese are not White.	Congressional intent Legal precedent
In re Knight 171 F. 299 (E.D.N.Y. 1909)	Persons half White, one- quarter Japanese, and one-quarter Chinese are not White.	Legal precedent

[a] Although the reasoning in this case is characterized as relying on "legal precedent," *Rodriguez* is unique in that the court relied on treaties rather than cases to hold the applicant admissible to naturalization.

TABLE 2
Racial Prerequisite Cases, 1909–1923

Case	Holding	Rationales
In re Balsara 171 F. 294 (C.C.S.D.N.Y. 1909)	Asian Indians are proba- bly not White.[a]	Congressional intent
In re Najour 174 F. 735 (N.D.Ga. 1909)	Syrians are White.	Scientific evidence
In re Halladjian 174 F. 834 (C.C.D.Mass. 1909)	Armenians are White.	Scientific evidence Legal precedent[b]
United States v. Dolla 177 F. 101 (5th Cir. 1910)	Asian Indians are White.	Ocular inspection of skin[c]
In re Mudarri 176 F. 465 (C.C.D.Mass. 1910)	Syrians are White.	Scientific evidence Legal precedent
Bessho v. United States 178 F. 245 (4th Cir. 1910)	Japanese are not White.	Congressional intent

TABLE 2 *Continued*

Case	Holding	Rationales
In re Ellis 179 F. 1002 (D.Or. 1910)	Syrians are White.	Common knowledge Congressional intent
United States v. Balsara 180 F. 694 (2nd Cir. 1910)	Asian Indians are White.	Scientific evidence Congressional intent
In re Alverto 198 F. 688 (E.D.Pa. 1912) White.	Persons three-quarters Filipino and one-quar- ter White are not White.	Legal precedent Congressional intent
In re Young 195 F. 645 (W.D. Wash. 1912)	Persons half German and half Japanese are not White.	Legal precedent
In re Young 198 F. 715 (W.D.Wash. 1912)	Persons half German and half Japanese are not White.	Common knowledge Legal precedent
Ex parte Shahid 205 F. 812 (E.D.S.C. 1913)	Syrians are not White.[d]	Common knowledge
In re Akhay Kumar Mozumdar 207 F. 115 (E.D.Wash. 1913)	Asian Indians are White.	Legal precedent[e]
Ex parte Dow 211 F. 486 (E.D.S.C. 1914)	Syrians are not White.	Common knowledge
In re Dow 213 F. 355 (E.D.S.C. 1914)	Syrians are not White.[f]	Common knowledge Congressional intent
Dow v. United States 226 F. 145 (4th Cir. 1915)	Syrians are White.	Scientific evidence Congressional intent Legal precedent
In re Lampitoe 232 F. 382 (S.D.N.Y. 1916)	Persons three-quarters Filipino and one-quar- ter White are not White.	Legal precedent
In re Mallari 239 F. 416 (D.Mass. 1916)	Filipinos are not White.	No explanation
In re Rallos 241 F. 686 (E.D.N.Y. 1917)	Filipinos are not White.	Legal precedent

TABLE 2 *Continued*

Case	Holding	Rationales
In re Sadar Bhagwab Singh 246 F. 496 (E.D.Pa. 1917)	Asian Indians are not White.	Common knowledge Congressional intent
In re Mohan Singh 257 F. 209 (S.D.Cal. 1919)	Asian Indians are White.	Scientific evidence Legal precedent
In re Thind 268 F. 683 (D.Or. 1920)	Asian Indians are White.	Legal precedent
Petition of Easurk Emsen Charr 273 F. 207 (W.D.Mo. 1921)	Koreans are not White.	Common knowledge Legal precedent
Ozawa v. United States 260 U.S. 178 (1922)	Japanese are not White.	Legal precedent Congressional intent Common knowledge Scientific evidence
United States v. Thind 261 U.S. 204 (1923)	Asian Indians are not White.	Common knowledge Congressional intent

[a] Despite concluding that Asian Indians probably were not White, the court noted the need for an authoritative pronouncement on this issue, as well as the government's willingness to appeal. For these reasons, the court ruled that Balsara could naturalize.

[b] Here, "legal precedent" refers not to case law but to prior government usage.

[c] *Dolla* is unique in two respects. First, at the appellate level, the Fifth Circuit refused to hear the government's objection to the naturalization of Dolla on the ground that naturalization proceedings do not constitute a "case" such that an appeal could be taken. Second, at least as the underlying case is summarized in the appellate decision, the district court did not rely on any of the four prevalent rationales, but instead inspected Dolla's skin minutely, going so far as to ask him to roll up his sleeve, in order to determine whether Dolla was White.

[d] This holding is dictum, as the court rested denial of the petition for citizenship on "personal disqualifications." 205 F. at 817.

[e] The court relied on legal precedent for the proposition that the terms "white person" and "caucasian" were synonymous. For the secondary postulate that a Hindu is a Caucasian, however, the court relied on the testimony of the petitioner himself, who claimed to be "a high-caste Hindu of pure blood, belonging to what is known as the warrior caste, or ruling caste." 207 F. at 116.

[f] The court limited its holding to the conclusion that Syrians are not White within the meaning of the prerequisite statute. The court specifically refused to answer the more general question of whether Syrians "belong to the 'white race.' " 213 F. at 356, 366–67.

TABLE 3
Racial Prerequisite Cases, 1923–1944

Case	Holding	Rationales
Sato v. Hall 191 Cal. 510 217 Pac. 520 (1923)	Japanese are not White.	Legal precedent

TABLE 3 *Continued*

Case	Holding	Rationales
United States v. Akhay Kumar Mozumdar 296 F. 173 (S.D.Cal. 1923)	Asian Indians are not White.	Legal precedent
United States v. Cartozian 6 F.2d 919 (D.Or. 1925)	Armenians are White.	Scientific evidence Common knowledge Legal precedent
United States v. Ali 7 F.2d 728 (E.D.Mich. 1925)	Punjabis (whether Hindu or Arabian) are not White.	Common knowledge
In re Fisher 21 F.2d 1007 (N.D.Cal. 1927)	Persons three-quarters Chinese and one-quarter White are not White.	Legal precedent
United States v. Javier 22 F.2d 879 (D.C. Cir. 1927)	Filipinos are not White.	Legal precedent
In re Feroz Din 27 F.2d 568 (N.D.Cal. 1928)	Afghanis are not White.	Common knowledge
United States v. Gokhale 26 F.2d 360 (2nd Cir. 1928)	Asian Indians are not White.	Legal precedent
De La Ysla v. United States 77 F.2d 988 (9th Cir. 1935)	Filipinos are not White.	Legal precedent
In re Cruz 23 F.Supp. 774 (E.D.N.Y. 1938)	Persons three-quarters Native American and one-quarter African are not African.	Legal precedent
Wadia v. United States 101 F.2d 7 (2nd Cir. 1939)	Asian Indians are not White.	Common knowledge
De Cano v. State 110 P.2d 627 (Wash. 1941)	Filipinos are not White.	Legal precedent
Kharaiti Ram Samras v. United States 125 F.2d 879 (9th Cir. 1942)	Asian Indians are not White.	Legal precedent
In re Ahmed Hassan 48 F.Supp. 843 (E.D.Mich. 1942)	Arabians are not White.	Common knowledge Legal precedent
Ex parte Mohriez 54 F.Supp. 941 (D.Mass. 1944)	Arabians are White.	Common knowledge Legal precedent

Appendix B
Excerpts from Selected Prerequisite Cases

In re Ah Yup

F.Cas. 223 (C.C.D.Cal. 1878)

SAWYER, Circuit Judge.

Ah Yup, a native and citizen of the empire of China, of the Mongolian race, presented a petition in writing, praying that he be permitted to make proof of the facts alleged, and upon satisfactory proof being made, and his taking the oath required in such cases, he be admitted as a citizen of the United States. The petition stated all the qualifications required by the statute to entitle the petitioner to be naturalized, provided the statute authorizes the naturalization of a native of China of the Mongolian race.

This being the first application made by a native Chinaman for naturalization, the members of the bar were requested by the court to make such suggestions as amici curiae as occurred to them upon either side of the question. . . . Is a person of the Mongolian race a "white person" within the meaning of the statute?

Words in a statute, other than technical terms, should be taken in their ordinary sense. The words "white person," as well argued by petitioner's counsel, taken in a strictly literal sense, constitute a very indefinite description of a class of persons, where none can be said to be literally white, and those called white may be found of every shade from the lightest blonde to the most swarthy brunette. But these words in this country, at least, have undoubtedly acquired a well settled meaning in common popular speech, and they are constantly used in the sense so acquired in the literature of the country, as well as in common parlance. As ordinarily used everywhere in the United States, one would scarcely fail to understand that the party employing the words "white person" would intend a person of the Caucasian race.

In speaking of the various classifications of races, Webster in his dictionary says, "The common classification is that of Blumenbach, who makes five. 1. The Caucasian, or white race, to which belong the greater part of the European nations and those of Western Asia; 2. The Mongolian, or yellow race, occupying Tartary, China, Japan, etc.; 3. The Ethiopian or Negro (black) race, occupying all Africa, except the north; 4. The American, or red race, containing the Indians of North and South America; and, 5. The Malay, or Brown race, occupying the islands of the Indian Archipelago," etc. This division was adopted from Buffon, with some changes in names, and is founded on the combined characteristics of complexion, hair and skull. Linnaeus makes four divisions, founded on the color of the skin: "1. European, whitish; 2. American, coppery; 3. Asiatic, tawny; and, 4. African, black." Cuvier makes three: Caucasian, Mongol, and Negro. Others make many more, but no one includes the white, or Caucasian, with the Mongolian or yellow race; and no one of those classifications recognizing color as one of the distinguishing characteristics includes the Mongolian in the white or whitish race.

Neither in popular language, in literature, nor in scientific nomenclature, do we ordinarily, if ever, find the words "white person" used in a sense so comprehensive as to include an individual of the Mongolian race. Yet, in all, color, notwithstanding its indefiniteness as a word of description, is made an important factor in the basis adopted for the distinction and classification of races. I am not aware that the term "white person," as used in the statutes as they have stood from 1802 till the late revision, was ever supposed to include a Mongolian. While I find nothing in the history of the country, in common or scientific usage, or in legislative proceedings, to indicate that congress intended to include in the term "white person" any other than an individual of the Caucasian race, I do find much in the proceedings of congress to show that it was universally understood in that body, in its recent legislation, that it excluded Mongolians. At the time of the amendment, in 1870, extending the naturalization laws to the African race, Mr. Sumner made repeated and strenuous efforts to strike the word "white" from the naturalization laws, or to accomplish the same object by other language. It was opposed on the sole ground that the effect would be to authorize the admission of Chinese to citizenship. Every senator, who spoke upon the subject, assumed that they were then excluded by the term "white person," and that the amendment would admit them, and the amendment was advocated on the one hand, and opposed on the other, upon that single idea. Senator Morton, in the course of the discussion said: "This amendment involves the whole Chinese problem . . . The country has just awakened to the question and to the enormous magnitude of the question, involving a possible immigration of many millions, involving another civilization; involving labor problems that no intellect can solve without study and time. Are you now prepared to settle the Chinese problem, thus in advance inviting that immigration?" Senator Sumner replied: "Senators undertake to disturb us in our judgment by reminding us of the possibility of large numbers swarming from China; but the answer to all this is very obvious and very simple. If the Chinese come here they will come for citizenship, or merely for labor. If they come for citizenship then in this desire do they give a pledge of loyalty to our institutions, and where is the peril in such vows? They are peaceful and industrious; how can their citizenship be the occasion of solicitude?"

Many other senators spoke pro and con on the question, this being the point of the contest, and these extracts being fair examples of the opposing opinions. It was finally defeated, and the amendment cited, extending the right of naturalization to the African only, was adopted. It is clear, from these proceedings that congress retained the word "white" in the naturalization laws for the sole purpose of excluding the Chinese from the right of naturalization.

Thus, whatever latitudinarian construction might otherwise have been given to the term "white person," it is entirely clear that congress intended by this legislation to exclude Mongolians from the right of naturalization. . . . I am, therefore, of the opinion that a native of China, of the Mongolian race, is not a white person within the meaning of the act of congress.

In re Najour

174 F. 735 (N.D.Ga. 1909)

NEWMAN, District Judge.

In admitting to naturalization the petitioner, Costa George Najour, I wish to say this: Although the term "free white person" is used in the statutes, this expression, I think, refers to race, rather than to color, and fair or dark complexion should not be allowed to control, provided the person seeking naturalization comes within the classification of the white or Caucasian race, and I consider the Syrians as belonging to what we recognize, and what the world recognizes, as the white race. The applicant comes from Mt. Lebanon, near Beirut. He is not particularly dark, and has none of the characteristics or appearance of the Mongolian race, but, so far as I can see and judge, has the appearance and characteristics of the Caucasian race.

Quite a recent work, which I have before me now, "The World's People," by Dr. A. H. Keane, classifies, without question or qualification in any way, Syrians as a part of the Caucasian or white race, and this they are, so far as my knowledge and information goes. Dr. Keane divides the world's people into four classes, the "Negro or black, in the Sudan, South Africa, and Oceania (Australasia); Mongol or yellow, in Central, North, and East Asia; Amerinds (red or brown), in the New World; and Caucasians (white and also dark), in North Africa, Europe, Irania, India, Western Asia, and Polynesia." Discussing the various nationalities and subdivisions of these four general divisions, he unhesitatingly places the Syrians in the Caucasian or white division.

The Assistant United States Attorney, representing the government, objecting to the naturalization of Najour, seems to attach some importance to the fact that the applicant was born within the dominions of Turkey, and was heretofore a subject of the Sultan of Turkey. I do not think this should cut any figure in the matter. If it did, the extension of the Turkish Empire over people unquestionably of the white race would deprive them of the privilege of naturalization.

In my opinion the applicant belongs to the white race within the meaning of statute, and the other requisites existing after careful examination, he is clearly entitled to naturalization.

Ex parte Shahid

205 F. 812 (E.D.S.C. 1913)

SMITH, District Judge.

This is an application for naturalization. The applicant has performed all the necessary formalities, and the matter now comes up first upon his right to naturalization, and next whether, conceding that he belongs to the class of persons entitled to the benefit of naturalization, he is a fit subject to be naturalized.

According to his statement he is now 59 years of age, and was born at Zahle, in Asia Minor, in Syria, and came to this country about 11 years ago, and is a Christian. He writes his name in Arabic, cannot read or write English, and speaks and understands English very imperfectly, and does not understand any questions relating to the manner and method of government in America, or of the responsibilities of a citizen. His answers to the questions whether he is a polygamist or a disbeliever in organized government were in the affirmative, and he could not be made to understand in English the purport of the questions asked.

In color, he is about that of walnut, or somewhat darker than is the usual mulatto of one-half mixed blood between the white and the negro races.

The first question that comes up for consideration is whether a Syrian of Asiatic birth and descent is entitled under the act of Congress to be admitted a citizen of the United States. This depends upon the construction of the provisions of the law, and practically upon the construction of the following clause, which limits the classes entitled to the benefit of the naturalization statute, viz.:

"The provisions of this title shall apply to aliens being free, white persons, and to aliens of African nativity and to persons of African descent."

The phrase "free white persons" was used in the first naturalization statute approved March 26, 1790, and the phrase "aliens of African nativity and to persons of African descent" was incorporated in the amendatory statute approved July 14, 1870. As so phrased, the language of the statute is about as open to many constructions as it possibly could be.

Who is a free white person? And who is a person of African nativity or of African descent? It has been decided that the Chinese, Japanese, Malays, and American Indians do not belong to the white race and are therefore excluded. Furthermore, by express additional statutory provision the Chinese are expressly excluded. This, however, leaves open the question: Suppose one of these people had been born in Africa, would the children of Chinese parents, for instance, or Japanese parents, because born in Africa, be of African nativity?

Next, what is the meaning of African descent? The Chinaman is not entitled to be admitted to citizenship, but would a half-breed, the child of a negro and a Chinese, be entitled to admission because by his mother's or his father's side he was of African descent? Then what is the limitation of African descent? For how many generations would that continue? If the son of an African man by a Chinese woman is entitled to admission by reason of African descent, would the great-great-grandson of an African, although one whose immediate ancestors were Chinese, and who had lived in China, be entitled to admission by reason of the infinitesimal portion of negro blood in him? Then, what is white? What degree of colorization, if it be referred to color, constitutes a white person as against a colored person, and is the court to take the responsibility by ocular inspection of determining the shades of different colorization where the dividing line comes between white and colored.

The statute as it stands is most uncertain, ambiguous, and difficult both of construction and application, and all that the court can do is to construe it under the test and control of the legal rules for the construction of statutes. There have been a number of decisions in which the question has been treated, and the conclusions arrived at in them are as unsatisfactory as they are varying.

After considering them all in an attempt to evolve, if possible, some definite rule for judicial decision, the conclusion that this court has arrived at is as follows: That the meaning of free white persons is to be such as would naturally have been given to it when used in the first naturalization act of 1790. Under such interpretation it would mean by the term "free white persons" all persons belonging to the European races, then commonly counted as white, and their descendants. It would not mean a "Caucasian" race; a term generally employed only after the date of the statute and in a most loose and indefinite way.

It would mean such persons as were in 1790 known as white Europeans, with their descendants, including as their descendants their descendants in other countries to which they have emigrated, such as the descendants of the English in Africa or Australia, or of the French and Germans and Russians in other countries.

This may not, ethnologically or physiologically speaking, be a very clear and logical construction. It includes all European Jews who are of Semitic descent, more or less intermixed with the peoples of European habitancy, viz., with peoples of Celtic, Scandinavian, Teutonic, Iberian, Latin, Greek, and Slavic descent. It includes Magyars, Lapps, and Finns, who are of Ugric stock, and the Basques and Albanians. It includes the mixed Latin, Celtic-Iberian, and Moorish inhabitants of Spain and Portugal, the mixed Greek, Latin, Phoenician, and North African inhabitants of Sicily, and the mixed Slav and Tartar inhabitants of South Russia. It includes peoples containing many of them blood of very mixed races, but the governing or controlling element or strain in all is supposed to be that of a fair-complexioned people of European descent. In 1790 the distinctions of race were not so well known or carefully drawn as they are to-day. At that date all Europeans were commonly classed as the white race, and the term "white" person in the statute then enacted must be construed accordingly. To hold that a pure-blooded Chinaman, because born in England or France, was included within the term, would be as far-fetched as to hold that a pure-blooded Englishman, Irishman, or German born in China was excluded.

To say that a very dark brown, almost black, inhabitant of India is en titled to rank as a white person, because of a possible or hypothetical infusion of white blood 30 or 40 centuries old, and to exclude a Chinese or Japanese, whose parent on one side was white, and who thus possesses manifestly at least one-half European blood, would seem highly inconsistent. If the matter were placed, as some decisions would indicate, on intellectual status and achievement, then the Japanese and certain of the Chinese would be clearly entitled to stand with many of the so-called white nations and with the Parsee, the Brahmin, and the Persian, and far above the negro races.

The law as enacted by Congress gives no place for the consideration of intellectual or moral qualifications or past achievements in a nation or people. It says that the privileges of citizenship of this country may be extended to "free white persons" and to persons of "African nativity" and "African descent." It may be that a highly educated and cultivated Japanese or Chinese or Malay or Siamese is better calculated to make a useful and desirable citizen than a savage from the Guinea coast, but it is not for the courts to give effect to such reasoning. It may also be that the statute as it stands is ambiguous and defective and most difficult of application. All such questions are for the lawmaking department, and the courts can only apply the law as it finds it on the statute book.

In the face of all these difficulties it is safest to follow the reasonable construction of the statute as it would appear to have been intended at the time of its passage, and understand it as restricting the words "free white persons" to mean persons as then understood to be of European habitancy or descent.

This construction of the statute would exclude from naturalization all inhabitants of Asia, Australia, the South Seas, the Malaysian Islands and territories, and of South America, who are not of European descent, or of mixed European and African descent. Under this definition the inhabitants of Syria would be excluded.

The argument that such a construction would exclude persons coming from the very cradle of the Jewish and Christian religions, as professed by the nations of Europe whose descendants form the great bulk of the citizens of the United States, is unworthy of consideration. Such arguments are of the emotional ad captandum order, that have no place in the judicial interpretation of a statute. If the people of the United States, through their representatives in Congress, see fit to exclude by law from citizenship the most worthy and spiritual inhabitants of the globe, it is not for the courts by judicial legislation to gainsay that law, and substitute for it what in their opinion may be more appropriate and reasonable legislation.

In the present case the applicant is not one the admission of whom to citizenship is likely to be for the benefit of the country and in favor of whom the court should exercise the power of discretion given under the statute, and in view of the great uncertainties resulting from the language of the statute and the unsatisfactory reasoning of most of the decisions, the court, without determining the general question of admissibility, will rest its conclusion that the present applicant should not be admitted upon his own personal disqualifications.

Ordered, that the application of the applicant be refused.

Takao Ozawa v. United States

260 U.S. 178 (1922)

Mr. Justice SUTHERLAND delivered the opinion of the Court.

The appellant is a person of the Japanese race born in Japan. He applied, on October 16, 1914, to the United States District Court for the Territory of Hawaii to be admitted as a citizen of the United States. His petition was opposed by the United States District Attorney for the District of Hawaii. Including the period of his residence in Hawaii, appellant had continuously resided in the United States for 20 years. He was a graduate of the Berkeley, California, High School, had been nearly three years a student in the University of California, had educated his children in American schools, his family had attended American churches and he had maintained the use of the English language in his home. That he was well qualified by character and education for citizenship is conceded.

The District Court of Hawaii, however, held that, having been born in Japan and being of the Japanese race, he was not eligible to naturalization under section 2169 of the Revised Statutes, and denied the petition. Thereupon the appellant brought the cause to the Circuit Court of Appeals for the Ninth Circuit and that court has certified the following questions, upon which it desires to be instructed: . . .

"2. Is one who is of the Japanese race and born in Japan eligible to citizenship under the naturalization laws?"

The language of the naturalization laws from 1790 to 1870 had been uniformly such as to deny the privilege of naturalization to an alien unless he came within the description "free white person." By section 7 of the Act of July 14, 1870, the naturalization laws were "extended to aliens of African nativity and to persons of African descent." Section 2169 of the Revised Statutes, as already pointed out, restricts the privilege to the same classes of persons, viz. "to aliens [being free white persons, and to aliens] of African nativity and persons of African descent." It is true that in the first edition of the Revised Statutes of 1873 the words in brackets, "being free white persons, and to aliens" were omitted, but this was clearly an error of the compilers and was corrected by the subsequent legislation of 1875. Is appellant, therefore, a "free white person," within the meaning of that phrase as found in the statute?

On behalf of the appellant it is urged that we should give to this phrase the meaning which it had in the minds of its original framers in 1790 and that it was employed by them for the sole purpose of excluding the black or African race and the Indians then inhabiting this country. It may be true that those two races were alone thought of as being excluded, but to say that they were the only ones within the intent of the statute would be to ignore the affirmative form of the legislation. The provision is not that Negroes and Indians shall be *excluded,* but it is, in effect, that only free white persons shall be *included.* The intention was to confer the privilege of citizenship upon that class of persons whom the fathers knew as white, and to deny it to all who could not be so classified. It is not enough to say that the framers did not have in mind the brown or yellow races of Asia. It is necessary to go farther and be able to say that had these particular races been suggested the language of the act would have been so varied as to include them within its privileges.

If it be assumed that the opinion of the framers was that the only persons who would fall outside the designation "white" were Negroes and Indians, this would go no farther than to demonstrate their lack of sufficient information to enable them to foresee precisely who would be excluded by that term in the subsequent administration of the statute. It is not important in construing their words to consider the extent of their ethnological knowledge or whether they thought that under the statute the only persons who would be denied naturalization would be Negroes and Indians. It is sufficient to ascertain whom they intended to include and having ascertained that it follows, as a necessary corollary, that all others are to be excluded.

The question then is, Who are comprehended within the phrase "free white persons?" Undoubtedly the word "free" was originally used in recognition of the fact that slavery then existed and that some white persons occupied that status. The word, however, has long since ceased to have any practical significance and may now be disregarded.

We have been furnished with elaborate briefs in which the meaning of the words "white person" is discussed with ability and at length, both from the standpoint of judicial decision and from that of the science of ethnology. It does not seem to us necessary, however, to follow counsel in their extensive researches in these fields. It is sufficient to note the fact that these decisions are, in substance, to the effect that the words import a racial and not an individual test, and with this conclusion, fortified as it is by reason and authority, we entirely agree. Manifestly, the test afforded by the mere color of the skin of each individual is impracticable, as that differs greatly among persons of the same race, even among Anglo-Saxons, ranging by imperceptible gradations from the fair blond to the swarthy brunette, the latter being darker than many of the lighter hued persons of the brown or yellow races. Hence to adopt the color test alone would result in a confused overlapping of races and a gradual merging of one into the other, without any practical line of separation. Beginning with the decision of Circuit Judge Sawyer, in *In re Ah Yup*, the federal and state courts, in an almost unbroken line, have held that the words "white person" were meant to indicate only a person of what is popularly known as the Caucasian race.

With the conclusion reached in these several decisions we see no reason to differ. Moreover, that conclusion has become so well established by judicial and executive concurrence and legislative acquiescence that we should not at this late day feel at liberty to disturb it, in the absence of reasons far more cogent than any that have been suggested.

The determination that the words "white person" are synonymous with the words "a person of the Caucasian race" simplifies the problem, although it does not entirely dispose of it. Controversies have arisen and will no doubt arise again in respect of the proper classification of individuals in border line cases. The effect of the conclusion that the words "white person" means a Caucasian is not to establish a sharp line of demarcation between those who are entitled and those who are not entitled to naturalization, but rather a zone of more or less debatable ground inside of which, upon the one hand, are those clearly eligible, and outside of which, upon the other hand, are those clearly ineligible for citizenship.

The appellant, in the case now under consideration, however, is clearly of a race which is not Caucasian and therefore belongs entirely outside the zone on the negative side. A large number of the federal and state courts have so decided and we find no reported case definitely to the contrary. These decisions are sustained by numerous scientific authorities, which we do not deem it necessary to review. We think these decisions are right and so hold.

The briefs filed on behalf of appellant refer in complimentary terms to the culture and enlightenment of the Japanese people, and with this estimate we have no reason to disagree; but these are matters which cannot enter into our consideration of the questions here at issue. We have no function in the matter other than to ascertain the will of Congress and declare it. Of course there is not implied—either in the legislation or in our interpretation of it—any suggestion of individual unworthiness or racial inferiority. These considerations are in no manner involved.

United States v. Bhagat Singh Thind

261 U.S. 204 (1923)

Mr. Justice SUTHERLAND delivered the opinion of the Court.

This cause is here upon a certificate from the Circuit Court of Appeals requesting the instruction of this Court in respect of the following questions:

"1. Is a high-caste Hindu of full Indian blood, born at Amrit Sar, Punjab, India, a white person within the meaning of section 2169, Revised Statutes?"

"2. Does the Act of February 5, 1917 (39 Stat. L. 875, section 3) disqualify from naturalization as citizens those Hindus now barred by that act, who had lawfully entered the United States prior to the passage of said act?"

Section 2169, Revised Statutes, provides that the provisions of the Naturalization Act "shall apply to aliens being free white persons and to aliens of African nativity and to persons of African descent."

If the applicant is a white person, within the meaning of this section, he is entitled to naturalization; otherwise not.

Following a long line of decisions of the lower Federal courts, we held [in *Ozawa v. United States*] that the words imported a racial and not an individual test and were meant to indicate only persons of what is *popularly* known as the Caucasian race. But, as there pointed out, the conclusion that the phrase "white persons" and the word "Caucasian" are synonymous does not end the matter. It enabled us to dispose of the problem as it was there presented, since the applicant for citizenship clearly fell outside the zone of debatable ground on the negative side; but the decision still left the question to be dealt with, in doubtful and different cases.

Mere ability on the part of an applicant for naturalization to establish a line of descent from a Caucasian ancestor will not *ipso facto* and necessarily conclude the inquiry. "Caucasian" is a conventional word of much flexibility, as a study of the literature dealing with racial questions will disclose, and while it and the words "white persons" are treated as synonymous for the purposes of that case, they are not of identical meaning—*idem per idem.*

In the endeavor to ascertain the meaning of the statute we must not fail to keep in mind that it does not employ the word "Caucasian," but the words "white persons," and these are words of common speech and not of scientific origin. The word "Caucasian," not only was not employed in the law but was probably wholly unfamiliar to the original framers of the statute in 1790.

But in this country, during the last half century especially, the word by common usage has acquired a popular meaning, not clearly defined to be sure, but sufficiently so to enable us to say that its popular as distinguished from its scientific application is of appreciably narrower scope. It is in the popular sense of the word, therefore, that we employ it as an aid to the construction of the statute. . . . The words of the statute are to be interpreted in accordance with the understanding of the common man from whose vocabulary they were taken.

They imply, as we have said, a racial test; but the term "race" is one which, for the practical purposes of the statute, must be applied to a group of living persons *now* possessing in common the requisite characteristics, not to groups of persons who are supposed to be or really are descended from some remote, common ancestor, but who, whether they both resemble him to a greater or less extent, have, at any rate, ceased altogether to resemble one another. It may be true that the blond Scandinavian and the brown Hindu have a common ancestor in the dim reaches of antiquity, but the average man knows perfectly well that there are unmistakable and profound differences between them to-day; and it is not impossible, if that common ancestor could be materialized in the flesh, we should discover that he was himself sufficiently differentiated from both of his descendants to preclude his racial classification with either. The question for determination is not, therefore, whether by the speculative processes of ethnological reasoning we may present a probability to the scientific mind that they have the same ori gin, but whether we can satisfy the common understanding that they are now the same or sufficiently the same to justify the interpreters of a statute—written in the words of common speech, for common under-standing, by unscientific men—in classifying them together in the statu-tory category as white persons.

The eligibility of this applicant for citizenship is based on the sole fact that he is of high caste Hindu stock, born in Punjab, one of the extreme northwestern districts of India, and classified by certain scientific author-ities as of the Caucasian or Aryan race.

The term "Aryan" has to do with linguistic and not at all with physical characteristics, and it would seem reasonably clear that mere resemblance in language, indicating a common linguistic root buried in remotely an-cient soil, is altogether inadequate to prove common racial origin. There is, and can be, no assurance that the so-called Aryan language was not spoken by a variety of races living in proximity to one another. Our own history has witnessed the adoption of the English tongue by millions of ne-groes, whose descendants can never be classified racially with the descen-dants of white persons notwithstanding both may speak a common root language.

The word "Caucasian" is in scarcely better repute. It is at best a con-ventional term, with an altogether fortuitous origin, which, under scien-tific manipulation, has come to include far more than the unscientific mind suspects. According to [A. H.] Keane, for example, it includes not only the Hindu, but some of the Polynesians, (that is the Maori, Tahi-tians, Samoans, Hawaiians and others), the Hamites of Africa, upon the ground of the Caucasic cast of their features, though in color they range from brown to black. We venture to think that the average well informed white American would learn with some degree of astonishment that the race to which he belongs is made up of such heterogeneous elements.

The various authorities are in irreconcilable disagreement as to what constitutes a proper racial division. For instance, Blumenbach has five races; Keane following Linnaeus, four; Deniker, twenty-nine. The expla-nation probably is that "the innumerable varieties of mankind run into one another by insensible degrees," and to arrange them in sharply bounded divisions is an undertaking of such uncertainty that common agreement is practically impossible. . .

It does not seem necessary to pursue the matter of scientific classification further. We are unable to agree with the District Court, or with other lower federal courts, in the conclusion that a native Hindu is eligible for naturalization under section 2169. The words of familiar speech, which were used by the original framers of the law, were intended to include only the type of man whom they knew as white. The immigration of that day was almost exclusively from the British Isles and Northwestern Europe, whence they and their forebears had come. When they extended the privilege of American citizenship to "any alien being a free white person" it was these immigrants—bone of their bone and flesh of their flesh—and their kind whom they must have had affirmatively in mind. The succeeding years brought immigrants from Eastern, Southern and Middle Europe, among them the Slavs and the dark-eyed, swarthy people of Alpine and Mediterranean stock, and these were received as unquestionably akin to those already here and readily amalgamated with them. It was the descendants of these, and other immigrants of like origin, who constituted the white population of the country when section 2169, re-enacting the naturalization test of 1790, was adopted; and there is no reason to doubt, with like intent and meaning.

What we now hold is that the words "free white persons" are words of common speech, to be interpreted in accordance with the understanding of the common man, synonymous with the word "Caucasian" only as that word is popularly understood. As so understood and used, whatever may be the speculations of the ethnologist, it does not include the body of people to whom the appellee belongs. It is a matter of familiar observation and knowledge that the physical group characteristics of the Hindus render them readily distinguishable from the various groups of persons in this country commonly recognized as white. The children of English, French, German, Italian, Scandinavian, and other European parentage, quickly merge into the mass of our population and lose the distinctive hallmarks of their European origin. On the other hand, it cannot be doubted that the children born in this country of Hindu parents would retain indefinitely the clear evidence of their ancestry. It is very far from our thought to suggest the slightest question of racial superiority or inferiority. What we suggest is merely racial difference, and it is of such character and extent that the great body of our people instinctively recognize it and reject the thought of assimilation.

It follows that a negative answer must be given to the first question, which disposes of the case and renders an answer to the second question unnecessary, and it will be so certified.

Notes

NOTES TO THE PREFACE TO THE REVISED
AND UPDATED EDITION

1. 29 HARVARD CIVIL RIGHTS-CIVIL LIBERTIES LAW REVIEW 1 (1994).

2. RACISM ON TRIAL: THE CHICANO FIGHT FOR JUSTICE (2003). This book focuses on the legal history of the Chicano movement in East Los Angeles in the late 1960s and early 1970s. In the spring of 1968, ten thousand Mexican high school students poured into the streets to protest the abysmal schools that served more to imprison than to educate. The Mexican community had long sought assimilation partly through the claim of a White racial identity, but these young activists instead embraced a politics of resistance largely predicated on a self-conception as racially brown. The protests were originally organized by student leaders who came together under the banner of the Young Citizens for Community Action—a name that positively reeks of White do-gooder assimilationism. Within months, though, as the Los Angeles Police Department set out to crush the nascent activism on the eastside, this group reconstituted itself as the Brown Berets, a militant cadre that emphasized pride "in our race and in the color of our skin." *Racism on Trial* advances the analysis in *White by Law* in two directions, documenting the informal legal construction of race, and exploring one of the few instances in which a community has affirmatively rejected White identity.

3. I am indebted to Devon Carbado for his insightful comments on the new material in this edition, and owe a million thanks each to Jamie Crook and Emily Bolt for their indispensable help as research assistants. Finally, I am deeply grateful to Deborah Gershenowitz at New York University Press: without her enthusiasm for a tenth anniversary edition of *White by Law*, this new volume would not exist.

NOTES TO CHAPTER 1

1. Act of March 26, 1790, ch. 3, 1 Stat. 103. Naturalization is the conferring of the nationality of a state upon a person after birth, by whatever means. *See* Immigration and Nationality Act of 1952, § 101(a)(23), 66 Stat. 169 (codified as amended at 8 U.S.C. § 1101[a][23] [1988]).

2. Immigration and Nationality Act of 1952, § 311, ch. 2, 66 Stat. 239 (codified as amended at 8 U.S.C. § 1422 [1988]).

3. Louis DeSipio and Harry Pachon, *Making Americans: Administrative Discretion and Americanization,* 12 CHICANO-LATINO L. REV. 52, 54 (1992) (giving the figure as 1,240,700 persons) (citing U.S. DEPT. OF JUSTICE, 1988 STATISTICAL YEARBOOK OF THE IMMIGRATION AND NATURALIZATION Service [1989]).

4. *Id. See also* DARRELL HEVENOR SMITH, THE BUREAU OF NATURALIZATION: ITS HISTORY, ACTIVITIES, AND Organization (1926).

5. Stanford Lyman provides a group-by-group analysis of the holdings in the prerequisite cases. Stanford Lyman, *The Race Question and Liberalism: Casuistries in American Constitutional Law,* 5 INT'L J. OF POL., CULTURE, AND SOC. 183, 206 (1991). On the role of race in the laws governing naturalization generally, *see* Charles Gordon, *The Racial Barrier to American Citizenship,* 93 U. PA. L. REV. 237 (1945) (arguing for removal of racial barriers in naturalization); George Gold, *The Racial Prerequisite in the Naturalization Law,* 15 B.U. L. REV. 462 (1935) (favorably reviewing racial prerequisites and advocating their continuance); and D. O. McGovney, *Race Discrimination in Naturalization,* 8 IOWA L. BULL. 129 (1923) (criticizing racial discrimination in naturalization).

6. Dred Scott v. Sandford, 60 U.S. (19 How.) 393 (1857).

7. His failed efforts are summarized in the first reported prerequisite decision. *See* In re Ah Yup, 1 F.Cas. 223, 224 (C.C.D.Cal. 1878).

8. YUJI ICHIOKA, THE ISSEI: THE WORLD OF THE FIRST GENERATION JAPANESE IMMIGRANTS, 1885–1924, at 212 (1988).

9. *Proceedings of the Asiatic Exclusion League* 8 (1910), *quoted in* RONALD TAKAKI, STRANGERS FROM A DIFFERENT SHORE: A HISTORY OF ASIAN AMERICANS 298 (1989).

10. ICHIOKA, *supra,* at 176–226.

11. John Wigmore, *American Naturalization and the Japanese,* 28 AM. L. REV. 818 (1894).

12. United States v. Cartozian, 6 F.2d 919 (D.Or. 1925). Franz Boas's contribution to anthropology is discussed in AUDREY SMEDLEY, RACE IN NORTH AMERICA: ORIGIN AND EVOLUTION OF A WORLDVIEW 274–82 (1993). *See also* Eric Wolf, *Perilous Ideas: Race, Culture, People,* 35 CURRENT ANTHROPOLOGY 1, 5–7 (1994).

13. *Ah Yup, supra,* 1 F.Cas. 223.

14. *Id.*

15. *Id.* at 223–24.

16. 260 U.S. 178, 198 (1922) (emphasis deleted).

17. 261 U.S. 204, 211 (1922).

18. *Id.*

19. *Id.*

20. *Id.* at 214–15.

21. MARK KELMAN, A GUIDE TO CRITICAL LEGAL STUDIES 253 (1987).

22. Cheryl Harris, *Whiteness as Property,* 106 HARV. L. REV. 1707, 1725 (1993).

23. A. LEON HIGGINBOTHAM, JR., IN THE MATTER OF COLOR: RACE AND THE AMERICAN LEGAL Process: THE COLONIAL PERIOD 20 (1978).

24. REPORT OF THE NATIONAL COMMISSION ON CIVIL DISOR DERS, REJECTION AND PROTEST: AN HISTORICAL SKETCH 95 (1968), *quoted in* DERRICK BELL, RACE, RACISM AND AMERICAN LAW 16 (3rd. ed. 1992).

25. This is not to say that all critical race theorists emphasize that race is human-made. Derrick Bell, for example, is commonly considered one of the founders of critical race theory, and yet, as discussed above, his writings treat races as natural categories. Nor is it to suggest that only critical race theorists have recognized the social origins of race; other writers have as well. *See, e.g.,* Paul Finkelman, *The Crime of Color,* 67 TUL. L. REV. 2063, 2106 (1993) ("American law-making bodies have never been very good at [defining who is a member of what race]. On one level race is clearly a social construct. There is no such thing as a Negro or Caucasian race. There are only people who have certain characteristics associated with people who predominate certain geographic locations."). Most of those writing about the legal construction of race, however, are critical race theorists.

Richard Delgado has compiled an anthology of critical race theory writings and has also published a bibliographic essay on the subject. RICHARD DEL-GADO, CRITICAL RACE THEORY: THE CUTTING EDGE (1995); Richard Delgado, *Bibliographic Essay: Critical Race Theory,* SAGE RACE RELATIONS ABSTRACTS, May 1994, at 3. Moreover, he and Jean Stefancic have compiled an annotated bibliography of the genre. Richard Delgado and Jean Stefancic, *Critical Race Theory: An Annotated Bibliography,* 79 VA. L. REV. 461 (1993). Angela Harris has explored the "modernist" and "postmodernist" tensions in critical race theory, offering an insightful survey of the literature. Angela Harris, *Forword: The Jurisprudence of Reconstruction,* 82 CAL. L. REV. 741 (1994). A brief history of critical race theory is also given in MARI MATSUDA, CHARLES R. LAWRENCE III, RICHARD DELGADO AND KIMBERLE W. CRENSHAW, WORDS THAT WOUND: CRITICAL RACE THEORY, ASSAULTIVE SPEECH, AND THE FIRST AMENDMENT 3–7 (1993).

26. Gerald Torres and Kathryn Milun, *Translating* Yonnondio *by Precedent and Evidence: The Mashpee Indian Case,* 1990 DUKE L.J. 625.

27. *Id.* at 634.

28. John Calmore, *Critical Race Theory, Archie Shepp, and Fire Music: Securing an Authentic Intellectual Life in a Multicultural World,* 65 SO. CAL. L. REV. 2129, 2160 (1992).

29. A large number of critical race theory articles now take race to be a legal

construction. The following stand out: Robert Chang, *Toward an Asian American Legal Scholarship: Critical Race Theory, Post-Structuralism, and Narrative Space,* 81 CAL. L. REV. 1241 (1993) (critiquing the legal and social construction of Asian American identity); Kimberlé Crenshaw, *Race, Reform, and Retrenchment: Transformation and Legitimation in Antidiscrimination Law,* 101 HARV. L. REV. 1331 (1988) (criticizing some critical legal scholars for insufficient concern with the oppositional construction of Black and White identity); Richard Delgado, *Rodrigo's Eighth Chronicle: Black Crime, White Fears—On the Social Construction of Threat,* 80 VA. L. REV. 503 (1994) (asserting that though Blacks have been constructed as a public threat, White criminality is in fact far more harmful to society); Richard Delgado and Jean Stefancic, *Images of the Outsider in American Law and Culture: Can Free Expression Remedy Systemic Social Ills?* 77 CORNELL L. REV. 1258 (1993) (criticizing free-speech advocates for ignoring the difficulty of correcting contemporaneous social understandings of race through speech); Richard Ford, *Urban Space and the Color Line: The Consequences of Demarcation and Disorientation in the Postmodern Metropolis,* 9 HARV. BLACKLETTER J. 117 (1992), and Richard Ford, *The Boundaries of Race: Political Geography in Legal Analysis,* 107 HARV. L. REV. 1841 (1994) (both arguing that to some extent legal segregation creates the races it purports to rely on); Neil Gotanda, *A Critique of "Our Constitution is Color-Blind,"* 44 STAN. L. REV. 1 (1991) (elaborating a taxonomy of the various ways in which the current Supreme Court deploys the idea of "race"); Ian Haney López, *The Social Construction of Race: Some Observations on Illusion, Fabrication, and Choice,* 29 HARV. CIVIL RIGHTS-CIVIL LIBERTIES L. REV. 1 (1994) (arguing for conceiving of race as a social construction); Cheryl Harris, *Whiteness as Property,* 106 HARV. L. REV. 1707 (1993) (examining the manner in which the racial and legal status of Whites was constructed in opposition to that of Blacks so that White status becomes akin to a property right); Lisa Ikemoto, *Traces of the Master Narrative in the Story of African American/Korean American Conflict: How We Constructed "Los Angeles,"* 66 SO. CAL. L. REV. 1581 (1993) (arguing that conflict between minority groups often masks the persistence of a racial system built on White supremacy); D. Marvin Jones, *Darkness Made Visible: Law, Metaphor, and the Racial Self,* 82 GEO. L.J. 437 (1993) (providing a language-based analysis of the courts as creators of symbols that treat Blacks as the "Other"); Jayne Chong-Soon Lee, *Navigating the Topology of Race,* 46 STAN. L. REV. 747 (1994) (advocating strategic deployment of the many nonexclusive meanings of "race," and criticizing the Supreme Court for failing to recognize the extent to which it not only responds to but also creates races); Judy Scales-Trent, *Commonalities: On Being Black and White, Different and the Same,* 2 YALE J.L. & FEMINISM 305 (1990) (exploring in autobiographical form the complexities of "being black and looking white"); Gerald Torres and Kathryn Milun, *Translating* Yonnondio *by Precedent and Evidence: The Mash-*

pee Indian Case, 1990 DUKE L.J. 625 (examining the incongruity of a Native American community having to prove they exist within the parameters of a legal understanding of "tribe" that relies on notions of race and identity unrelated to those of the community); and Patricia Williams, *The Obliging Shell: An Informal Essay on Formal Equal Opportunity,* 87 MICH. L. REV. 2128 (1989) (arguing that legal understandings of race should be grounded in the complexity of social experience, rather than in the false simplicity of formal abstraction).

30. Haney López, *supra,* at 7, 39–53.

31. Immigration Act of 1924, ch. 190, § 13(c), 43 Stat. 162; Immigration and Nationality Act of 1952, ch. 2, § 311, 66 Stat. 239 (codified as amended at 8 U.S.C. § 1422 [1988]).

32. Act of Sept. 22, 1922, ch. 411, § 3, 42 Stat. 1021. *See generally* CHARLES GORDON AND STANLEY MAILMAN, IMMIGRATION LAW AND PROCEDURE § 95.03[6] (rev. ed. 1992).

33. Henry Louis Gates, Jr., *Writing "Race" and the Difference It Makes,* "RACE," WRITING, AND DIFFERENCE 1, 6 (Henry Louis Gates, Jr., ed., 1985).

34. Patrick Buchanan, *This Week with David Brinkley* (ABC television broadcast, Dec. 8, 1991), *quoted in* Bill Ong Hing, *Beyond the Rhetoric of Assimilation and Cultural Pluralism: Addressing the Tension of Separatism and Conflict in an Immigration-Driven Multiracial Society,* 81 CAL. L. REV. 863, 863–64 (1993).

35. Walter Benn Michaels, *Race into Culture: A Critical Genealogy of Cultural Identity,* 18 CRITICAL INQUIRY 655, 663 (1992).

36. Robin Barnes argues that race-consciousness is a core theme running through critical race theory works. Robin Barnes, *Race Consciousness: The Thematic Content of Racial Distinctiveness in Critical Race Scholarship,* 103 HARV. L. REV. 1864 (1990).

37. *See, e.g.,* Crenshaw, *supra* (criticizing the "color-blind, process-oriented" vision of antidiscrimination law); Gotanda, *supra* (arguing that "color-blindness" is a legal construct that ignores the relevance of race in American society and concomitantly fosters White supremacy). Several scholars have argued in favor of "color-blindness." *See, e.g.,* ANDREW KULL, THE COLOR-BLIND CONSTITUTION (1992).

38. *See, e.g.,* Charles Lawrence, *The Id, the Ego, and Equal Protection: Reckoning with Unconscious Racism,* 39 STAN. L. REV. 317 (1987) (author prefaces his critique of equal protection law with a description of his own experience as a victim of unconscious racism); Mari Matsuda, *Looking to the Bottom: Critical Legal Studies and Reparations,* 22 HARV. CIVIL RIGHTS-CIVIL LIBERTIES L. REV. 323, 326 (1987) (arguing for a jurisprudence informed by the experiences of minorities because "the victims of racial oppression have distinct normative insights"). *But see* Stephen Carter, *Academic Tenure and "White Male" Standards:*

Some Lessons from Patent Law, 100 YALE L.J. 2065 (1991) (criticizing the trend in scholarship toward assigning relevance to an author's race); Daniel Farber and Suzanna Sherry, *Telling Stories Out of School: An Essay on Legal Narratives,* 45 STAN. L. REV. 807 (1993) (criticizing narrative methodology and also the idea that there exists a "voice of color").

39. *See, e.g.,* Richard Delgado, *The Imperial Scholar: Reflections on a Review of Civil Rights Literature,* 132 U. PA. L. REV. 561, 577 (1984) ("The time has come for white liberal authors who write in the field of civil rights to redirect their efforts and to encourage their colleagues to do so as well."). *But see* Richard Delgado, *The Imperial Scholar Revisited: How to Marginalize Outsider Writing, Ten Years Later,* 140 U. PA. L. REV. 1349, 1355 (1992) ("The field of civil rights has not been given over entirely to minority and feminist scholars. . . . Nor am I arguing that it should be. For one thing, white males are affected to some degree by issues of racial justice. Moreover, we certainly do not need ghettoization; the cross fertilization resulting from integrated scholarship can be as beneficial as the recognition of long-neglected voices.").

40. *See* Rennard Strickland, *Scholarship in the Academic Circus or the Balancing Act at the Minority Side Show,* 20 U.S.F. L. REV. 491 (1986) (counseling minority law professors not to allow themselves to be shunted into a sideshow in the academic circus).

41. *See* Randall Kennedy, *Racial Critiques of Legal Academia,* 102 HARV. L. REV. 1745, 1818–19 (1989) ("I suspect that another reason [for the lack of engagement by White scholars] is that some observers do not have much confidence in the abilities, or perhaps even the capacities, of minority intellectuals. . . . The contempt that springs from that belief is manifested by silence, a powerful rhetorical weapon."); Jerome Culp, *Posner on Duncan Kennedy and Racial Difference: White Authority in the Legal Academy,* 1991 DUKE L.J. 1095 (denouncing White scholars' assertion of control over legal discourse, even as it applies to Blacks).

42. *See* T. Alexander Aleinikoff, *A Case for Race-Consciousness,* 91 COLUM. L. REV. 1060 (1991); Gary Peller, *Race Consciousness,* 1990 DUKE L.J. 758, 847 (1990); Barbara Flagg, *"Was Blind, But Now I See": White Race Consciousness and the Requirement of Discriminatory Intent,* 91 MICH. L. REV. 953 (1993).

43. Two of the three White authors writing on race-consciousness explicitly acknowledge their intellectual debt to critical race theory. *See* Peller, *supra,* at 758; Flagg, *supra,* at 955–56. An increasing number of White scholars are now writing critically about race or critiquing critical race theory arguments. *See, e.g.,* Francis Lee Ansley, *Race and the Core Curriculum in Legal Education,* 79 CAL. L. REV. 1511 (1991); Duncan Kennedy, *A Cultural Pluralist Case for Affirmative Action in Legal Academia,* 1990 DUKE L.J. 705. *See also* Farber and Sherry, *supra.*

44. Aleinikoff, *supra.*

45. *Id.* at 1066.

46. *Id.* at 1062.

47. *Id.*

48. Like Aleinikoff, Gary Peller discusses race-consciousness only in terms of Blacks. Peller, *supra.* Despite an almost exclusive focus on Blacks, however, Peller does suggest that Whites should examine the constructed nature of their identity. "We should, I think, reinterpret our role in race relations so that we might self-consciously understand ourselves as *whites,* as having a particular identity that was historically constructed through the economy of race relations." *Id.* at 847. Unfortunately, this statement comes in the form of a concluding remark on the last page of Peller's article, rather than as a point he explores at length.

49. Flagg, *supra,* at 956–57.

50. *Id.* at 957 (emphasis in original).

51. *Id.* at 961.

52. 205 F. 812, 813 (E.D.S.C. 1913).

53. *Id.*

54. McIlwaine 479 (Sept. 1630), *reprinted in* HIGGINBOTHAM, *supra,* at 23.

55. HIGGINBOTHAM, *supra,* at 23.

56. Flagg, *supra,* at 969.

57. RUTH FRANKENBERG, WHITE WOMEN, RACE MATTERS: THE SOCIAL CONSTRUCTION OF WHITENESS 9 (1993). Frankenberg suggests that "the extent to which white women were 'missing' or 'not getting' the significance of race in our or anyone else's experience had everything to do with standpoint: because we were race privileged . . . we were not in a structural position to see the effects of racism on our lives, nor the significance of race in the shaping of U.S. society." *Id.* (citation omitted).

58. *Shahid, supra,* 205 F. at 814.

59. VIRGINIA DOMINGUEZ, WHITE BY DEFINITION: SOCIAL CLASSI-FICATION IN CREOLE LOUISIANA 54 (1986).

60. *Shahid, supra,* 205 F. at 814.

61. *Thind, supra,* 261 U.S. at 211. The holding in *Shahid* differs from that in *Thind,* though in a manner not relevant to the above discussion, in concluding that Whiteness should be defined in terms of common knowledge as it existed in 1790, rather than as it existed contemporaneously.

62. *Shahid, supra,* 205 F. at 814 (emphasis added).

63. F. JAMES DAVIS, WHO IS BLACK? ONE NATION'S DEFINITION 5 (1991).

64. Gotanda, *supra,* at 26.

65. *Thind, supra,* 261 U.S. at 215.

66. Crenshaw, *supra,* at 1373.

67. Drawing on a wider range of cases, Neil Gotanda also notes the close link-age of non-Black minority identities with foreignness. Neil Gotanda, *"Other Non-Whites" in American Legal History: A Review of* Justice at War, 85 COLUM. L. REV. 1186, 1190–92 (1985).

68. Ford, *Urban Space, supra,* at 134 (citation omitted). *See also* JOEL KOVEL, WHITE RACISM: A PSYCHOHISTORY (1970).

69. TONI MORRISON, PLAYING IN THE DARK: WHITENESS AND THE LITERARY IMAGINATION 52 (1993).

70. Flagg, *supra,* at 957.

71. *Id.* at 1017.

72. *Id.* at 957 (White identity should be "neither founded on the implicit ac-ceptance of white racial domination nor productive of distributive effects that sys-tematically advantage whites"); *id.* at 977–78 ("the development of a positive white racial identity [should] not posit whites as superior to blacks").

73. In re Halladjian, 174 F. 834 (C.C.D. Mass. 1909).

74. Scholars in many fields have recently begun to scrutinize Whiteness. Sev-eral recent works stand out. *See* THEODORE ALLEN, THE INVENTION OF THE WHITE RACE, VOLUME ONE: RACIAL OPPRESSION AND SOCIAL CONTROL (1994) (history); FRANKENBERG, *supra* (women's studies); MOR-RISON, *supra* (literary criticism); DAVID ROEDIGER, TOWARDS THE ABO-LITION OF WHITENESS (1994), and THE WAGES OF WHITENESS: RACE AND THE MAKING OF THE AMERICAN WORKING CLASS (1992) (labor history); ALEXANDER SAXTON, THE RISE AND FALL OF THE WHITE RE-PUBLIC: CLASS POLITICS AND MASS CULTURE IN NINETEENTH-CENTURY AMERICA (1990) (history); VRON WARE, BEYOND THE PALE: WHITE WOMEN, RACISM AND HISTORY (1992) (historiography); and ROB-ERT YOUNG, WHITE MYTHOLOGIES: WRITING HISTORY AND THE WEST (1990) (historiography).

The laws defining Whites and Blacks in relation to each other are summarized in Paul Finkelman, *The Color of Law,* 87 NW. U. L. REV. 937, 952–57 (1993), and Finkelman, *The Crime of Color, supra. See also* Harris, *supra,* at 1737–41. Several interesting contemporary cases exploring legal definitions of White identity are excerpted in LESLIE BENDER AND DAAN BRAVEMAN, POWER, PRIVILEGE AND LAW: A CIVIL RIGHTS READER 150–57 (1995). For his-torical works on this subject, *see generally* PAUL MURRAY, STATES' LAWS ON RACE AND COLOR (1950); CHARLES M. MAGNUM, JR., THE LEGAL STA-TUS OF THE NEGRO (1940); and GILBERT T. STEPHENSON, RACE DIS-TINCTIONS IN AMERICAN LAW (1910). More recent though not specifically legal works include DAVIS, *supra,* and DOMINGUEZ, *supra.*

75. David Roediger has recently provided one such study, assessing the devel-opment of White identity among the working class. ROEDIGER, THE WAGES OF WHITENESS, *supra.* Similarly, Ruth Frankenberg has provided another such

study, though focused on the construction of race among White women. FRANKENBERG, *supra*.

76. ALEXANDER BICKEL, THE MORALITY OF CONSENT 33 (1975).

77. H.R.J. Res. 129, 103d Cong., 1st Sess. (1993).

78. *Proposition 187: Text of Proposed Law*, CALIFORNIA BALLOT PAMPHLET, GENERAL ELECTION, NOVEMBER 8, 1994, at 91.

NOTES TO CHAPTER 2

1. U.S. COMMISSION ON CIVIL RIGHTS, THE TARNISHED GOLDEN DOOR: CIVIL RIGHTS ISSUES IN IMMIGRATION 1–12 (1990).

2. Chinese Exclusion Act, ch. 126, 22 Stat. 58 (1882). *See generally* Harold Hongju Koh, *Bitter Fruit of the Asian Immigration Cases*, 6 CONSTITUTION 69 (1994). For a sobering account of the many lynchings of Chinese in the western United States during this period, *see* John R. Wunder, *Anti-Chinese Violence in the American West, 1850–1910*, LAW FOR THE ELEPHANT, LAW FOR THE BEAVER: ESSAYS IN THE LEGAL HISTORY OF THE NORTH AMERICAN WEST 212 (John McLaren, Hamar Foster, and Chet Orloff eds., 1992). Charles McClain, Jr., discusses the historical origins of anti-Chinese prejudice and the legal responses undertaken by that community on the West Coast. Charles McClain, Jr., *The Chinese Struggle for Civil Rights in Nineteenth Century America: The First Phase, 1850–1870*, 72 CAL. L. REV. 529 (1984). For a discussion of contemporary racial violence against Asian Americans, *see* Note, *Racial Violence against Asian Americans*, 106 HARV. L. REV. 1926 (1993); Robert Chang, *Toward an Asian American Legal Scholarship: Critical Race Theory, Post-Structuralism, and Narrative Space*, 81 CAL. L. REV. 1241, 1251–58 (1993).

3. Act of July 9, 1884, ch. 220, 23 Stat. 115; Act of May 5, 1892, ch. 60, 27 Stat. 25; Act of April 29, 1902, ch. 641, 32 Stat. 176; Act of April 27, 1904, ch. 1630, 33 Stat. 428.

4. Act of Feb. 5, 1917, ch. 29, 39 Stat. 874.

5. U.S. COMMISSION ON CIVIL RIGHTS, *supra*, at 9.

6. *Id. See* Act of May 19, 1921, ch. 8, 42 Stat. 5; Act of May 26, 1924, ch. 190, 43 Stat. 153.

7. U.S. COMMISSION ON CIVIL RIGHTS, *supra*, at 10.

8. *Id.* at 11. *See generally* JUAN RAMON GARCIA, OPERATION WETBACK: THE MASS DEPORTATION OF MEXICAN UNDOCUMENTED WORKERS IN 1954 (1980).

9. Act of Oct. 2, 1965, 79 Stat. 911.

10. Chae Chan Ping v. United States, 130 U.S. 581 (1889). The Court reasoned in part that if "the government of the United States, through its legislative department, considers the presence of foreigners of a different race in this coun-

try, who will not assimilate with us, to be dangerous to its peace and security, their exclusion is not to be stayed." For a critique of this deplorable result, *see* Louis Henkin, *The Constitution and United States Sovereignty: A Century of Chinese Exclusion and Its Progeny,* 100 HARV. L. REV. 853 (1987).

11. For efforts to encourage Irish immigration, *see, e.g.,* Immigration Act of 1990, § 131, 104 Stat. 4978 (codified as amended at 8 U.S.C. §1153 (c) [1994]). Bill Ong Hing argues that Congress continues to discriminate against Asians. "Through an examination of past exclusion laws, previous legislation, and the specific provisions of the Immigration Act of 1990, the conclusion can be drawn that Congress never intended to make up for nearly 80 years of Asian exclusion, and that a conscious hostility towards persons of Asian descent continues to pervade Congressional circles." Bill Ong Hing, *Asian Americans and Present U.S. Immigration Policies: A Legacy of Asian Exclusion,* ASIAN AMERICANS AND THE SUPREME COURT: A DOCUMENTARY HISTORY 1106, 1107 (Hyung-Chan Kim ed., 1992).

12. Louis DeSipio and Harry Pachon, *Making Americans: Administrative Discretion and Americanization,* 12 CHICANO-LATINO L. REV. 52, 53 (1992).

13. CHARLES GORDON AND STANLEY MAILMAN, IMMIGRATION LAW AND PROCEDURE § 92.03[1][b] (rev. ed. 1992).

14. Dred Scott v. Sandford, 60 U.S. (19 How.) 393 (1857). For an insightful discussion of the role of *Dred Scott* in the development of American citizenship, *see* JAMES KETTNER, THE DEVELOPMENT OF AMERICAN CITIZEN-SHIP, 1608–1870, at 300–333 (1978); *see also* KENNETH L. KARST, BE-LONGING TO AMERICA: EQUAL CITIZENSHIP AND THE CONSTITU-TION 43–61 (1989).

15. Civil Rights Act of 1866, ch. 31, 14 Stat. 27.

16. U.S. Const. amend. XIV.

17. 169 U.S. 649 (1898).

18. 112 U.S. 94 (1884).

19. Act of June 2, 1924, ch. 233, 43 Stat. 253.

20. Nationality Act of 1940, § 201(b), 54 Stat. 1138. *See generally* GOR-DON AND MAILMAN, *supra,* at § 92.03[3][e].

21. Pete Wilson, *Crack Down on Illegals,* USA TODAY, Aug. 20, 1993, at 12A.

22. H.R.J. Res. 129, 103d Cong., 1st Sess. (1993). An earlier, scholarly call to revamp the Fourteenth Amendment can be found in PETER SCHUCK and ROGER SMITH, CITIZENSHIP WITHOUT CONSENT: ILLEGAL ALIENS IN THE AMERICAN POLITY (1985).

23. Koh, *supra,* at 69–70.

24. Bill Ong Hing, *Beyond the Rhetoric of Assimilation and Cultural Pluralism: Addressing the Tension of Separatism and Conflict in an Immigration-Driven Multiracial Society,* 81 CAL. L. REV. 863, 866 (1993).

25. Gerald Neuman warns against amending the Citizenship Clause. Gerald Neuman, *Back to* Dred Scott? 24 SAN DIEGO L. REV. 485, 500 (1987). *See also* Note, *The Birthright Citizenship Amendment: A Threat to Equality,* 107 HARV. L. REV. 1026 (1994).

26. U.S. Const. art. I, sec. 8, cl. 4.

27. Act of March 26, 1790, ch. 3, 1 Stat. 103.

28. KETTNER, *supra,* at 215–16.

29. One exception exists. In revisions undertaken in 1870, the "white person" limitation was omitted. However, this omission is regarded as accidental, and the prerequisite was reinserted in 1875 by "an act to correct errors and to supply omissions in the Revised Statutes of the United States." Act of Feb. 18, 1875, ch. 80, 18 Stat. 318. *See* In re Ah Yup, 1 F.Cas. 223 (C.C.D.Cal. 1878) ("Upon revision of the statutes, the revisors, probably inadvertently, as Congress did not contemplate a change of the laws in force, omitted the words 'white persons.' ").

30. Statement of Senator Hendricks, 59 CONG. GLOBE, 42nd Cong., 1st Sess. 2939 (1866). *See also* John Guendelsberger, *Access to Citizenship for Children Born Within the State to Foreign Parents,* 40 AM. J. COMP. L. 379, 407–9 (1992).

31. Statement of Senator Cowan, 57 CONG. GLOBE, 42nd Cong., 1st Sess. 499 (1866). For a discussion of the role of anti-Asian prejudice in the laws governing naturalization, *see generally* Elizabeth Hull, *Naturalization and Denaturalization,* ASIAN AMERICANS AND THE SUPREME COURT: A DOCUMENTARY HISTORY 403 (Hyung-Chan Kim ed., 1992)

32. The Senate rejected an amendment that would have allowed Chinese persons to naturalize. The proposed amendment read: "That the naturalization laws are hereby extended to aliens of African nativity, and to persons of African descent, and to persons born in the Chinese empire." BILL ONG HING, MAKING AND REMAKING ASIAN AMERICA THROUGH IMMIGRATION POLICY, 1850–1990, at 239 n.34 (1993).

33. Act of July 14, 1870, ch. 255, § 7, 16 Stat. 254.

34. Chinese Exclusion Act, ch. 126, § 14, 22 Stat. 58 (1882).

35. Fong Yue Ting v. United States, 149 U.S. 698, 716 (1893).

36. Neil Gotanda contends that separate racial ideologies function with respect to "other non-Whites," meaning non-Black racial minorities such as Asians, Native Americans, and Latinos. Neil Gotanda, *"Other Non-Whites" in American Legal History: A Review of* Justice at War, 85 COLUM. L. REV. 1186 (1985). Gotanda explicitly identifies the operation of this separate ideology in the Supreme Court's jurisprudence regarding Asians and citizenship. Neil Gotanda, *Asian American Rights and the "Miss Saigon Syndrome,"* ASIAN AMERICANS AND THE SUPREME COURT: A DOCUMENTARY HISTORY 1087, 1096–97 (Hyung-Chan Kim ed., 1992).

37. Charles Gordon, *The Racial Barrier to American Citizenship,* 93 U. PA. L. REV. 237, 252 (1945).

38. MILTON KONVITZ, THE ALIEN AND THE ASIATIC IN AMERICAN LAW 80–81 (1946) (citation omitted).

39. Act of Oct. 14, 1940, ch. 876, § 303, 54 Stat. 1140.

40. Note, *The Nationality Act of 1940*, 54 HARV. L. REV. 860, 865 n.40 (1941).

41. Act of Dec. 17, 1943, ch. 344, § 3, 57 Stat. 600.

42. Act of July 2, 1946, ch. 534, 60 Stat. 416.

43. *Id.*

44. Immigration and Nationality Act of 1952, ch. 2, § 311, 66 Stat. 239 (codified as amended at 8 U.S.C. 1422 [1988]).

45. Arguably, the continued substantial exclusion of Asians from immigration, not remedied until 1965, rendered their eligibility for naturalization relatively meaningless. "[T]he national quota system for admitting immigrants which was built into the 1952 Act gave the grant of eligibility a hollow ring." Chin Kim and Bok Lim Kim, *Asian Immigrants in American Law: A Look at the Past and the Challenge Which Remains*, 26 AM. U. L. REV. 373, 390 (1977).

46. *See generally* Ursula Vogel, *Is Citizenship Gender-Specific?* THE FRONTIERS OF CITIZENSHIP 58 (Ursula Vogel and Michael Moran eds., 1991).

47. Act of Feb. 10, 1855, ch. 71, § 2, 10 Stat. 604. Because gender-based laws in the area of citizenship were motivated by the idea that a woman's citizenship should follow that of her husband, no naturalization law has explicitly targeted unmarried women. GORDON AND MAILMAN, *supra,* at § 95.03[6] ("An unmarried woman has never been [statutorily] barred from naturalization.").

48. PRENTISS WEBSTER, LAW OF NATURALIZATION IN THE UNITED STATES OF AMERICA AND OTHER COUNTRIES 80 (1895).

49. Act of Feb. 10, 1855, ch. 71, § 2, 10 Stat. 604.

50. Kelly v. Owen, 74 U.S. 496, 498 (1868).

51. GORDON AND MAILMAN, *supra* at § 95.03[6].

52. Act of Sept. 22, 1922, ch. 411, § 2, 42 Stat. 1021.

53. GORDON AND MAILMAN, *supra* at § 100.03[4][m].

54. Act of March 2, 1907, ch. 2534, § 3, 34 Stat. 1228. This act was upheld in MacKenzie v. Hare, 239 U.S. 299 (1915) (expatriating a U.S.-born woman upon her marriage to a British citizen).

55. Act of Sept. 22, 1922, ch. 411, § 3, 42 Stat. 1021.

56. *Id.* The Act also stated that "[n]o woman whose husband is not eligible to citizenship shall be naturalized during the continuance of the marriage."

57. Act of March 3, 1931, ch. 442, § 4(a), 46 Stat. 1511.

58. The loss of birthright citizenship was particularly harsh for those women whose race made them unable to regain citizenship through naturalization, especially after 1924, when the immigration laws of this country barred entry to any alien ineligible to citizenship. Immigration Act of 1924, ch. 190, § 13(c), 43 Stat. 162. *See, e.g.,* Ex parte (Ng) Fung Sing, 6 F.2d 670 (W.D.Wash. 1925). In that

case, a U.S. birthright citizen of Chinese descent was expatriated because of her marriage to a Chinese citizen, and was subsequently refused admittance to the United States as an alien ineligible to citizenship

NOTES TO CHAPTER 3

1. In re Ah Yup, 1 F.cas. 223 (C.C.D.Cal. 1878).

2. The only reported case in which a petitioner sought to naturalize as a person of African nativity came in 1938. In re Cruz, 23 F.Supp. 774 (E.D.N.Y. 1938). The court held that persons one-quarter African and three-quarters Native American are not eligible to citizenship as a person of "African descent."

3. JAMES KETTNER, THE DEVELOPMENT OF AMERICAN CITIZEN-SHIP, 1608–1870, at 343 (1978).

4. Chin Kim and Bok Lim Kim, *Asian Immigrants in American Law: A Look at the Past and the Challenge Which Remains,* 26 AM. U. L. REV. 373, 380 (1977).

5. RONALD TAKAKI, IRON CAGES: RACE AND CULTURE IN 19TH CENTURY AMERICA 101 (1990). *See also* GARY OKIHIRO, MARGINS AND MAINSTREAMS: ASIANS IN AMERICAN HISTORY AND CULTURE 31–63 (1994); Dan Caldwell, *The Negroization of the Chinese Stereotype in California,* 53 SO. CAL. Q. 123 (June 1971).

6. People v. Hall, 4 Cal. 399 (1854).

7. *Id.* at 400–402.

8. Rice v. Gong Lum, 139 Miss. 760, 104 So. 105 (1925), discussed in Stanford Lyman, *The Race Question and Liberalism: Casuistries in American Constitutional Law,* 5 INT'L J. OF POL., CULTURE, AND SOC. 183, 206 (1991).

9. *See, e.g.,* Gilbert Stephenson, *Race Distinctions in American Law,* 43 AM. L. REV. 29, 37–46 (1909) (addressing "What is a Negro?"); *see generally* F. JAMES DAVIS, WHO IS BLACK? ONE NATION'S DEFINITION (1991). Of course, as I argue in chapter 6, the legal definitions of Black identity in the slave codes and the Jim Crow laws served at least by default to define who was White.

10. *See generally* STANLEY LIEBERSON, A PIECE OF THE PIE: BLACKS AND WHITE IMMIGRANTS SINCE 1880 (1980).

11. *Ah Yup, supra,* 1 F.Cas. at 224–25.

12. *Id.* at 223.

13. *Id.*

14. *Id.* at 224.

15. Terrace v. Thompson, 274 F. 841, 849 (W.D.Wash. 1921), *aff'd,* 263 U.S. 197 (1923). *Terrace* is not directly a racial prerequisite case, but instead concerns the ability of a person racially barred from citizenship to own land under state law. Statutes barring aliens racially ineligible for naturalization from owning land, referred to collectively as alien land laws, are discussed in chapter 6. Note that one

ation here:

legal scholar cites the quoted passage to support his contention that racial barriers to naturalization were "not without foundation in reason." George Gold, *The Racial Prerequisite in Naturalization Law,* 15 B.U. L. REV. 462 (1935).

16. AUDREY SMEDLEY, RACE IN NORTH AMERICA: ORIGIN AND EVOLUTION OF A WORLDVIEW 280 (1993).

17. In re Po, 28 N.Y. Supp. 383, 384 (City Ct. 1894).

18. *Id.*

19. In re Camille, 6 F. 256, 258 (C.C.D.Or. 1880).

20. Ex parte Shahid, 205 F. 812, 815 (E.D.S.C. 1913).

21. Thomas Ross, *The Rhetorical Tapestry of Race: White Innocence and Black Abstraction,* 32 WM & MARY L. REV. 1 (1990). Ross's thesis is that little has changed: he argues that "the rhetorical themes of the nineteenth-century cases on race are still the essential themes of our contemporary legal rhetoric of race." *Id.* at 7.

22. Randall Kennedy, *Race Relations Law and the Tradition of Celebration: The Case of Professor Schmidt,* 86 COLUM. L. REV. 1622 (1986).

23. *Id.*

24. Charles Gordon, *The Racial Barrier to American Citizenship,* 93 U. PA. L. REV. 237, 246 (1945).

25. *See generally* Peter Fitzpatrick, *Racism and the Innocence of Law,* ANATOMY OF RACISM 247 (David Theo Goldberg ed., 1990).

26. In re Knight, 171 F. 299, 300 (E.D.N.Y. 1909).

27. *Id.*

28. *Id.* at 301.

29. In re Gee Hop, 71 F. 274 (N.D.Cal. 1895).

30. *Id.* at 275.

31. *Id.*

32. *See, e.g.,* In re Buntaro Kumagai, 163 F. 922, 923 (W.D.Wash. 1908). The court wrote:

This applicant for naturalization is an educated Japanese gentleman, and, in support of his petition to be admitted to citizenship, he presents a certificate showing that at the expiration of a term for which he enlisted as a soldier in the regular army of the United States he was honorably discharged. There appears to be no objection to his admission on personal grounds, and the court has given no consideration to any questions which might be raised of a formal character; the intention of the court being to rest its decision denying the application on the single ground that Congress has not extended to Japanese people not born within the United States the privilege of becoming adopted citizens of this country.

33. *See, e.g., Camille, supra,* 6 F. 256. Camille moved to the United States in 1847 at age seventeen, and was denied naturalization in 1880 when he was fifty years old, after having lived in the country for thirty-three years.

34. *See, e.g.,* In re Hong Yen Chang, 84 Cal. 163, 165 (1890). The court held that the certificate of naturalization and license to practice law issued by New York courts to Hong Yen Chang were "issued without authority of law, and . . . void" in California because the holder was "a person of Mongolian nativity." *See also* In re Yamashita, 30 Wash. 234, 236 (1902). The court denied Yamashita's application to practice law and declared that the order admitting him to citizenship was void on its face and subject to attack at any time and in any proceeding because he was of the "Japanese race."

35. In re Rodriguez, 81 F. 337, 349 (W.D.Tex. 1897).

36. *Id.* at 354. Despite the admission of Rodriguez to citizenship, Mexicans in the Southwest suffered considerable legal repression in the decades after the U.S. conquest of that region. *See generally* RODOLFO ACUÑA, OCCUPIED AMER-ICA: A HISTORY OF CHICANOS (3rd. ed. 1988). The history of legal resistance to such repression is examined in George Martínez, *Legal Indeterminacy, Judicial Discretion and the Mexican-American Litigation Experience: 1930–1980,* 27 U.C. DAVIS L. REV. 555 (1994).

37. The Supreme Court subsequently drew into question the holding in *Rodriguez.* Morrison v. California, 291 U.S. 82, 95 n.5 (1933). The Court wrote: "Whether a person of [Mexican] descent may be naturalized in the United States is still an unsettled question. The subject was considered in *Matter of Rodriguez,* but not all that was there said is consistent with later decisions of this court." For a commentator's criticism of *Rodriguez* on the grounds that Mexicans are not "white persons," *see* Gold, *supra,* at 499–501.

38. John Wigmore, *American Naturalization and the Japanese,* 28 AM. L. REV. 818 (1894).

39. *Id.* at 827.

40. *Id.*

41. Chester Rowell, *Chinese and Japanese Immigrants—A Comparison,* 34 ANNALS OF AM. ACAD. 223, 224 (July-Dec. 1909).

42. *Ah Yup, supra,* 1 F.Cas. at 223. The appearance of common knowledge and scientific evidence rationales in *Ah Yup* is discussed at greater length in chapter 1.

43. *Id.* at 223–24.

44. *Id.* at 224–25.

45. *Hong Yen Chang, supra,* 84 Cal. at 164.

46. *Ah Yup, supra,* 1 F.Cas. at 223.

47. FREDERICK VAN DYNE, A TREATISE ON THE LAW OF NATURAL-IZATION OF THE UNITED STATES 42 (1907).

48. In re Saito, 62 F. 126, 127 (C.C.D.Mass. 1894).

49. *Id.*

50. *See* VAN DYNE, *supra,* at 41.

51. In re Halladjian, 174 F. 735 (C.C.D.Mass. 1909).

52. In re Najour, 174 F. 735 (N.D.Ga. 1909); In re Mudari, 176 F. 465 (C.C.D.Mass. 1910); In re Ellis, 179 F. 1003 (D.Or. 1910); Dow v. United States, 226 F. 145 (4th Cir. 1915); *Shahid, supra,* 205 F. 812; Ex parte Dow, 211 F. 486 (E.D.S.C. 1914); In re Dow, 213 F. 355 (E.D.S.C. 1914).

53. United States v. Dolla, 177 F. 101 (5th Cir. 1910); United States v. Balsara, 180 F. 694 (2nd Cir. 1910); In re Akhay Kumar Mozumdar, 207 F. 114 (E.D.Wash. 1913); In re Mohan Singh, 257 F. 209 (S.D.Cal. 1919); In re Thind, 268 F. 683 (D.Or. 1920), In re Balsara, 171 F. 294 (C.C.S.D.N.Y. 1909); In re Sadar Bhagwar Singh, 246 F. 496 (E.D.Pa. 1917); United States v. Thind, 261 U.S. 204 (1923).

54. *Najour, supra,* 174 F. 735. *Najour* is not the first case during this period to rule in favor of an applicant for citizenship. The court in *In re Balsara* did so as well. However, the court in that case granted naturalization despite concluding that the Asian Indian applicant was not White. *In re Balsara, supra,* 171 F. 294. The court in *Rodriguez* also naturalized the applicant despite concluding that he was not White. *Rodriguez, supra,* 81 F. 337.

55. *Id.* (citation omitted).

56. *Halladjian, supra,* 174 F. 735; *Mudarri, supra,* 176 F. 465; *United States v. Balsara, supra,* 180 F. 694.

57. In re Young, 198 F. 715 (W.D.Wash. 1912); *Shahid, supra,* 205 F. 812; *Ex parte Dow, supra,* 211 F. 486; *In re Dow, supra,* 213 F. 355.

58. *Shahid, supra,* 205 F. at 813.

59. *Ex parte Dow, supra,* 211 F. at 487.

60. *Najour, supra,* 174 F. at 735.

61. *Halladjian, supra,* 174 F. at 835.

62. *Najour, supra,* 174 F. at 735 (quoting A. H. KEANE, THE WORLD'S PEOPLE: A Popular ACCOUNT OF THEIR BODILY AND MENTAL CHARACTERS, BELIEFS, TRADITIONS, Political AND SOCIAL INSTITUTIONS 5 [1908]).

63. THOMAS GOSSETT, RACE: THE HISTORY OF AN IDEA IN NORTH AMERICA 82 (1963).

64. KEANE, *supra,* at 13–26, *passim.*

65. *Id.* at 416–17.

66. *Mudarri, supra,* 176 F. 465 (Syrians are White); *Halladjian, supra,* 174 F. 834 (Armenians are White); and *United States v. Balsara, supra,* 180 F. 694 (Asian Indians are White).

67. *Shahid, supra,* 205 F. at 812–13.

68. *Id.* at 813.

69. *Id.*

70. *Id.* at 814.

71. *Id.*

72. *Id.*

73. *Id.* at 815.
74. *Id.* at 814.
75. *Id.* at 817.
76. *Ex parte Dow, supra,* 211 F. 486.
77. *In re Dow, supra,* 213 F. 355.
78. *Id.* at 357.
79. *Ex parte Dow, supra,* 211 F. at 486–87.
80. *In re Dow, suptra,* 213 F. at 363–64.
81. *Id.* at 364.
82. *Id.* at 358.
83. *Id.*
84. GOSSETT, *supra,* at 37–39.
85. *In re Dow, supra,* 213 F. at 358–59 (reference omitted).
86. *Id.* at 360.
87. *Ex parte Dow, supra,* 211 F. at 489.
88. *Shahid, supra,* 205 F. at 815. *See, e.g., Akhay Kumar Mozumdar, supra,* 207 F. 115; *Mohan Singh, supra,* 257 F. 209; *In re Thind, supra,* 268 F. 683.
89. *In re Dow, supra,* 211 F. at 488.

NOTES TO CHAPTER 4

1. Ozawa v. United States, 260 U.S. 178, 197 (1927) (emphasis in original).
2. *Id.* at 198. *See generally* Yuji Ichioka, *The Early Japanese Immigrant Quest for Citizenship: The Background of the 1922 Ozawa Case,* 4 AMERASIA 1 (1977); Robert C. Yamashita and Peter Park, *The Politics of Race: The Open Door, Ozawa and the Case of Japanese in America,* 17 REV. RADICAL POL. ECON. 135 (1985); Raymond Leslie Buell, *Some Legal Aspects of the Japanese Question,* 17 AM. J. INT'L. L. 29 (1923).
3. Ichioka, *supra,* at 12.
4. *Quoted in id.* at 11.
5. *Id.*
6. *Ozawa, supra,* 260 U.S. at 198.
7. Ichioka, *supra,* at 9–17.
8. *Ozawa, supra,* 260 U.S. at 184.
9. Brief for Petitioner at 55, 57, 71, Takao Ozawa vs. United States, 260 U.S. 178 (1922).
10. *Ozawa, supra,* 260 U.S. at 197.
11. THOMAS GOSSETT, RACE: THE HISTORY OF AN IDEA IN NORTH AMERICA 69 (1963) (citation omitted).
12. *Ozawa, supra,* 260 U.S. at 197.
13. GOSSETT, *supra,* at 65–83.
14. *Id.* at 69.

15. *Ozawa, supra,* 260 U.S. at 189 (citations omitted).

16. *But see* John Wigmore, *American Naturalization and the Japanese,* 28 AM. L. REV. 818 (1894) (articulating the ethnological argument that the Japanese are Caucasian).

17. *Ozawa, supra,* 260 U.S. at 198.

18. *Id.*

19. Ichioka, *supra,* at 17.

20. *Id.*

21. YUJI ICHIOKA, THE ISSEI: THE WORLD OF THE FIRST GENERATION JAPANESE IMMIGRANTS, 1885–1924, at 1–2 (1988).

22. *See* James Lesser, *Always "Outsiders": Asians, Naturalization, and the Supreme Court,* 12 AMERASIA 83 (1985–86) (the prerequisite cases "had the effect of defining Asian immigrants as perpetual 'outsiders,' as aliens ineligible for citizenship").

23. United States v. Thind, 261 U.S. 204 (1923). *See generally* JOAN JENSEN, PASSAGE FROM INDIA: ASIAN INDIAN IMMIGRANTS IN NORTH AMERICA 246–69 (1988).

24. In re Thind, 268 F. 683 (D.Or. 1920).

25. RONALD TAKAKI, STRANGERS FROM A DIFFERENT SHORE: A HISTORY OF ASIAN AMERICANS 294 (1989); JENSEN, *supra,* at 256.

26. *In re Thind, supra,* 268 F. 683.

27. *Id.* at 684 (citing In re Mohan Singh, 257 F. 209 [S.D.Cal. 1919]; In re Halladjian, 174 F. 834 [C.C.D.Mass. 1909]; and United States v. Balsara, 180 F. 694 [2d Cir. 1910]).

28. *Thind, supra,* 261 U.S. at 206.

29. TAKAKI, *supra,* at 295.

30. *See* United States v. Dolla, 177 F. 101 (5th Cir. 1910) (Asian Indians are White); *Balsara, supra,* 180 F. 694 (same); In re Akhay Kumar Mozumdar, 207 F. 115 (E.D.Wash. 1913) (same); *Mohan Singh, supra,* 257 F. 209 (same); *but see* In re Sadar Bhagwab Singh, 246 F. 496 (E.D.Pa. 1917) (Asian Indians are not White).

31. *Thind, supra,* 261 U.S. at 209.

32. *Id.* at 210–11.

33. *Id.* at 211.

34. *Id.*

35. *Id.* (citation omitted).

36. *Id.*

37. *Id.* at 214–15.

38. *Id.* at 210.

39. *Id.* at 215.

40. JENSEN, *supra,* at 258 (citation omitted).

41. DAVID ROEDIGER, TOWARDS THE ABOLITION OF WHITENESS

182 (1994). To their credit, some courts resisted these efforts, usually on jurisdictional grounds. *See, e.g.,* United States v. Sakharam Ganesh Pandit, 15 F.2d 285 (9th Cir. 1926).

42. TAKAKI, *supra,* at 300 (citation omitted).

43. Quoted in JENSEN, *supra,* at 258–59.

44. *Id.*

45. Justice Sutherland's tenure on the Supreme Court is reviewed in David Burner, *George Sutherland,* THE JUSTICES OF THE UNITED STATES SUPREME COURT 1789–1969: THEIR LIVES AND WORKS, VOL. 3, 2133–43 (Leon Friedman and Fred Israel eds., 1969), and in JOEL F. PASCHAL, MR. JUSTICE SUTHERLAND: A MAN AGAINST THE STATE (1951). Neither of these sources discuss Justice Sutherland's decisions in *Ozawa* and *Thind.* Justice Sutherland is best remembered for his opposition to many of the New Deal initiatives.

46. *Thind, supra,* 261 U.S. at 215. In a sense, the Court's words about popular prejudice against Asian Indians continue to ring true today. Apparently, some still violently "reject the thought of assimilation" with Asian Indians. Robert Chang discusses recent attacks on Asian Indians in New Jersey, linking this violence to the larger history of racial terror against Asians. Robert Chang, *Toward an Asian American Legal Scholarship: Critical Race Theory, Post-Structuralism, and Narrative Space,* 81 CAL. L. REV. 1241, 1253–55 (1993).

47. Judge Leon Higginbotham notes that "at least one Justice of the Supreme Court [in 1923] was a 'white supremacist,' who referred to Blacks as 'niggers.' " A. Leon Higginbotham, Jr., *An Open Letter to Justice Clarence Thomas from a Federal Judicial Colleague,* 140 U. PA. L. REV. 1007, 1008 n.4 (1992) (citations omitted).

48. OLIVER WENDELL HOLMES, THE COMMON LAW 1 (1881).

49. AUDREY SMEDLEY, RACE IN NORTH AMERICA: ORIGIN AND EVOLUTION OF A WORLDVIEW 26 (1993).

50. Janet Halley, *Sexual Orientation and the Politics of Biology: A Critique of the Argument from Immutability,* 46 STAN. L. REV. 503, 505 (1994).

51. A. H. KEANE, THE WORLD'S PEOPLE: A Popular ACCOUNT OF THEIR BODILY AND MENTAL CHARACTERS, BELIEFS, TRADITIONS, Political AND SOCIAL INSTITUTIONS 16 (1908).

52. *Id.* at 18.

53. *Id.* at 22.

54. *Id.* at 25.

55. Indeed, the lack of any objective, scientifically ascertainable basis for race was increasingly recognized by the scientists of the times. *See generally* ELAZAR BARKAN, THE RETREAT OF SCIENTIFIC RACISM: CHANGING CONCEPTS OF RACE IN BRITAIN AND THE UNITED STATES BETWEEN THE WORLD WARS (1992).

56. In re Feroz Din, 27 F.2d 568, 568 (N.D.Cal. 1928).

57. *Halladjian, supra,* 174 F. at 843.

58. Morrison v. California, 291 U.S. 82, 94 (1933).

59. *See generally* NANCY STEPAN, THE IDEA OF RACE IN SCIENCE: GREAT BRITAIN, 1800–1960 (1982); STEPHEN GOULD, THE MISMeasure OF MAN (1981).

60. Alice Littlefield, Leonard Lieberman, and Larry T. Reynolds, *Redefining Race: The Potential Demise of a Concept in Physical Anthropology,* 23 CURRENT ANTHROPOLOGY 641 (1982).

61. *See* Sharon Begley, *Three Is Not Enough: Surprising Lessons from the Controversial Science of Race,* NEWSWEEK, Feb. 13, 1995, at 67.

62. An example of such thinking appears in Pat Shipman, *Facing Racial Differences—Together,* THE CHRONICLE OF HIGHER EDUCATION, Aug. 3, 1994, at B1, B2. Shipman argues that "modern races . . . must at the very least include Mongoloids, Caucasoids, Negroids, and Australoids: the native people of Asia, Europe, Africa, and Australia respectively." She asserts that these groups developed into races 100,000 to 200,000 years ago, upon the occasion of their initial contact with each other. "Predictably," Shipman writes, "these encounters solidified people's identification with their own group, in the same way that colonials in foreign lands later would cling to the ways of their native countries." She adds that this "need to identify with a group is surely among the most basic and ancient human instincts." *Id.* Efforts to rebiologize race are reviewed and critiqued in Martin Barker, *Biology and the New Racism,* ANATOMY OF RACISM 18 (David Theo Goldberg ed., 1990).

63. Jason DeParle, *Daring Research or 'Social Science Pornography'?* NEW YORK TIMES MAGAZINE, Oct. 9, 1994, at 48, 50, reviewing CHARLES MURRAY and RICHARD HERRNSTEIN, THE BELL CURVE (1994).

64. Genocide Convention Implementation Act of 1987, 18 U.S.C. § 1093 (1988).

65. Saint Francis College v. Al-Khazraji, 481 U.S. 604 (1987).

66. *Id.* at 610 n.4.

67. *Id.* at 613.

68. Neil Gotanda, *A Critique of "Our Constitution is Color-Blind,"* 44 STAN. L. REV. 1, 32 (1991) (citing Ruth Marcus, *FCC Defends Minority License Policies: Case Before High Court Could Shape Future of Affirmative Action,* WASHINGTON POST, Mar. 29, 1990, at A8).

69. *Id.*

70. Barbara Fields, *Ideology and Race in American History,* REGION, RACE, AND RECONSTRUCTION: ESSAYS IN HONOR OF C. VANN WOODWARD 143, 150 (J. Morgan Kousser and James McPherson eds., 1982).

71. As Paul Gilroy writes: "Accepting that skin 'colour,' however meaningless we know it to be, has a strictly limited material basis in biology, opens up the pos-

sibility of engaging with theories of signification which can highlight the elasticity and the emptiness of 'racial' signifiers as well as the ideological work which has to be done in order to turn them into signifiers in the first place." PAUL GILROY, 'THERE AIN'T NO BLACK IN THE Union JACK': THE CULTURAL POLITICS OF RACE AND NATION 38–39 (1987).

72. The census of 1910 recorded the presence of 420 naturalized citizens of Japanese descent. Ichioka, *supra,* at 2.

73. *Thind, supra,* 261 U.S. at 213.

74. *Id.*

75. GOSSETT, *supra,* at 353–63; SMEDLEY, *supra,* at 257–58, 271 n.2.

76. SMEDLEY, *supra,* at 271 n.2 (citation omitted).

77. STANLEY LIEBERSON, A PIECE OF THE PIE: BLACKS AND WHITE IMMIGRANTS SINCE 1880, at 31 (1980).

78. U.S. COMMISSION ON CIVIL RIGHTS, THE TARNISHED GOLDEN DOOR: CIVIL RIGHTS ISSUES IN IMMIGRATION 9–10 (1990).

79. F. JAMES DAVIS, WHO IS BLACK? ONE NATION'S DEFINITION 161 (1991) (citation omitted). *See also Al-Khazraji, supra,* 481 U.S. 604.

80. Donald Tricario, *Guido: Fashioning an Italian-American Youth Style,* 19 J. OF ETHNIC STUDIES 41 (Spring 1991).

81. Ex parte Shahid, 205 F. 812, 813 (E.D.S.C. 1913).

82. Buck v. Bell, 274 U.S. 200 (1927).

83. Act of March 20, 1924, ch. 394, 1924 Va. Acts 569, 570.

84. Paul Lombardo, *Three Generations, No Imbeciles: New Light on* Buck v. Bell, 60 N.Y.U. L. REV. 30, 48–50 (1985).

85. *Id.* at 49–59.

86. Mary Dudziak, *Oliver Wendell Holmes as a Eugenic Reformer: Rhetoric in the Writing of Constitutional Law,* 71 IOWA L. REV. 833, 848 (1986).

87. John Conley, *"The First Principle of Real Reform": The Role of Science in Constitutional Jurisprudence,* 65 N.C. L. REV. 935, 939 (1987).

88. *Buck, supra,* 274 U.S. at 207.

89. *Id.* John Conley concludes that the "Supreme Court relied explicitly on the eugenics research program in upholding the Virginia statute" in *Buck v. Bell.* Conley, *supra,* at 938.

90. Lombardo, *supra,* at 31.

91. *Id. See also* GOULD, *supra,* at 335.

NOTES TO CHAPTER 5

1. Brown v. Board of Education, 347 U.S. 483 (1954).

2. This three-level analysis is more fully developed in the section on the legal construction of race in chapter 1.

3. The Supreme Court declared antimiscegenation laws unconstitutional in

Loving v. Virginia, 388 U.S. 1 (1967). *See generally* ROBERT J. SICKELS, RACE, MARRIAGE, AND THE LAW (1972).

4. *See* VIRGINIA DOMINGUEZ, WHITE BY DEFINITION: SOCIAL CLASSIFICATION IN CREOLE LOUISIANA 56–62 (1986); Paul Finkelman, *The Crime of Color*, 67 TUL. L. REV. 2063, 2081–87 (1993).

5. Martha Hodes, *The Sexualization of Reconstruction Politics: White Women and Black Men in the South after the Civil War*, 3 J. OF THE HIST. OF SEXUALITY 402, 415 (1993).

6. Finkelman, *supra*, at 2088. According to Finkelman, "This act also made the first stab at defining who was actually black. The law declared that anyone who was a child, grandchild, or great grandchild of a black was a mulatto under the statute. This meant that persons who were of one-eighth African ancestry were black for purposes of Virginia law." *See generally* A. Leon Higginbotham, Jr., and Barbara K. Kopytoff, *Racial Purity and Interracial Sex in the Law of Colonial and Antebellum Virginia*, 77 GEO. L.J. 1967 (1989).

7. *See* Raymond T. Diamond and Robert J. Cottrol, *Codifying Caste: Louisiana's Racial Classification Scheme and the Fourteenth Amendment*, 29 LOY. L. REV. 255, 265 (1983) They argue that "[s]tate supported or initiated discrimination required racial definitions. The law could not separate what it failed to categorize."

8. Paul Finkelman, *The Color of Law*, 87 NW. U. L. REV. 937, 955 n.96 (citing PAUL MURRAY, STATES' LAWS ON RACE AND COLOR [1950]).

9. Richard Ford, *Urban Space and the Color Line: The Consequences of Demarcation and Disorientation in the Postmodern Metropolis*, 9 HARV. BLACK-LETTER J. 117, 130 (1992).

10. Judy Scales-Trent, *Commonalities: On Being Black and White, Different, and the Same*, 2 YALE J. L. & FEMINISM 305, 307 (1990).

11. Robert Cover, *Violence and the Word*, 95 YALE L.J. 1601 (1986).

12. James Baldwin, *On Being 'White' . . . And Other Lies*, ESSENCE, April 1984, at 90.

13. MARK KELMAN, A GUIDE TO CRITICAL LEGAL STUDIES 253–57 (1987).

14. Robert Gordon, *Critical Legal Histories*, 36 STAN. L. REV. 57, 109 (1984).

15. Kimberlé Crenshaw, *Race, Reform, and Retrenchment: Transformation and Legitimation in Antidiscrimination Law*, 101 HARV. L. REV. 1331, 1351–52 (1988).

16. *See, e.g.,* Janet Halley, *The Construction of Heterosexuality*, FEAR OF A QUEER PLANET: QUEER POLITICS AND SOCIAL THEORY 82 (Michael Warner ed., 1993).

17. KELMAN, *supra*, at 244.

18. Korematsu v. United States, 323 U.S. 214 (1944).

19. DOMINGUEZ, *supra*, at 5.

20. *See, e.g.*, Richard Delgado and Vicky Palacios, *Mexican Americans as a Legally Cognizable Class Under Rule 23 and the Equal Protection Clause*, 50 NOTRE DAME LAW. 393 (1975); Gary A. Greenfield and Don B. Kates, Jr., *Mexican Americans, Racial Discrimination, and the Civil Rights Act of 1866*, 63 CAL. L. REV. 662 (1975).

21. KELMAN, *supra*, 255. *See also* Martha Minow, *Identities*, 3 YALE J. L. & HUMAN. 97, 111 (1991) Minow writes, "The use of a specific notion of identity to resolve a legal dispute can obscure the complexity of lived experiences while imposing the force of the state behind the selected notion of identity."

22. In re Halladjian, 174 F. 834, 843 (C.C.D.Mass. 1909).

23. Carol Greenhouse, *Just in Time: Temporality and the Cultural Legitimation of Law*, 98 YALE L.J. 1631, 1640 (1989).

24. Mashpee Tribe v. Town of Mashpee, 447 F. Supp. 940 (D.Mass. 1978), *aff'd sub nom.* Mashpee Tribe v. New Seabury Corp., 592 F.2d 575 (1st Cir. 1979), *cert. denied*, 444 U.S. 866. *See generally* Gerald Torres and Kathryn Milun, *Translating* Yonnondio *by Precedent and Evidence: The Mashpee Indian Case*, 1990 DUKE L.J. 625; Minow, *supra*, at 112–16; JAMES CLIFFORD, THE PREDICAMENT OF CULTURE: TWENTIETH CENTURY ETHNOGRAPHY, LITERATURE, AND ART 277–346 (1988).

25. The original act provided that "no person shall be permitted to carry on any trade or intercourse with the Indian tribes, without a license for that purpose under the hand and seal of the superintendent of the department." Act of July 22, 1790, ch. 33, § 1, 1 Stat. 137.

26. Montoya v. United States, 180 U.S. 261, 266 (1901).

27. Torres and Milun, *supra*, at 649.

28. Act of Sept. 22, 1922, ch. 411, § 3, 42 Stat. 1021.

29. Act of May 26, 1924, ch. 190, § 13(c), 43 Stat. 153.

30. Dudley O. McGovney, *The Anti-Japanese Land Laws of California and Ten Other States*, 35 CAL. L. REV. 7 (1947). *See also* T. R. Powell, *Alien Land Law Cases in the Supreme Court*, 12 CAL. L. REV. 259 (1924); Edwin E. Ferguson, *The California Alien Land Law and the Fourteenth Amendment*, 35 CAL. L. REV. 61 (1947).

31. Act of Feb. 13, 1943, No. 47, §§ 1–2, 1943 Ark. Acts 75.

32. *See* Terrace v. Thompson, 263 U.S. 197 (1923) (upholding Washington's alien land law); Porterfield v. Webb, 263 U.S. 225 (1923) (upholding California's alien land law); *but see* Oyama v. California, 332 U.S. 633 (1947) (striking down California's alien land law).

33. *Oyama, supra*, 332 U.S. at 656.

34. *Id.* at 660.

35. *See generally* Peter Gabel, *Reification in Legal Reasoning*, 3 RES. IN L. & SOC. 25 (1980).

36. *See Halladjian, supra,* 174 F. 834.
37. RONALD TAKAKI, STRANGERS FROM A DIFFERENT SHORE: A HISTORY OF ASIAN AMERICANS 15 (1989).
38. *See generally* DOUGLAS MASSEY and NANCY DENTON, AMERICAN APARTHEID: SEGREGATION AND THE MAKING OF THE UNDERCLASS (1993).
39. *See* Richard Ford, *The Boundaries of Race: Political Geography in Legal Analysis,* 107 HARV. L. REV. 1841 (1994); Margalynne Armstrong, *Protecting Privilege: Race, Residence and Rodney King,* 12 L. & Inequality 351 (1994).
40. In re Po, 28 N.Y. Supp. 383, 384 (City Ct. 1894).
41. Ozawa v. United States, 260 U.S. 178, 198 (1922).
42. United States v. Thind, 261 U.S. 204, 215 (1923).
43. *See* Edward Greer, *Antonio Gramsci and "Legal Hegemony,"* THE POLITICS OF LAW: A PROGRESSIVE CRITIQUE 304 (David Kairys ed., 1982).
44. Richard Delgado and Jean Stefancic, *Norms and Narratives: Can Judges Avoid Serious Moral Error?* 69 TEX. L. REV. 1929, 1957 (1991) (citations omitted).
45. Charles Lawrence, *The Id, the Ego, and Equal Protection: Reckoning with Unconscious Racism,* 39 STAN. L. REV. 317, 322 (1987). *See also* Peggy Davis, *Law as Microaggression,* 98 YALE L.J. 1559 (1989).
46. For a short but insightful critique of psychological explanations of racism, *see* ALEXANDER SAXTON, THE RISE AND FALL OF THE WHITE REPUBLIC: CLASS POLITICS AND MASS CULTURE IN NINETEENTH-CENTURY AMERICA 8–13 (1990).
47. *See, e.g.,* Daniel E. Georges-Abeyie, *Race, Ethnicity, and the Spatial Dynamic: Toward a Realistic Study of Black Crime, Crime Victimization, and Criminal Justice Processing of Blacks,* 16 SOC. JUST. 35 (1989); Susan Welch, John Gruhl, and Cassia Spohn, *Dismissal, Conviction, and Incarceration of Hispanic Defendants: A Comparison with Anglos and Blacks,* 65 SOC. SCI. Q. 257 (1984); Malcolm Holmes and Howard Daudistel, *Ethnicity and Justice in the Southwest: The Sentencing of Anglo, Black, and Mexican Origin Defendants,* 65 SOC. SCI. Q. 265 (1984).
48. Robert García, *Latinos and Criminal Justice,* 14 CHICANO-LATINO L. REV. 6, 14 (1994) (citation omitted).
49. Christopher Smith, *Plea Bargaining Favors Whites as Blacks, Hispanics Pay the Price,* SAN JOSE MERCURY NEWS, Dec. 8, 1994, at A1.
50. *Id.*
51. McCleskey v. Kemp, 481 U.S. 279, 313 (1987).
52. Davis, *supra,* at 1576.
53. In analyzing *McCleskey v. Kemp,* Stephen Carter and Randall Kennedy both emphasize the criminal justice system's relative lack of interest in pursuing

criminals who victimize Blacks and comment on the implications of this in terms of Black social worth. Stephen Carter, *When Victims Happen to be Black,* 97 YALE L.J. 420 (1988), Randall Kennedy, *McCleskey v. Kemp: Race, Capital Punishment, and the Supreme Court,* 101 HARV. L. REV. 1388 (1988).

54. H.R.J. Res. 129, 103d Cong., 1st Sess. (1993). See chapter 2.

55. *Proposition 187: Text of Proposed Law,* CALIFORNIA BALLOT PAMPHLET, GENERAL ELECTION, NOVEMBER 8, 1994, at 91.

56. *Illegal Aliens. Ineligibility for Public Services. Verification and Reporting. Initiative Statute,* CALIFORNIA BALLOT PAMPHLET, GENERAL ELECTION, NOVEMBER 8, 1994, at 54.

57. Elizabeth Kadetsky, *Bashing Illegals in California,* THE NATION, Oct. 17, 1994, at 416, 421.

58. Elizabeth Martínez, *Seeing More Than Black and White: Latinos, Racism, and Cultural Divides,* Z MAGAZINE, May 1994, at 56, 58.

59. Amy Chance, *Controls Defended as Economic, Not Racist,* SACRAMENTO BEE, Jan. 24, 1993, at A10, *quoted in* Kevin Johnson, Los Olvidados: *Images of the Immigrant, Political Power of Noncitizens, and Immigration Law and Enforcement,* 1993 B.Y.U. L. REV. 1139, 1165 n.95.

60. Amy Chance, *Illegal Aliens Increasingly Blamed for State's Problems,* SACRAMENTO BEE, Jan. 24, 1993, at A1 (quoting John Tanton), *quoted in* Johnson, *supra,* at 1165 n.95.

61. Bill Ong Hing, *Beyond the Rhetoric of Assimilation and Cultural Pluralism: Addressing the Tension of Separatism and Conflict in an Immigration-Driven Multiracial Society,* 81 CAL. L. REV. 863, 870 (1993) (quoting David Duke) (citation omitted).

62. Gerald López, *Undocumented Mexican Migration: In Search of a Just Immigration Law and Policy,* 28 UCLA L. REV. 615, 713 (1981).

63. *Illegal Aliens. Ineligibility for Public Services. Verification and Reporting. Initiative Statute, supra,* at 54.

64. Lawrence, *supra,* at 322–23 (citation omitted).

65. Act of April 30, 1855, ch. 175, § 2, 1855, Cal. Stat. 217, *excerpted in* ROBERT F. HEIZER and ALAN J. ALMQUIST, THE OTHER CALIFORNIANS: PREJUDICE AND DISCRIMINATION UNDER SPAIN, MEXICO, AND THE UNITED STATES 151 (1971).

66. Richard Delgado and Jean Stefancic, *Images of the Outsider in American Law and Culture: Can Free Expression Remedy Systemic Social Ills?* 77 CORNELL L. REV. 1258, 1284 (1992).

67. KELMAN, *supra,* at 263.

68. Crenshaw, *supra,* at 1357.

69. *Thind, supra,* 261 U.S. at 204, 205–6.

70. DOMINGUEZ, *supra,* at 53. As Dominguez observes more generally,

"the law play[s] two seemingly contradictory roles . . . it's as if the individual were pitted against society, and sought recourse through the very legal system which caused the trouble in the first place."

71. Minow, *supra*, at 114.

72. YUJI ICHIOKA, THE ISSEI: THE WORLD OF THE FIRST GENERATION JAPANESE IMMIGRANTS, 1885–1924, at 190–92 (1988).

73. Kiyoshi K. Kawakami, *The Naturalization of the Japanese*, 185 N. AM. REV. 394 (1907).

74. *Id.* at 399.

75. *Id.* at 401.

76. KIYOSHI K. KAWAKAMI, ASIA AT THE DOOR 78–79 (1914), *quoted in* ICHIOKA, *supra*, at 193.

77. KAWAKAMI, *supra*, at 79, *quoted in* ICHIOKA, *supra*, at 192.

78. Derrick Bell has made this argument in a number of different forms and forums. For example, he as argued that "litigation—while perhaps a guaranteed employment program for lawyers—is a never-ending detour for blacks, at least for those seeking protection of their own rights as opposed to lawyers seeking new and more exciting cases." DERRICK BELL, AND WE ARE NOT SAVED: THE ELUSIVE QUEST FOR RACIAL JUSTICE 69 (1987).

79. Crenshaw, *supra*, at 1358.

80. *Id.*

NOTES TO CHAPTER 6

1. Ex parte Shahid, 205 F. 812, 813 (E.D.S.C. 1913).

2. Angela Harris, *Race and Essentialism in Feminist Legal Theory*, 42 STAN. L. REV. 582, 604 (1990).

3. Julie Ann Su, *Race, Identity and Diversity at Harvard Law School: A Memo to the HLS Community* (1993) (unpublished manuscript).

4. *See, e.g.*, Martha Mahoney, *Whiteness and Women, In Practice and Theory: A Reply to Catherine McKinnon*, 5 YALE J. L. & FEMINISM 217 (1993); Francis Lee Ansley, *Stirring the Ashes: Race, Class and the Future of Civil Rights Scholarship*, 74 CORNELL L. REV. 993 (1989); Marlee Kline, *Race, Racism and Feminist Theory*, 12 HARV. WOMEN'S L.J. 115 (1989).

5. Barbara Flagg, *"Was Blind, But Now I See": White Race Consciousness and the Requirement of Discriminatory Intent*, 91 MICH. L. REV. 953, 969 (1993) (citations omitted).

6. Trina Grillo and Stephanie Wildman, *Obscuring the Importance of Race: The Implication of Making Comparisons Between Racism and Sexism (or Other-Isms)*, 1991 DUKE L.J. 397, 405.

7. *Id.*

8. *See, e.g.*, ELLIS COSE, THE RAGE OF A PRIVILEGED CLASS (1993).

9. RUTH FRANKENBERG, WHITE WOMEN, RACE MATTERS: THE SOCIAL CONSTRUCTION OF WHITENESS 9 (1993).

10. In re Knight, 171 F. 299 (E.D.N.Y. 1909).

11. *Id.* at 301.

12. These distinctions are suggested by Audrey Smedley. AUDREY SMEDLEY, RACE IN NORTH AMERICA: ORIGIN AND EVOLUTION OF A WORLDVIEW 27 (1993).

13. Sharon M. Lee, *Racial Classifications in the US Census: 1890–1990,* 16 ETHNIC AND RACIAL STUDIES 75, 83 (1993).

14. *Should the Census be Less Black and White?* BUSINESS WEEK, July 4, 1994, at 40.

15. Lawrence Wright, *One Drop of Blood,* THE NEW YORKER, July 25, 1994, at 46, 49.

16. SMEDLEY, *supra,* at 27.

17. Terrace v. Thompson, 274 F. 841, 849 (W.D.Wash. 1921).

18. FRANCIS PARKMAN: REPRESENTATIVE SELECTIONS 380–82 (William Schram ed., 1938), *quoted in* THOMAS GOSSETT, RACE: THE HISTORY OF AN IDEA IN NORTH AMERICA 95 (1963).

19. SMEDLEY, *supra,* at 27.

20. In re Camille, 6 F. 256, 258 (C.C.D.Or. 1880).

21. U.S. v. Thind, 261 U.S. 204, 211 (1923).

22. *Id.* at 214.

23. *Id.* at 215.

24. *Id.* at 211.

25. Stuart Alan Clarke, *Fear of a Black Planet: Race, Identity Politics, and Common Sense,* 21 SOCIALIST REV. 37, 40 (1991).

26. FRANKENBERG, *supra,* at 236–237.

27. Janet Halley, *The Construction of Heterosexuality,* FEAR OF A QUEER PLANET: QUEER POLITICS AND SOCIAL THEORY 82, 83 (Michael Warner ed., 1993).

28. Richard Ford, *Urban Space and the Color Line: The Consequences of Demarcation and Disorientation in the Postmodern Metropolis,* 9 HARV. BLACKLETTER J. 117, 125 (1992).

29. *See* Lisa Ikemoto, *Traces of the Master Narrative in the Story of African American/Korean American Conflict: How We Constructed "Los Angeles,"* 66 SO. CAL. L. REV. 1581 (1993); David Palumbo-Liu, *Los Angeles, Asians, and Perverse Ventriloquisms: On the Functions of Asian America in the Recent American Imaginary,* 6 PUB. CULTURE 365 (1994).

30. Jayne Chong-Soon Lee, *Navigating the Topology of Race,* 46 STAN. L. REV. 747, 762 (1994).

31. Kevin Johnson analyzes the recent images of immigrants being circulated by nascent restrictionist organizations, finding many of the images to be blatantly

racist. Kevin Johnson, Los Olvidados: *Images of the Immigrant, Political Power of Noncitizens, and Immigration Law and Enforcement,* 1993 B.Y.U. L. REV. 1139, 1162–74.

32. DAVID ROEDIGER, TOWARDS THE ABOLITION OF WHITENESS 13 (1994).

33. FRANKENBERG, *supra,* at 231 (citation omitted). Frankenberg adds, however, that "whiteness *does* have content inasmuch as it generates norms, ways of understanding history, ways of thinking about the self and other, and even ways of thinking about the notion of culture." *Id.* (emphasis in original).

34. ROEDIGER, *supra,* at 13.

35. RICHARD ALBA, ETHNIC IDENTITY: THE TRANSFORMATION OF WHITE AMERICA 292 (1990).

36. *Id.* at 12, 13.

37. *Id.* at 3 (emphasis in original).

38. *Id.* at 312.

39. MARY WATERS, ETHNIC OPTIONS: CHOOSING IDENTITIES IN AMERICA 157 (1990).

40. ALBA, *supra,* at 316.

41. *Id.* at 3 n.5.

42. Flagg, *supra,* at 957.

43. *Id.* at 957 n.20.

44. *Id.* at 978.

45. *Id.* at 1017.

46. Patricia Williams, *The Obliging Shell: An Informal Essay on Formal Equal Opportunity,* 87 MICH L. REV. 2128, 2143 (1989).

47. *Id.* at 2143–44.

48. FRANTZ FANON, BLACK SKIN, WHITE MASKS 188–89 (1967) (emphasis in original).

49. Flagg, *supra,* at 991–92. *See also* Barbara Flagg, *Enduring Principle: On Race, Process, and Constitutional Law,* 82 CAL. L. REV. 935, 968–80 (1994).

50. Anthony Appiah, *The Conservation of "Race,"* 23 BLACK. AM. LIT. F. 36, 48 (1989).

51. Lewis Killian, *Black Power and White Reactions: The Revitalization of Race-Thinking in the United States,* 454 ANNALS AM. ACAD. POL. & SOC. SCI. 43, 53 (1981).

52. University of California Regents v. Bakke, 438 U.S. 265, 407 (1978) (Blackmun, J., writing separately).

53. Cheryl Harris, *Whiteness as Property,* 106 HARV. L. REV. 1707, 1768 (1993).

54. Richmond v. J. A. Croson Co., 488 U.S. 469 (1989).

55. Presley v. Etowah County Commission, 502 U.S. 491 (1992).

56. LANI GUINIER, THE TYRANNY OF THE MAJORITY: FUNDA-MENTAL FAIRNESS IN REPRESENTATIVE DEMOCRACY 8 (1994).

57. Neil Gotanda, *A Critique of "Our Constitution is Color-Blind,"* 44 STAN. L. REV. 1, 16–18 (1991).

58. *See* Flagg, *"Was Blind," supra,* at 1012–13.

59. FRANKENBERG, *supra,* at 142.

60. D. Marvin Jones, *Darkness Made Visible: Law, Metaphor, and the Racial Self,* 82 GEO. L.J. 437, 446 (1993).

61. TERRY EAGLETON, NATIONALISM, IRONY AND COMMITMENT (1988), *quoted without page attribution in* ROEDIGER, *supra,* at 83.

62. Adrian Piper, *Passing for White, Passing for Black,* 58 TRANSITION 4, 20–21 (1992).

63. Ford, *supra,* at 138 (citation omitted).

64. Richard Delgado has written recently on the social construction of criminality in terms of Black and White. Richard Delgado, *Rodrigo's Eighth Chronicle: Black Crime, White Fears—On the Social Construction of Threat,* 80 VA. L. REV. 503 (1994). Rather than challenging White innocence indirectly, Delgado tackles this construction head on, compiling statistical data showing that crime by Whites is "more serious, more common, *and* more hurtful." *Id.* at 531 (emphasis in original).

65. Michael Van Sistine contributed the insight that Whiteness is opaque to the extent it prevents those constructed as White from seeing clearly either themselves or others.

66. Robert Terry makes a similar argument using the language of authenticity. Robert Terry, *The Negative Impact on White Values,* IMPACTS OF RACISM ON WHITE AMERICANS 119 (Benjamin Bowser and Raymond Hunt eds., 1981).

67. James Baldwin, *On Being 'White' . . . And Other Lies,* ESSENCE, April 1984, at 92.

68. "Pursuing critical race projects," John Calmore writes, "entails a number of very tricky moves, such as impugning the integrity of America for its racist ways without coming across as antiwhite because you reduce all white individuals to fungible parts of a collective evil, injustice, and oppression." He adds: "Inducing White guilt is not really the objective." John Calmore, *Critical Race Theory, Archie Shepp, and Fire Music: Securing an Authentic Intellectual Life in a Multicultural World,* 65 SO. CAL. L. REV. 2129, 2146 (1992).

69. Ford, *supra,* at 144.

70. ROEDIGER, *supra,* at 12.

71. Grillo and Wildman, *supra,* at 398.

72. Flagg, *"Was Blind," supra,* at 972 (citations omitted).

73. *Treason to Whiteness Is Loyalty to Humanity: An Interview with Noel Ig-*

natiev of Race Traitor *Magazine,* THE BLAST!, June/July 1994, *excerpted in* UTNE READER, Nov./Dec. 1994, at 82.

74. Noel Ignatiev, *How to Be a Race Traitor: Six Ways to Fight Being White,* UTNE READER, Nov./Dec. 1994, at 85.

75. Barbara Fields, *Slavery, Race and Ideology in the United States of America,* 181 NEW LEFT REVIEW 95, 117 (1990).

76. HENRY LOUIS GATES, JR., LOOSE CANONS: NOTES ON THE CULTURE WARS 34 (1992).

77. These terms are developed more fully in Ian Haney López, *The Social Construction of Race: Some Observations on Illusion, Fabrication, and Choice,* 29 HARV. CIVIL RIGHTS-CIVIL LIBERTIES L. REV. 1, 39–53 (1994).

78. *See* KATHY RUSSELL, MIDGE WILSON, and RONALD HALL, THE COLOR COMPLEX: THE POLITICS OF SKIN COLOR AMONG AFRICAN AMERICANS (1992).

79. *Id.* at 51.

80. Anthony Appiah, *The Uncompleted Argument: DuBois and the Illusion of Race,* "RACE," WRITING, AND DIFFERENCE 21, 26 (Henry Louis Gates ed., 1985).

81. Renato Rosaldo, *Others of Invention: Ethnicity and Its Discontents,* VILLAGE VOICE, Feb. 13, 1990, at 27.

82. *See* DERRICK BELL, CONFRONTING AUTHORITY: REFLECTIONS OF AN ARDENT PROTESTER (1994).

83. HOWARD WINANT, RACIAL CONDITIONS: POLITICS, THEORY, COMPARISONS xiii (1994).

84. *Id.* at 21.

NOTES TO CHAPTER 7

1. Randall Kennedy, *Race Relations Law and the Tradition of Celebration: The Case of Professor Schmidt,* 86 COLUM. L. REV. 1622, 1653–56 (1986).

2. ANDREW HACKER, TWO NATIONS: BLACK AND WHITE, SEPARATE, HOSTILE, UNEQUAL 32 (1992).

3. Adrian Piper, *Passing for White, Passing for Black,* 58 TRANSITION 4, 25 (1992).

4. Joshua Solomon, *Skin Deep: My Own Journey into the Heart of Race-Conscious America,* WASHINGTON POST, Oct. 30, 1994 at C1.

5. *Id.* at C4.

6. *See also* GREGORY WILLIAMS, LIFE ON THE COLOR LINE: THE TRUE STORY OF A WHITE BOY WHO DISCOVERED HE WAS BLACK (1995).

7. HACKER, *supra,* at 217.

8. DERRICK BELL, FACES AT THE BOTTOM OF THE WELL: THE PER-MANENCE OF RACISM v (1992).

9. Francis Lee Ansley, *Stirring the Ashes. Race, Class and the Future of Civil Rights Scholarship,* 74 CORNELL L. REV. 993, 1035 (1989) (note omitted).

10. *See* HOWARD WINANT, RACIAL CONDITIONS: POLITICS, THE-ORY, COMPARISONS 88–89 (1994).

NOTES TO CHAPTER 8

1. In a helpful discussion, Jennifer Hochschild sees six possible racial futures in the United States: White exceptionalism, Black exceptionalism, a South African model, complex regional divides, skin-color hierarchy, and multiracial mélange. Jennifer Hochschild, *Looking Ahead: Racial Trends in the United States,* 134 DAEDALUS 70, 80–81 (2005) [hereinafter Hochschild, *Looking Ahead*].

2. THOMAS F. GOSSETT, RACE: THE HISTORY OF AN IDEA IN AMER-ICA (1963); AUDREY SMEDLEY, RACE IN NORTH AMERICA: ORIGINS AND EVOLUTION OF A WORLDVIEW (2d ed. 1999). *See also* Ian F. Haney López, *The Social Construction of Race,* 29 HARV. C.R.-C.L. L. REV. 1 (1994).

3. Barbara Jeanne Fields, *Slavery, Race and Ideology in the United States of America,* 181 NEW LEFT REV. 95 (1990).

4. Elizabeth M. Grieco & Rachel C. Cassidy, *US Bureau of the Census: Overview of Race and Hispanic Origin, Census Brief 2000,* at 3 (March 2001); Kim M. Williams, *Multiracialism and the Civil Rights Future,* 134 Daedalus 53 (2005); KIM WILLIAMS, RACE COUNTS: AMERICAN MULTIRACIALISM AND THE CIVIL RIGHTS MOVEMENT (forthcoming 2006).

5. Jessica Barnes & Claudette Bennett, *The Asian Population: 2000: Census 2000 Brief,* at 3 (Feb. 2002).

6. Betsy Guzmán, *US Bureau of the Census: The Hispanic Population, Census Brief 2000,* at 2 (May 2001).

7. *New Latino Nation,* Newsweek, May 30, 2005, at 28–29.

8. MICHAEL LIND, THE NEXT AMERICAN NATION: THE NEW NA-TIONALISM AND THE FOURTH AMERICAN REVOLUTION 151, 161 (1995).

9. VICTOR DAVIS HANSON, MEXIFORNIA: A STATE OF BECOMING (2003); SAMUEL P. HUNTINGTON, WHO ARE WE? THE CHALLENGES TO AMERICA'S NATIONAL IDENTITY (2004).

10. NATHAN GLAZER, WE ARE ALL MULTICULTURALISTS NOW 149 (1998) [hereinafter GLAZER, MULTICULTURALISTS]. *See also* Nathan Glazer, *The Future of Race in the United States, in* RACE IN 21st CENTURY AMERICA 73 (Curtis Stokes et al. eds., 2001) [hereinafter Glazer, *Future of Race*]; GEORGE YANCEY, WHO IS WHITE? LATINOS, ASIANS, AND THE NEW BLACK/

NONBLACK DIVIDE 14 (2003) ("[I]nstead of 'whites' becoming a numerical minority group in the near future, we are heading toward a black/nonblack society wherein African Americans remain anchored to the bottom of the racial hierarchy in the United States.").

11. GLAZER, MULTICULTURALISTS, *supra,* at 159.

12. *See* HUGH DAVIS GRAHAM, COLLISION COURSE: THE STRANGE CONVERGENCE OF AFFIRMATIVE ACTION AND IMMIGRATION POLICY IN AMERICA (2002); David A. Hollinger, *Amalgamation and Hypodescent: The Question of Ethnoracial Mixture in the History of the United States,* 108 AM. HIST. REV. 1 (2003); John D. Skrentny, *Inventing Race,* 46 PUB. INT. 97 (Winter 2002).

13. DAVID HOLLINGER, POST-ETHNIC AMERICA: BEYOND MULTICULTURALISM (1995); Roberto Suro, *Mixed Doubles,* AM. DEMOGRAPHICS, Nov. 1999, at 57, 58. As others note, however, relatively little racial mixing involves African Americans, suggesting that intermarriage is not breaking down all racial lines. See Matthijs Kalmijn, *Trends in Black/White Intermarriage,* 72 SOC. FORCES 119 (1993); Michael Lind, *The Beige and the Black,* N.Y. TIMES MAF., Aug. 16, 1998, at 38.

14. Gregory Rodriguez, *Mongrel America,* ATLANTIC MONTHLY, Jan./Feb. 2003, at 95, 97. *See also* Gregory Rodriguez, *Dining at the Ethnicity Café,* L.A. TIMES, May 18, 2003, at M3, and the comments by Jorge Klor de Alva in *Our Next Race Question,* HARPER'S, Apr. 1996, at 55 (printing a conversation among Jorge Klor de Alva, Earl Shorris, and Cornel West).

15. Not all who predict an erosion of putatively biologically defined racial lines also predict the decline of social conflict. George Fredrickson, for instance, sees "racism"—which he defines as group conflict justified in terms of differences believed to be "hereditary and unalterable"—declining, even as he predicts increasing culturally-based conflicts. GEORGE M. FREDRICKSON, RACISM: A SHORT HISTORY 141, 170 (2002).

16. RICHARD RODRIGUEZ, BROWN, THE LAST DISCOVERY OF AMERICA (2002).

17. Jennifer Hochschild, *From Nominal to Ordinal to Interval: Reconceiving Racial and Ethnic Hierarchy in the United States,* paper delivered as Wesson Lectures, Stanford University, May 5 and 6, 2003.

18. *See* William H. Frey, *Immigration, Domestic Migration, and Demographic Balkanization in America: New Evidence from the 1990s,* 22 POPULATION & DEVELOPMENT REV. 741 (1996). *See also* Hochschild, *Looking Ahead, supra.*

19. George Fredrickson defines White supremacy as "the attitudes, ideologies, and policies associated with the rise of blatant forms of white or European dominance over 'nonwhite' populations." Thus defined, the term "applies with particular force to the historical experience of two nations—South Africa and the

United States." GEORGE FREDRICKSON, WHITE SUPREMACY: A COM-
PARATIVE STUDY IN AMERICAN AND SOUTH AFRICAN HISTORY xi
(1981) [hereinafter FREDERICKSON, WHITE SUPREMACY] On the resur-
gence of White supremacist groups in the United States, see MICHAEL
BARKUN, RELIGION AND THE RACIST RIGHT: THE ORIGINS OF THE
CHRISTIAN IDENTITY MOVEMENT (1997 ed.); HOWARD BUSHART ET
AL., SOLDIERS OF GOD: WHITE SUPREMACISTS AND THEIR HOLY WAR
FOR AMERICA (1998); BETTY DOBRATZ & STEPHANIE SHANKS-MEILE,
THE WHITE SEPARATIST MOVEMENT IN THE UNITED STATES (1997).

20. Robert Cleveland, *US Bureau of the Census: Alternative Income Estimates in the United States: 2003: Current Population Reports,* 6 (June 2005).

21. Joe Dalaker, *US Bureau of the Census: Alternative Poverty Estimates in
the United States: 2003: Current Population Reports,* 7 (June 2005).

22. Carmen DeNavas-Walt et al., *US Bureau of the Census: Income, Poverty,
and Health Insurance Coverage in the United States: 2003: Current Population
Reports,* 18 (August 2004).

23. Human Rights Watch, *Race and Incarceration in the United States,*
http://www.hrw.org/backgrounder/usa/race. *See generally,* HUMAN RIGHTS
WATCH, PUNISHMENT AND PREJUDICE: RACIAL DISPARITIES IN THE
WAR ON DRUGS (2000); MARC MAUER, RACE TO INCARCERATE (1999).

24. Adam Liptak, *Study Suspects Thousands of False Convictions,* NEW
YORK TIMES, April 19, 2004.

25. *See, e.g.,* RICHARD L. ZWEIGENHAFT & G. WILLIAM DOMHOFF,
DIVERSITY IN THE POWER ELITE: HAVE WOMEN AND MINORITIES
REACHED THE TOP? (1998).

26. *See* MATTHEW FRYE JACOBSON, WHITENESS OF A DIFFERENT
COLOR: EUROPEAN IMMIGRANTS AND THE ALCHEMY OF RACE
(1998). Of course, as previous chapters demonstrate, the anthropological notion
of a "Caucasian" race was sometimes rejected, as by the Supreme Court, when it
proved too capacious.

27. STEPHEN STEINBERG, TURNING BACK: THE RETREAT FROM
RACIAL JUSTICE IN AMERICAN THOUGHT AND POLICY (2001) [hereinafter
STEINBERG, TURNING BACK].

28. Frederick Douglass, *West India Emancipation,* Speech Delivered at
Canandaigua, New York (Aug. 4, 1857), *in* FREDERICK DOUGLASS, SE-
LECTED SPEECHES AND WRITINGS 358, 367 (Philip S. Foner ed., 1999).

29. DAVID R. ROEDIGER, COLORED WHITE: TRANSCENDING THE
RACIAL PAST (2003).

30. *See* JACOBSON, *supra. See also* Richard Alba, *Assimilation's Quite Tide,*
119 PUB. INT. 1, 3 (1995).

31. So opined Francis Walker, head of the American Economic Association,
in an essay in the *Atlantic Monthly.* Francis A. Walker, *Restriction of Immigra-*

tion, ATLANTIC MONTHLY, June 1896, at 828 (*quoted* in GOSSETT, *supra,* at 303).

32. On the intricacies of passing, see PASSING AND THE FICTIONS OF IDENTITY (Elaine K. Ginsberg ed., 1996), especially Adrian Piper's chapter, *Passing for White, Passing for Black.*

33. KAREN BRODKIN, HOW JEWS BECAME WHITE FOLKS AND WHAT THAT SAYS ABOUT RACE IN AMERICA (1999); NOEL IGNATIEV, HOW THE IRISH BECAME WHITE (1996).

34. MASAKO OSADA, SANCTIONS AND HONORARY WHITES: DIPLOMATIC POLICIES AND ECONOMIC REALITIES IN RELATIONS BETWEEN JAPAN AND SOUTH AFRICA (2002).

35. For the argument that the boundaries of Whiteness are expanding, see Jonathan Warren & France Winddance Twine, *White Americans, the New Minority?* 28 J. BLACK STUD. 200 (1997).

36. YANCEY, *supra,* at 42.

37. Of course, one cannot talk of Asian Americans as a whole, for the experience of Asian American sub-groups differs dramatically. For a discussion of the extent to which honorary White status does and does not apply to Asian Americans, see MIA TUAN, FOREVER FOREIGNERS OR HONORARY WHITES? THE ASIAN ETHNIC EXPERIENCE TODAY (2001).

38. Neil Foley, *Becoming Hispanic: Mexican Americans and the Faustian Pact with Whiteness, in* REFLEXIONES 1997, at 57 (Neil Foley ed., 1998); Ian Haney López, *Race, Ethnicity, Erasure: The Salience of Race to LatCrit Theory,* 85 CALIF. L. REV. 1143 (1997).

39. For an extended discussion of the racial politics of the Chicano movement, see IAN HANEY LÓPEZ, RACISM ON TRIAL: THE CHICANO FIGHT FOR JUSTICE (2003). For background on the Young Lords, see MIGUEL MELENDEZ, WE TOOK THE STREETS: FIGHTING FOR LATINOS WITH THE YOUNG LORDS (2003); PALANTE: THE YOUNG LORDS PARTY (1971).

40. John R. Logan, *How Race Counts for Hispanic Americans* (Albany, NY: Lewis Mumford Center for Comparative Urban and Regional Research, University at Albany, SUNY), Jul. 14, 2003 (analyzing census numbers); Pew Hispanic Center/Kaiser Family Foundation, 2002 *National Survey of Latinos, Summary of Findings* (December 2002), 31 (concluding that only twenty percent of Latinos accept a white racial identity).

41. For further discussion of Latino racial identity, see Ian Haney López, *Race on the 2010 Census: Hispanics and the Shrinking White Majority,* 134 DAEDALUS 42 (2005); Haney López, *Race, Ethnicity, Erasure, supra;* HANEY LÓPEZ, RACISM ON TRIAL, *supra.*

42. Jessica Barnes & Claudette Bennett, *The Asian Population: 2000: Census 2000 Brief,* at 3 (Feb. 2002); Betsy Guzmán, *US Bureau of the Census: The Hispanic Population, Census Brief 2000,* at 2 (May 2001).

43. Frank Hobbs & Nicole Stoops, *US Bureau of the Census: Demographic Trends in the 20th Century: Census 2000 Special Reports,* 74 (November 2002).

44. Lisa Richardson & Robin Fields, *Latinos Account for Majority of Births in California,* L.A. TIMES, Feb. 6, 2003, at A1.

45. US Bureau of the Census, 2004, *US Interim Projections by Age, Sex, Race, and Hispanic Origin,* http://www.census.gov/ipc/www/usinterimproj/, March 18, 2004. *See generally* Antonio McDaniel, *The Dynamic Racial Composition of the Untied States,* 124 DAEDALUS 179 (1995).

46. THOMAS HOLT, THE PROBLEM OF RACE IN THE 21st CENTURY 107 (2000).

47. *See, e.g.,* Adrienne Davis, *Identity Notes Part One: Playing in the Light,* 45 AM. U. L. REV. 695 (1996); Michael Elliot, *Telling the Difference: Nineteenth Century Legal Narratives of Racial Taxonomy,* 24 LAW & SOC. INQUIRY 611 (1999); Ariela Gross, *Litigating Whiteness: Trials of Racial Determination in the Nineteenth Century South,* 108 YALE L.J. 109 (1998); Daniel Sharfstein, *The Secret History of Race in the United States,* 112 YALE. L.J. 1473 (2003); Teresa Zackodnik, *Fixing the Color Line: The Mulatto, Southern Courts, and Racial Identity,* 53 AM. Q. 420 (2001).

48. Devon Carbado & Mitu Gulati, *Working Identity,* 85 CORNELL L. REV. 1259 (2000); Ariella Gross, *Beyond Black and White: Cultural Approaches to Race and Slavery,* 101 COLUM. L. REV. 640 (2001); John Tehranian, *Performing Whiteness: Naturalization Litigation and the Construction of Racial Identity in America,* 109 YALE L.J. 817 (2000).

49. On the need to overhaul civil rights laws in order to respond more effectively to color discrimination, see Taunya Banks, *Colorism: A Darker Shade of Pale,* 47 UCLA L. REV. 1705 (2000); Trina Jones, *Shades of Brown: The Law of Skin Color,* 49 DUKE L.J. 1487 (2000).

50. Reginald Robinson, *The Shifting Race-Consciousness Matrix and the Multiracial Category Movement: A Critical Reply to Professor Hernandez,* 20 B.C. THIRD WORLD L.J. 231, 276 (2000).

51. Those persons of African descent who can claim a "foreign" identity, for instance as recent immigrants from Africa or from the Caribbean, or as Latinos, may find that this assists them in distancing themselves in socio-racial terms from Blackness, and so makes an honorary White identity more accessible.

52. *See, e.g.,* Thomas Skidmore, *Biracial USA vs. Multiracial Brazil: Is the Contrast Still Valid?,* 25 J. LATIN AM. STUD. 373 (1993) (exploring evidence of systematic and pervasive racial discrimination in Brazil and repudiating earlier studies lauding a supposed commitment to "racial democracy," including his own *Toward a Comparative Analysis of Race Relations Since Abolition in Brazil and the United States,* 4 J. LATIN AM. STUD. 1 (1972)).

53. Tanya Katerí Hernández, *Multiracial Matrix: The Role of Race Ideology*

in the Enforcement of Antidiscrimination Laws, A United States-Latin America Comparison, 87 CORNELL L. REV. 1093 (2002).

54. EDUARDO BONILLA-SILVA, RACISM WITHOUT RACISTS: COLOR-BLIND RACISM AND THE PERSISTENCE OF RACIAL INEQUALITY IN THE UNITED STATES (2003). Bonilla-Silva understands colorblindness as a new form of racism. George Fredrickson, in contrast, objects when scholars and others use "racism" to describe social practices not predicated on beliefs associated more or less directly with White supremacy. FREDRICKSON, WHITE SUPREMACY, *supra,* at xii. I would argue that White supremacy is but one form of racism, where, as Fredrickson himself emphasizes, "race relations are not so much a fixed pattern as a changing set of relationships that can only be understood within a broader historical context that is itself constantly evolving and thus altering the terms under which whites and non-whites interact." *Id.* at xvii. Without fully engaging the debate about whether colorblindness constitutes racism, my claim is that, at a minimum, colorblindness now encapsulates the most powerful rationalizations for a continued racial hierarchy that places Whites at the top.

55. Plessy v. Ferguson, 163 U.S. 537, 559 (1896) (Harlan, J., dissenting).

56. The larger quote from which the "colorblindness" excerpt is taken reads as follows:

> The white race deems itself to be the dominant race in this country. And so it is, in prestige, in achievements, in education, in wealth, and in power. So, I doubt not, it will continue to be for all time, if it remains true to its great heritage, and holds fast to the principles of constitutional liberty. But in view of the constitution, in the eye of the law, there is in this country no superior, dominant, ruling class of citizens. There is no caste here. Our constitution is colorblind, and neither knows nor tolerates classes among citizens.

163 U.S. at 559. Given his invocation of perpetual White dominance, it's no surprise that Harlan's reference to colorblindness is often presented in highly excerpted form. Harlan also wrote the opinion for a unanimous Court in *Cumming v. Board of Education,* 175 U.S. 528 (1899), which upheld racial segregation in public high schools.

57. Brief for Petitioner at 27, Sipuel v. Bd. of Regents of the Univ. of Okla., 332 U.S. 814 (1947) (No. 369).

58. Briggs v. Elliott, 132 F. Supp. 776, 777 (E.D.S.C. 1955) ("The Constitution, in other words, does not require integration. It merely forbids discrimination. It does not forbid such segregation as occurs as the result of voluntary action. It merely forbids the use of governmental power to enforce segregation."); *but see* United States v. Jefferson County Bd. of Educ., 372 F.2d 836, 876 (5th Cir. 1966) (rejecting the school board's interpretation of the Fourteenth Amendment as forbidding any consideration of race).

59. Regents of the Univ. of Cal. v. Bakke, 438 U.S. 265, 402 (Marshall, J., concurring in part and dissenting in part).

60. McCleskey v. Kemp, 401 U.S. 279, 327 (1986).

61. City of Richmond v. Croson, 488 U.S. 469, 534 (1989).

62. Adarand Constructors, Inc., v. Pena, 515 U.S. 200, 240–41 (1995) (Thomas, J., concurring) (citations omitted).

63. *Bakke,* 438 U.S. at 292 (Powell, J.). Powell made this claim about the United States as it stood at the end of World War II, though most proponents of color-blindness tie the defeat of White racism to the triumphs of the early civil rights movement. *See* DINESH D'SOUZA, THE END OF RACISM (1995); STEPHAN & ABIGAIL THERNSTROM, AMERICA IN BLACK AND WHITE: ONE NA-TION INDIVISIBLE (1997).

64. One of the first efforts to harness race-as-ethnicity to colorblindness can be found in NATHAN GLAZER, AFFIRMATIVE DISCRIMINATION: ETH-NIC INEQUALITY AND PUBLIC POLICY (1975). Alan Freeman has criticized the Court for its "startling claim of 'ethnic fungibility'—the notion that each of us bears an 'ethnicity' with an equivalent legal significance and with an identical claim to protection." Alan Freeman, *Antidiscrimination Law: The View From 1989,* 64 TUL. L. REV. 1407, 1412 (1990). *See also* Reva Siegel, *Discrimination in the Eyes of the Law: How "Color Blindness" Discourse Disrupts and Ratio-nalizes Social Stratification,* 88 CALIF. L. REV. 77, 103–105 (2000); STEPHEN STEINBERG, THE ETHNIC MYTH: RACE, ETHNICITY, AND CLASS IN AMERICA (2001).

65. *Bakke,* 438 U.S. at 296 (Powell, J.).

66. *Id. See also* Cheryl Harris, *Equal Treatment and the Reproduction of In-equality,* 69 FORDHAM L. REV. 1753, 1771 (2001).

67. Hernandez v. New York, 500 U.S. 352, 404 (1991) (The prosecutor testi-fied: "I felt there was a great deal of uncertainty as to whether they could accept the interpreter as the final arbiter of what was said by each of the witnesses, es-pecially where there were going to be Spanish-speaking witnesses, and I didn't feel, when I asked them whether or not they could accept the interpreter's trans-lation of it, I didn't feel that they could.").

68. *Id.* at 375 (O'Connor, J., concurring) (emphasis added).

69. STEINBERG, TURNING BACK, *supra,* at 214 ("Through . . . code words it is possible to play on racial stereotypes, appeal to racial fears, and heap blame on blacks without naming them. Thus, in this cryptic vernacular we have a new and insidious form of racebaiting.").

70. HUNTINGTON, *supra.*

71. Lawrence Bobo et al., *Laissez Faire Racism, in* RACIAL ATTITUDES IN THE 1990s 15 (Steven Tuch & Jack Martin eds., 1997). *See also* Lawrence Bobo & James Kluegel, *Status, Ideology, and Dimensions of Whites' Racial Beliefs and Attitudes: Progress and Stagnation,* in RACIAL ATTITUDES IN THE 1990s at 93.

Bibliography

ACUÑA, RODOLFO, OCCUPIED AMERICA: A HISTORY OF CHICANOS (3rd. ed. 1988).

AFTER IDENTITY: A READER IN LAW AND CULTURE (Dan Danielson and Karen Engle eds., 1995).

ALBA, RICHARD, ETHNIC IDENTITY: THE TRANSFORMATION OF WHITE AMERICA (1990).

Aleinikoff, T. Alexander, *A Case for Race-Consciousness*, 91 COLUM. L. REV. 1060 (1991).

Aleinikoff, T. Alexander, *The Constitution in Context: The Continuing Significance of Racism*, 63 U. COLO. L. REV. 325 (1992).

ALLEN, THEODORE, THE INVENTION OF THE WHITE RACE, VOLUME ONE: RACIAL OPPRESSION AND SOCIAL CONTROL (1994).

Alva, Jorge Klor de, *Our Next Race Question*, HARPER'S, Apr. 1996.

ANATOMY OF RACISM (David Theo Goldberg ed., 1990).

ANDERSON, BENEDICT, IMAGINED COMMUNITIES: REFLECTIONS ON THE ORIGIN AND SPREAD OF NATIONALISM (rev. ed. 1991).

Ansley, Francis Lee, *A Civil Rights Agenda for the Year 2000: Confessions of an Identity Politician*, 59 TENN L. REV. 593 (1992).

Ansley, Francis Lee, *Race and the Core Curriculum in Legal Education*, 79 CAL. L. REV. 1511 (1991).

Ansley, Francis Lee, *Stirring the Ashes: Race, Class and the Future of Civil Rights Scholarship*, 74 CORNELL L. REV. 993 (1989).

Appiah, Anthony, *Are We Ethnic? The Theory and Practice of American Pluralism*, 20 BLACK AM. LIT. F. 209 (1986).

Appiah, Anthony, *The Conservation of "Race,"* 23 BLACK. AM. LIT. F. 36 (1989).

APPIAH, ANTHONY, IN MY FATHER'S House: AFRICA IN THE PHILOSOPHY OF CULTURE (1992).

Appiah, Anthony, *The Uncompleted Argument: DuBois and the Illusion of Race*, "RACE," WRITING, AND DIFFERENCE 21 (Henry Louis Gates ed., 1985).

Armstrong, Margalynne, *Protecting Privilege: Race, Residence and Rodney King*, 12 L. & INEQUALITY 351 (1994).

ASIAN AMERICANS AND THE SUPREME COURT: A DOCUMENTARY HISTORY (Hyung-Chan Kim ed., 1992).

Austin, Regina, *"The Black Community," Its Lawbreakers, and a Politics of Identification*, 65 SO. CAL. L. REV. 1769 (1992).

Austin, Regina, *Sapphire Bound!* 1989 WIS. L. REV. 539.

Baldwin, James, *On Being "White" . . . And Other Lies*, ESSENCE, April 1984, at 90.

Banks, Taunya, *Colorism: A Darker Shade of Pale*, 47 UCLA L. REV. 1705 (2000).

BARKAN, ELAZAR, THE RETREAT OF SCIENTIFIC RACISM: CHANGING CONCEPTS OF RACE IN BRITAIN AND THE UNITED STATES BETWEEN THE WORLD WARS (1992).

Barker, Martin, *Biology and the New Racism*, ANATOMY OF RACISM 18 (David Theo Goldberg ed., 1990).

BARKUN, MICHAEL, RELIGION AND THE RACIST RIGHT: THE ORIGINS OF THE CHRISTIAN IDENTITY MOVEMENT (1997 ed.).

Barnes, Robin, *Race Consciousness: The Thematic Content of Racial Distinctiveness in Critical Race Scholarship*, 103 HARV. L. REV. 1864 (1990).

Barnes, Jessica and Claudette Bennett, *The Asian Population: 2000: Census 2000 Breif*, at 3 (Feb. 2002).

Begley, Sharon, *Three Is Not Enough: Surprising Lessons from the Controversial Science of Race*, NEWSWEEK, Feb. 13, 1995, at 67.

BELL, DERRICK, AND WE ARE NOT SAVED: THE ELUSIVE QUEST FOR RACIAL JUSTICE (1987).

BELL, DERRICK, CONFRONTING AUTHORITY: REFLECTIONS OF AN ARDENT PROTESTER (1994).

BELL, DERRICK, FACES AT THE BOTTOM OF THE WELL: THE PERMANENCE OF RACISM (1992).

BELL, DERRICK, RACE, RACISM AND AMERICAN LAW (3rd. ed. 1992).

Bell, Derrick, *White Superiority in America: Its Legal Legacy, Its Economic Costs*, 33 VILL. L. REV. 767 (1988).

BENDER, LESLIE, and BRAVEMAN, DAAN, POWER, PRIVILEGE AND LAW: A CIVIL RIGHTS READER (1995).

BERGER, PETER, and LUCKMAN, THOMAS, THE SOCIAL CONSTRUCTION OF REALITY: A TREATISE IN THE SOCIOLOGY OF KNOWLEDGE (1966).

BICKEL, ALEXANDER, THE MORALITY OF CONSENT (1975).

Bobo, Lawrence et al., *Laissez Faire Racism*, RACIAL ATTITUDES IN THE 1990s (Steven Tuch & Jack Martin eds., 1997).

Bobo, Lawrence and Kluegel, James, *Status, Ideology, and Dimensions of Whites' Racial Beliefs and Attitudes: Progress and Stagnation*, RACIAL ATTITUDES IN THE 1990s (Steven Tuch & Jack Martin eds., 1997).

BONILLA-SILVA, EDUARDO, RACISM WITHOUR RACISTS: COLORBLIND RACISM AND THE PERSISTENCE OF RACIAL INEQUALITY IN THE UNITED STATES (2003).

THE BOUNDS OF RACE: PERSPECTIVES ON HEGEMONY AND RESIS-
TANCE (Dominick LaCapra ed., 1991).

Bower, Bruce, *Race Falls from Graoo*, 140 SCI. NEWS 380 (1991)

BRODKIN, KAREN, HOW JEWS BECAME WHITE FOLKS AND WHAT
THAT SAYS ABOUT RACE IN AMERICA (1999).

BROOKS, ROY L., RETHINKING THE AMERICAN RACE PROBLEM (1990).

Buell, Raymond Leslie, *Some Legal Aspects of the Japanese Question*, 17 AM. J.
INT'L. L. 29 (1923).

BUSHART, HOWARD ET AL., SOLDIERS OF GOD: WHITE SUPREMACISTS
AND THEIR HOLY WAR FOR AMERICA (1998).

Burner, David, *George Sutherland*, THE JUSTICES OF THE UNITED STATES
SUPREME COURT 1789–1969: THEIR LIVES AND WORKS, VOL. 3, at
2133 (Leon Friedman and Fred Israel eds., 1969).

Bush, Jonathan, *Free to Enslave: The Foundations of Colonial American Slave
Law*, 5 YALE J. L. & HUMANITIES 417 (1993).

Cabranes, José, *Citizenship and the American Empire: Notes on the Legislative
History of the United States Citizenship of Puerto Ricans*, 127 U. PA. L. REV.
391 (1978).

Caldwell, Dan, *The Negroization of the Chinese Stereotype in California*, 53 SO.
CAL. Q. 123 (June 1971).

Caldwell, Paulette, *A Hair Piece: Perspectives on the Intersection of Race and
Gender*, 1991 DUKE L.J. 365.

Calmore, John, *Critical Race Theory, Archie Shepp, and Fire Music: Securing an
Authentic Intellectual Life in a Multicultural World*, 65 SO. CAL. L. REV.
2129 (1992).

Calmore, John, *Spatial Equality and the Kerner Commission Report: A Back-to-
the-Future Essay*, 71 N.C. L. Rev. 1487 (1993).

Carbado, Devon & Mitu Gulati, *Working Identity*, 85 CORNELL L. REV. 1259
(2000)

Carter, Stephen, *Academic Tenure and "White Male" Standards: Some Lessons
from Patent Law*, 100 YALE L.J. 2065 (1991).

Carter, Stephen, *When Victims Happen to be Black*, 97 YALE L.J. 420 (1988).

Chang, Robert, *Toward an Asian American Legal Scholarship: Critical Race Theory, Post-Structuralism, and Narrative Space*, 81 CAL. L. REV. 1241 (1993).

Chew, Pat, *Asian Americans: The "Reticent" Minority and Their Paradoxes*, 36
WILLIAM & MARY L. REV. 1 (1994).

CHUMAN, FRANK, THE BAMBOO PEOPLE: THE LAW AND JAPANESE-
AMERICANS (1976).

Clarke, Stuart Alan, *Fear of a Black Planet: Race, Identity Politics, and Common
Sense*, 21 SOCIALIST REV. 37 (1991).

Cleveland, Robert, *US Bureau of the Census: Alternative Income Estimates in the
United States: 2003: Current Population Reports* (June 2005).

CLIFFORD, JAMES, THE PREDICAMENT OF CULTURE: TWENTIETH-CENTURY ETHNOGRAPHY, LITERATURE, AND ART (1988).

Conley, John, *"The First Principle of Reform": The Role of Science in Constitutional Jurisprudence,* 65 N.C. L. REV. 935 (1987).

COSE, ELLIS, THE RAGE OF A PRIVILEGED CLASS (1993).

Cottrol, Robert, *The Historical Definition of Race Law,* 21 LAW & SOC. REV. 865 (1988).

Cover, Robert, *Violence and the Word,* 95 YALE L.J. 1601 (1986).

Crenshaw, Kimberlé, *Mapping the Margins: Intersectionality, Identity Politics, and Violence Against Women of Color,* 43 STAN. L. REV. 1241 (1991).

Crenshaw, Kimberlé, *Race, Reform, and Retrenchment: Transformation and Legitimation in Antidiscrimination Law,* 101 HARV. L. REV. 1331 (1988).

Culp, Jerome McCristal, Jr., *The Michael Jackson Pill: Equality, Race, and Culture,* 92 MICH. L. REV. 2613 (1994).

Culp, Jerome McCristal, Jr., *Posner on Duncan Kennedy and Racial Difference: White Authority in the Legal Academy,* 1991 DUKE L.J. 1095.

Cutler, Stephen, *A Trait-Based Approach to National Origin Claims Under Title VII,* 94 YALE L.J. 1164 (1985).

Dalaker, Joe, *US Burau of the Census: Alternative Poverty Estimates in the United States: 2003: Current Population Reports* (June 2005).

DAVIS, F. JAMES, WHO IS BLACK? ONE NATION'S DEFINITION (1991).

Davis, Adrienne, *Identity Notes Part One: Playing in the Light,* 45 AM. U. L. REV. 695 (1996).

Davis, Peggy, *Law as Microaggression,* 98 YALE L.J. 1559 (1989).

Delgado, Richard, *Bibliographic Essay: Critical Race Theory,* SAGE RACE RELATIONS ABSTRACTS, May 1994, at 3.

DELGADO, RICHARD, CRITICAL RACE THEORY: THE CUTTING EDGE (1995).

Delgado, Richard, *The Imperial Scholar: Reflections on a Review of Civil Rights Literature,* 132 U. PA. L. REV. 561 (1984).

Delgado, Richard, *The Imperial Scholar Revisited: How to Marginalize Outsider Writing, Ten Years Later,* 140 U. PA. L. REV. 1349 (1992).

Delgado, Richard, *Rodrigo's Eighth Chronicle: Black Crime, White Fears—On the Social Construction of Threat,* 80 VA. L. REV. 503 (1994).

Delgado, Richard, and Palacios, Vicky, *Mexican Americans as a Legally Cognizable Class under Rule 23 and the Equal Protection Clause,* 50 NOTRE DAME LAW 393 (1975).

Delgado, Richard, and Stefancic, Jean, *Critical Race Theory: An Annotated Bibliography,* 79 VA. L. REV. 461 (1993).

Delgado, Richard, and Stefancic, Jean, *Images of the Outsider in American Law and Culture: Can Free Expression Remedy Systemic Social Ills?* 77 CORNELL L. REV. 1258 (1992).

Delgado, Richard, and Stefancic, Jean, *Norms and Narratives: Can Judges Avoid Serious Moral Error?* 69 TEX. L. REV. 1929 (1991).

Denavas-Walt, Carmen, et al., *US Bureau of the Census: Income, Poverty, and Health Insurance Coverage in the United States: 2003: Current Population Reports* (August 2004).

DeParle, Jason, *Daring Research or "Social Science Pornography"?* NEW YORK TIMES MAGAZINE, Oct. 9, 1994, at 48.

DeSipio, Louis, and Pachon, Harry, *Making Americans: Administrative Discretion and Americanization,* 12 CHICANO-LATINO L. REV. 52 (1992).

Developments in the Law: Race and the Criminal Process, 101 HARV. L. REV. 1472 (1988).

Diamond, Raymond T., and Cottrol, Robert J., *Codifying Caste: Louisiana's Racial Classification Scheme and the Fourteenth Amendment,* 29 LOY. L. REV. 255 (1983).

DOBRATZ, BETTY and SHANKS-MEILE, STEPHANIE, THE WHITE SEPARATIST MOVEMENT IN THE UNITED STATES (1997).

DOMINGUEZ, VIRGINIA, WHITE BY DEFINITION: SOCIAL CLASSIFICATION IN CREOLE LOUISIANA (1986).

Douglass, Frederick, *West India Emancipation,* Speech Delivered at Canandaigua, New York (Aug. 4, 1857), FREDERICK DOUGLASS, SELECTED SPEECHES AND WRITINGS (Philip S. Foner ed., 1999).

D'SOUZA, DINESH, THE END OF RACISM (1995).

Dudziak, Mary, *Oliver Wendell Holmes as a Eugenic Reformer: Rhetoric in the Writing of Constitutional Law,* 71 IOWA L. REV. 833 (1986).

Elliot, Michael, *Telling the Difference: Nineteenth Century Legal Narratives of Racial Taxonomy,* 24 LAW & SOC. INQUIRY 611 (1999).

FANON, FRANTZ, BLACK SKIN, WHITE MASKS (1967).

Farber, Daniel, and Sherry, Suzanna, *Telling Stories Out of School: An Essay on Legal Narratives,* 45 STAN. L. REV. 807 (1993).

Ferguson, Edwin E., *The California Alien Land Law and the Fourteenth Amendment,* 35 CAL. L. REV. 61 (1947).

Fields, Barbara, *Ideology and Race in American History,* REGION, RACE, AND RECONSTRUCTION: ESSAYS IN HONOR OF C. VANN WOODWARD 143 (J. Morgan Kousser and James McPherson eds., 1982).

Fields, Barbara, *Slavery, Race and Ideology in the United States of America,* 181 NEW LEFT REVIEW 95 (1990).

Finkelman, Paul, *The Centrality of the Peculiar Institution in American Legal Development,* 68 CHICAGO-KENT L. REV. 1009 (1993).

Finkelman, Paul, *The Color of Law,* 87 NW. U. L. REV. 937 (1993).

Finkelman, Paul, *The Crime of Color,* 67 TUL. L. REV. 2063 (1993).

FINKELMAN, PAUL, THE LAW OF FREEDOM AND BONDAGE: A CASEBOOK (1986).

Fitzpatrick, Peter, *Racism and the Innocence of Law*, ANATOMY OF RACISM 247 (David Theo Goldberg ed., 1990).

Flagg, Barbara, *Enduring Principle: On Race, Process, and Constitutional Law*, 82 CAL. L. REV. 935 (1994).

Flagg, Barbara, *"Was Blind, But Now I See": White Race Consciousness and the Requirement of Discriminatory Intent*, 91 MICH. L. REV. 953 (1993).

Foley, Neil, *Becoming Hispanic: Mexican Americans and the Faustian Pact with Whiteness*, REFLEXIONES 1997.

Forbes, Jack D., *The Manipulation of Race, Caste, and Identity: Classifying Afroamericans, Native Americans and Red-Black People*, 17 J. ETHNIC STUDIES 1 (1990).

Ford, Richard, *The Boundaries of Race: Political Geography in Legal Analysis*, 107 HARV. L. REV. 1841 (1994).

Ford, Richard, *The Repressed Community: Locating the New Communitarianism*, 65 TRANSITION 96 (1995).

Ford, Richard, *Urban Space and the Color Line: The Consequences of Demarcation and Disorientation in the Postmodern Metropolis*, 9 HARV. BLACK-LETTER J. 117 (1992).

FRANKENBERG, RUTH, WHITE WOMEN, RACE MATTERS: THE SOCIAL CONSTRUCTION OF WHITENESS (1993).

FREDRICKSON, GEORGE, WHITE SUPREMACY: A COMPARATIVE STUDY IN AMERICAN AND SOUTH AFRICAN HISTORY (1981).

FREDRICKSON, GEORGE M., RACISM: A SHORT HISTORY (2002).

FREDRICKSON, GEORGE, WHITE SUPREMACY: A COMPARATIVE STUDY IN AMEICAN AND SOUTH AFRICAN HISTORY (1981).

Freeman, Alan, *Legitimizing Racial Discrimination Through Antidiscrimination Law: A Critical Review of Supreme Court Doctrine*, 62 MINN. L. REV. 1049 (1978).

Freeman, Alan, *Antidiscrimination Law: The View From 1989*, 64 TUL. L. REV. 1407 (1990).

Frey, William H., *Immigration, Domestic Migration, and Domegraphic Balkanization in America: New Evidence from the 1990s*, 22 POPULATION AND DEVELOPMENT REV. 741 (1996).

FROM DIFFERENT SHORES: PERSPECTIVES ON RACE AND ETHNICITY IN AMERICA (Ronald Takaki ed., 1987).

FUSS, DIANA, ESSENTIALLY SPEAKING: FEMINISM, NATURE AND DIFFERENCE (1989).

Gabel, Peter, *Reification in Legal Reasoning*, 3 RES. IN L. & SOC. 25 (1980).

GARCIA, JUAN RAMON, OPERATION WETBACK: THE MASS DEPORTATION OF MEXICAN UNDOCUMENTED WORKERS IN 1954 (1980).

García, Robert, *Latinos and Criminal Justice*, 14 CHICANO-LATINO L. REV. 6 (1994).

GATES, HENRY LOUIS, JR., LOOSE CANONS: NOTES ON THE CULTURE WARS (1992).

Gates, Henry Louis, Jr., *Writing "Race" and the Difference It Makes,* "RACE," WRITING, AND DIFFERENCE 1 (Henry Louis Gates, Jr., ed., 1985).

GEERTZ, CLIFFORD, LOCAL KNOWLEDGE: FURTHER ESSAYS IN INTERPRETIVE ANTHROPOLOGY (1983).

Georges-Abeyie, Daniel E., *Race, Ethnicity, and the Spatial Dynamic: Toward a Realistic Study of Black Crime, Crime Victimization, and Criminal Justice Processing of Blacks,* 16 SOC. JUST. 35 (1989).

GILROY, PAUL, "THERE AIN'T NO BLACK IN THE Union JACK": THE CULTURAL POLITICS OF RACE AND NATION (1987).

GLAZER, NATHAN, AFFIRMATIVE DISCRIMINATION: ETHNIC INEQUALITY AND PUBLIC POLICY (1975).

Glazer, Nathan, *The Future of Race in the United States,* RACE IN 21ST CENTURY AMERICA (Curtis Stokes et al. eds., 2001).

GLAZER, NATHAN, WE ARE ALL MULTICULTURALISTS NOW (1998).

Gold, George, *The Racial Prerequisite in the Naturalization Law,* 15 B.U. L. REV. 462 (1935).

GOLDBERG, DAVID THEO, RACIST CULTURE: PHILOSOPHY AND THE POLITICS OF MEANING (1993).

Goldberg, David Theo, *The Semantics of Race,* 15 ETHNIC AND RACIAL STUD. 543 (1992).

Goldberg, Gary, and Greer, Colin, *American Visions, Ethnic Dreams: Public Ethnicity and the Sociological Imagination,* 15 SAGE RACE RELATIONS ABSTRACTS 5 (1990).

Gordon, Avery, and Newfield, Christopher, *White Philosophy,* 20 CRITICAL INQUIRY 737 (1994).

Gordon, Charles, *The Racial Barrier to American Citizenship,* 93 U. PA. L. REV. 237 (1945).

GORDON, CHARLES, and MAILMAN, STANLEY, IMMIGRATION LAW AND PROCEDURE (rev. ed. 1992).

Gordon, Robert, *Critical Legal Histories,* 36 STAN. L. REV. 57 (1984).

GOSSETT, THOMAS, RACE: THE HISTORY OF AN IDEA IN NORTH AMERICA (1963).

Gotanda, Neil, *Asian American Rights and the "Miss Saigon Syndrome,"* ASIAN AMERICANS AND THE SUPREME COURT: A DOCUMENTARY HISTORY 1087 (Hyung-Chan Kim ed., 1992).

Gotanda, Neil, *A Critique of "Our Constitution is Color-Blind,"* 44 STAN. L. REV. 1 (1991).

Gotanda, Neil, *"Other Non-Whites" in American Legal History: A Review of Justice at War,* 85 COLUM. L. REV. 1186 (1985).

GOULD, STEPHEN, THE MISMEASURE OF MAN (1981).

GRAHAM, HUGH DAVIS, COLLISION COURSE: THE STRANGE CON-
VERGENCE OF AFFIRMATIVE ACTION AND IMMIGRATION POLICY
IN AMERICA (2002).

Greenfield, Gary A., and Kates, Don B., Jr., *Mexican Americans, Racial Discrimination, and the Civil Rights Act of 1866*, 63 CAL. L. REV. 662
(1975).

Greenhouse, Carol, *Just in Time: Temporality and the Cultural Legitimation of
Law*, 98 YALE L.J. 1631 (1989).

Greer, Edward, *Antonio Gramsci and "Legal Hegemony,"* THE POLITICS OF
LAW: A PROGRESSIVE CRITIQUE 304 (David Kairys ed., 1982).

Grieco, Elizabeth M., and Cassidy, Rachel C, *US Bureau of the Census: Overview
of Race and Hispanic Origin, Census Brief 2000* (March 2001).

Grillo, Trina, and Wildman, Stephanie, *Obscuring the Importance of Race: The
Implication of Making Comparisons Between Racism and Sexism (or Other-
Isms)*, 1991 DUKE L.J. 397.

Gross, Ariella, *Beyond Black and White: Cultural Approaches to Race and Slavery*, 101 COLUM. L. REV. 640 (2001)

Gross, Ariella, *Litigating Whiteness: Trials of Racial Determination in the Nineteenth Century South*, 108 YALE L.J. 109 (1998)

Guendelsberger, John, *Access to Citizenship for Children Born Within the State
to Foreign Parents*, 40 AM. J. COMP. L. 379 (1992).

GUINIER, LANI, THE TYRANNY OF THE MAJORITY: FUNDAMENTAL
FAIRNESS IN REPRESENTATIVE DEMOCRACY (1994).

Guzman, Betsy, *US Bureau of the Census: The Hispanic Population, Census Brief
2000* (May 2001).

HACKER, ANDREW, TWO NATIONS: BLACK AND WHITE, SEPARATE,
HOSTILE, UNEQUAL (1992).

Hall, Stuart, and Held, David, *Citizens and Citizenship*, NEW TIMES: THE
CHANGING FACE OF POLITICS IN THE 1990S 173 (Stuart Hall and Martin Jacques eds., 1990).

Halley, Janet, *The Construction of Heterosexuality*, FEAR OF A QUEER
PLANET: QUEER POLITICS AND SOCIAL THEORY 82 (Michael Warner
ed., 1993).

Halley, Janet, *Reasoning about Sodomy: Act and Identity In and After* Bowers v.
Hardwick, 79 VA. L. REV. 1721 (1993).

Halley, Janet, *Sexual Orientation and the Politics of Biology: A Critique of the
Argument from Immutability*, 46 STAN. L. REV. 503 (1994).

Haney López, Ian, *Community Ties and Law School Faculty Hiring: The Case for
Professors Who Don't Think White*, BEYOND A DREAM DEFERRED:
MULTICULTURAL EDUCATION AND THE POLITICS OF EXCELLENCE
100 (Becky Thompson and Sangeeta Tyagi eds., 1993).

Haney López, Ian, *The Social Construction of Race: Some Observations on Illu-*

sion, Fabrication, and Choice, 29 HARV. CIVIL RIGHTS-CIVIL LIBERTIES L. REV. 1 (1994).

Hancy López, Ian, *Race on the 2010 Census: Hispanics and the Shrinking White Majority*, 134 DAEDALUS 42 (2005).

Haney López, Ian, *Race, Ethnicity, Erasure: The Salience of Race to LatCrit Theory*, 85 CALIF. L. REC. 1143 (1997).

HANEY LÓPEZ, IAN, RACISM ON TRIAL: THE CHICANO FIGHT FOR JUSTICE (2003).

HANSON, VICTOR DAVIS, MEXIFORNIA: A STATE OF BECOMING (2003).

Harris, Cheryl, *Equal Treatment and the Reproduction of Inequality*, 69 FORDHAM L. REV. 1753 (2001).

Harris, Angela, *Foreword: The Jurisprudence of Reconstruction*, 82 CAL. L. REV. 741 (1994).

Harris, Angela, *Race and Essentialism in Feminist Legal Theory*, 42 STAN. L. REV. 582 (1990).

Harris, Cheryl, *Whiteness as Property*, 106 HARV. L. REV. 1707 (1993).

HEIZER, ROBERT F., and ALMQUIST, ALAN J., THE OTHER CALIFORNIANS: PREJUDICE AND DISCRIMINATION UNDER SPAIN, MEXICO, AND THE UNITED STATES (1971).

Henkin, Louis, *The Constitution and United States Sovereignty: A Century of Chinese Exclusion and Its Progeny*, 100 HARV. L. REV. 853 (1987).

Hernández, Tanya Katerí, *Multiracial Matrix: The Role of Race Ideology in the Enforcement of Antidiscrimination Laws, A United States-Latin America Comparison*, 87 CORNELL L. REV. 1093 (2002).

Higginbotham, A. Leon, Jr., *An Open Letter to Justice Clarence Thomas from a Federal Judicial Colleague*, 140 U. PA. L. REV. 1007 (1992).

HIGGINBOTHAM, A. LEON, JR., IN THE MATTER OF COLOR: RACE AND THE AMERICAN LEGAL PROCESS: THE COLONIAL PERIOD (1978).

Higginbotham, A. Leon, Jr., *Racism in American and South African Courts: Similarities and Differences*, 65 N.Y.U. L. REV. 479 (1990).

Higginbotham, A. Leon, Jr., and Kopytoff, Barbara K., *Racial Purity and Interracial Sex in the Law of Colonial and Antebellum Virginia*, 77 GEO. L.J. 1967 (1989).

HIGHAM, JOHN, STRANGERS IN THE LAND: PATTERNS OF AMERICAN NATIVISM, 1860–1925 (1966).

Hing, Bill Ong, *Asian Americans and Present U.S. Immigration Policies: A Legacy of Asian Exclusion*, ASIAN AMERICANS AND THE SUPREME COURT: A DOCUMENTARY HISTORY 1106 (Hyung-Chan Kim ed., 1992).

Hing, Bill Ong, *Beyond the Rhetoric of Assimilation and Cultural Pluralism: Addressing the Tension of Separatism and Conflict in an Immigration-Driven Multiracial Society*, 81 CAL. L. REV. 863 (1993).

HING, BILL ONG, MAKING AND REMAKING ASIAN AMERICA THROUGH IMMIGRATION POLICY, 1850–1990 (1993).

Hobbs, Frank & Nicole Stoops, *US Bureau of the Census: Demographic Trends in the 20th Century: Census 2000 Special Reports* (Nov. 2002).

Hochschild, Jennifer, *Looking Ahead: Racial Trends in the United States*, 134 DAEDALUS 70 (2005).

Hochschild, Jennifer, *From Nominal to Ordinal to Interval: Reconceiving Racial and Ethnic Hierarchy in the United States*, paper delivered as Wesson Lectures, Stanford University, May 5 and 6, 2003.

Hodes, Martha, *The Sexualization of Reconstruction Politics: White Women and Black Men in the South after the Civil War*, 3 J. OF THE HIST. OF SEXUALITY 402 (1993).

HOLLINGER, DAVID, POST-ETHNIC AMERICA: BEYOND MULTICULTURALISM (1995).

Hollinger, David A., *Amalgamation and Hypo descent: The Question of Ethnoracial Mixture in the History of the United States*, 108 AM. HIST. REV. 1 (2003).

Holmes, Malcolm, and Daudistel, Howard, *Ethnicity and Justice in the Southwest: The Sentencing of Anglo, Black, and Mexican Origin Defendants*, 65 SOC. SCI. Q. 265 (1984).

HOLMES, OLIVER WENDELL, THE COMMON LAW (1881).

HOLT, THOMAS, THE PROBLEM OF RACE IN THE 21ST CENTURY (2000).

HORSMAN, REGINALD, RACE AND MANIFEST DESTINY: THE ORIGINS OF AMERICAN RACIAL ANGLO-SAXONISM (1981).

HOSOKAWA, BILL, NISEI: THE QUIET AMERICANS (1969).

Hull, Elizabeth, *Naturalization and Denaturalization*, ASIAN AMERICANS AND THE SUPREME COURT: A DOCUMENTARY HISTORY 403 (Hyung-Chan Kim ed., 1992).

HUMAN RIGHTS WATCH, PUNISHMENT AND PREJUDICE: RACIAL DISPARITIES IN THE WAR ON DRUGS (2000).

HUNTINGTON, SAMUEL P., WHO ARE WE? THE CHALLENGES TO AMERICA'S NATIONAL IDENTITY (2004).

Ichioka, Yuji, *The Early Japanese Immigrant Quest for Citizenship: The Background of the 1922 Ozawa Case*, 4 AMERASIA 1 (1977).

ICHIOKA, YUJI, THE ISSEI: THE WORLD OF THE FIRST GENERATION JAPANESE IMMIGRANTS, 1885–1924 (1988).

Ignatiev, Noel, *How to Be a Race Traitor: Six Ways to Fight Being White*, UTNE READER, Nov./Dec. 1994, at 85.

IGNATIEV, NOEL, HOW THE IRISH BECAME WHITE (1996).

Ikemoto, Lisa, *Traces of the Master Narrative in the Story of African American/Korean American Conflict: How We Constructed "Los Angeles,"* 66 SO. CAL. L. REV. 1581 (1993).

IMPACTS OF RACISM ON WHITE AMERICANS (Benjamin Bowser and Raymond Hunt eds., 1981).

THE INVENTION OF ETHNICITY (Werner Sollors ed., 1989).

JACOBSON, MATTHEW FRYE, WHITENESS OF A DIFFERENT COLOR: EUROPEAN IMMIGRANTS AND THE ALCHEMY OF RACE (1998).

JENSEN, JOAN, PASSAGE FROM INDIA: ASIAN INDIAN IMMIGRANTS IN NORTH AMERICA (1988).

Johnson, Alex, Jr., *The New Voice of Color*, 100 YALE L.J. 2007 (1991).

Johnson, Barbara, *Thresholds of Difference: Structures of Address in Zora Neale Hurston*, "RACE," WRITING, AND DIFFERENCE 322 (Henry Louis Gates ed., 1985).

Johnson, Kevin, Los Olvidados: *Images of the Immigrant, Political Power of Noncitizens, and Immigration Law and Enforcement*, 1993 B.Y.U. L. REV. 1139.

Jones, D. Marvin, *Darkness Made Visible: Law, Metaphor, and the Racial Self*, 82 GEO. L.J. 437 (1993).

Jones, Trina, *Shades of Brown: The Law of Skin Color*, 49 DUKE L.J. 1487 (2000).

JORDAN, WINTHROP, WHITE OVER BLACK: AMERICAN ATTITUDES TOWARD THE NEGRO, 1550–1812 (1968).

Kadetsky, Elizabeth, *Bashing Illegals in California*, THE NATION, Oct. 17, 1994, at 416.

KARST, KENNETH L., BELONGING TO AMERICA: EQUAL CITIZENSHIP AND THE CONSTITUTION (1989).

Karst, Kenneth, *Citizenship, Race, and Marginality*, 30 WILLIAM & MARY L. REV. 1 (1988).

Kawakami, Kiyoshi K., *The Naturalization of the Japanese*, 185 N. AM. REV. 394 (1907).

KEANE, A. H., THE WORLD'S PEOPLE: A Popular ACCOUNT OF THEIR BODILY AND MENTAL CHARACTERS, BELIEFS, TRADITIONS, POLITICAL AND SOCIAL INSTITUTIONS (1908).

KELMAN, MARK, A GUIDE TO CRITICAL LEGAL STUDIES (1987).

Kennedy, Duncan, *A Cultural Pluralist Case for Affirmative Action in Legal Academia*, 1990 DUKE L.J. 705.

KENNEDY, DUNCAN, SEXY DRESSING, ETC.: ESSAYS ON THE POWER AND POLITICS OF CULTURAL IDENTITY (1993).

Kennedy, Randall, McCleskey v. Kemp: *Race, Capital Punishment, and the Supreme Court*, 101 HARV. L. REV. 1388 (1988).

Kennedy, Randall, *Race Relations Law and the Tradition of Celebration: The Case of Professor Schmidt*, 86 COLUM. L. REV. 1622 (1986).

Kennedy, Randall, *Racial Critiques of Legal Academia*, 102 HARV. L. REV. 1745 (1989).

KETTNER, JAMES, THE DEVELOPMENT OF AMERICAN CITIZENSHIP, 1608–1870 (1978).

Killian, Lewis, *Black Power and White Reactions: The Revitalization of Race-Thinking in the United States,* 454 ANNALS AM. ACAD. POL. & SOC. SCI. 43 (1981).

Kim, Chin, and Kim, Bok Lim, *Asian Immigrants in American Law: A Look at the Past and the Challenge Which Remains,* 26 AM. U. L. REV. 373 (1977).

Kline, Marlee, *Race, Racism and Feminist Theory,* 12 HARV. WOMEN'S L.J. 115 (1989).

Koh, Harold Hongju, *Bitter Fruit of the Asian Immigration Cases,* 6 CONSTITUTION 69 (1994).

KONVITZ, MILTON, THE ALIEN AND THE ASIATIC IN AMERICAN LAW (1946).

KOVEL, JOEL, WHITE RACISM: A PSYCHOHISTORY (1970).

KULL, ANDREW, THE COLOR-BLIND CONSTITUTION (1992).

LAW FOR THE ELEPHANT, LAW FOR THE BEAVER: ESSAYS IN THE LEGAL HISTORY OF THE NORTH AMERICAN WEST (John McLaren, Hamar Foster, and Chet Orloff eds., 1992).

Lawrence, Charles, *The Id, the Ego, and Equal Protection: Reckoning with Unconscious Racism,* 39 STAN. L. REV. 317 (1987).

Lee, Jayne Chong-Soon, *Navigating the Topology of Race,* 46 STAN. L. REV. 747 (1994).

Lee, Sharon M., *Racial Classifications in the US Census: 1890–1990,* 16 ETHNIC AND RACIAL STUDIES 75 (1993).

Lesser, James, *Always "Outsiders": Asians, Naturalization, and the Supreme Court,* 12 AMERASIA 83 (1985–86).

LIEBERSON, STANLEY, A PIECE OF THE PIE: BLACKS AND WHITE IMMIGRANTS SINCE 1880 (1980).

LIND, MICHAEL, THE NEXT AMERICAN NATION: THE NEW NATIONALISM AND THE FOURTH AMERICAN REVOLUTION (1995).

Lind, Michael, *The Beige and the Black,* N.Y. TIMES MAG., Aug. 16, 1998.

Littlefield, Alice, Lieberman, Leonard, and Reynolds, Larry T., *Redefining Race: The Potential Demise of a Concept in Physical Anthropology,* 23 CURRENT ANTHROPOLOGY 641 (1982).

Logan, John R., *How Race Counts for Hispanic Americans* (Albany, NY: Lewis Mumford Center for Comparative Urban and Regional Research, University at Albany, SUNY), Jul. 14, 2003.

Lombardo, Paul, *Miscegenation, Eugenics, and Racism: Historical Footnotes to Loving v. Virginia,* 21 U.C. DAVIS L. REV. 421 (1988).

Lombardo, Paul, *Three Generations, No Imbeciles: New Light on Buck v. Bell,* 60 N.Y.U. L. REV. 30 (1989).

López, Gerald, *Undocumented Mexican Migration: In Search of a Just Immigration Law and Policy,* 28 UCLA L. REV. 615 (1981).

López, Gerald, *The Work We Know So Little About,* 42 STAN. L. REV. 1 (1989).

LURE AND LOATHING: ESSAYS ON RACE, IDENTITY, AND THE AMBIVALENCE OF ASSIMILATION (Gerald Early ed., 1993).

Lyman, Stanford, *The Race Question and Liberalism: Casuistries in American Constitutional Law,* 5 INT'L J. OF POL., CULTURE, AND SOC. 183 (1991).

Macarthur, Walter, *Opposition to Oriental Immigration,* 34 ANNALS OF AM. ACAD. 239 (July–Dec. 1909).

MAGNUM, CHARLES M., JR., THE LEGAL STATUS OF THE NEGRO (1940).

Mahoney, Martha, *Whiteness and Women, In Practice and Theory: A Reply to Catherine McKinnon,* 5 YALE J. L. & FEM. 217 (1993).

Martínez, Elizabeth, *Seeing More Than Black and White: Latinos, Racism, and Cultural Divides,* Z MAGAZINE, May 1994, at 56.

Martínez, George, *Legal Indeterminacy, Judicial Discretion and the Mexican-American Litigation Experience: 1930–1980,* 27 U.C. DAVIS L. REV. 555 (1994).

MARTINEZ, RUBEN, THE OTHER SIDE: FAULT LINES, GUERRILLA SAINTS, AND THE TRUE HEART OF ROCK 'N' ROLL (1992).

MASSEY, DOUGLAS S., and DENTON, NANCY A., AMERICAN APARTHEID: SEGREGATION AND THE MAKING OF THE UNDERCLASS (1993).

Matsuda, Mari, *Voices of America: Accent, Antidiscrimination Law, and a Jurisprudence for the Last Reconstruction,* 100 YALE L.J. 1329 (1991).

Matsuda, Mari, *Looking to the Bottom: Critical Legal Studies and Reparations,* 22 HARV. CIVIL RIGHTS-CIVIL LIBERTIES L. REV. 323 (1987).

MATSUDA, MARI, LAWRENCE, CHARLES R., III, DELGADO, RICHARD, AND CRENSHAW, KIMBERLE W., WORDS THAT WOUND: CRITICAL RACE THEORY, ASSAULTIVE SPEECH, AND THE FIRST AMENDMENT (1993).

MAUER, MARC, RACE TO INCARCERATE (1999).

McClain, Charles, Jr., *The Chinese Struggle for Civil Rights in Nineteenth Century America: The First Phase, 1850–1870,* 72 CAL. L. REV. 529 (1984).

McDaniel, Antonio, *The Dynamic Racial Composition of the Untied States,* 124 DAEDALUS 179 (1995).

McGovney, Dudley O., *The Anti-Japanese Land Laws of California and Ten Other States,* 35 CAL. L. REV. 7 (1947).

McGovney, D. O., *Race Discrimination in Naturalization,* 8 IOWA L. BULL. 129 (1923).

MELENDEZ, MIGUEL, WE TOOK THE STREETS: FIGHTING FOR LATINOS WITH THE YOUNG LORDS (2003).

MERCER, KOBENA, WELCOME TO THE JUNGLE: NEW POSITIONS IN BLACK CULTURAL STUDIES (1994).

Mezey, Naomi, *Legal Radicals in Madonna's Closet: The Influence of Identity Politics, Popular Culture, and a New Generation on Critical Legal Studies*, 46 STAN L. REV 1835 (1994).

Michaels, Walter Benn, *Race into Culture: A Critical Geneaology of Cultural Identity*, 18 CRITICAL INQUIRY 655 (1992).

Minow, Martha, *Foreword: Justice Engendered*, 101 HARV. L. REV. 10 (1987).

Minow, Martha, *Identities*, 3 YALE J. L. & HUMAN. 97 (1991).

Morganthau, Tom, *What Color Is Black?* NEWSWEEK, Feb. 13, 1995, at 63.

MORRISON, TONI, PLAYING IN THE DARK: WHITENESS AND THE LITERARY IMAGINATION (1993).

Morrison, Toni, *Unspeakable Things Unspoken: The Afro-American Presence in American Literature*, 28 MICHIGAN Q. REV. 1 (1989).

MURRAY, PAUL, STATES' LAWS ON RACE AND COLOR (1950).

Nan, Carlos, *Adding Salt to the Wound: Affirmative Action and Critical Race Theory*, 12 LAW & INEQUALITY 553 (1994).

Nei, Masatoshi, and Roychoudhury, Arun, *Genetic Relationship and Evolution of Human Races*, 14 EVOLUTIONARY BIOLOGY 1 (1982).

Neuman, Gerald, *Back to* Dred Scott? 24 SAN DIEGO L. REV. 485 (1987).

Note, *The Birthright Citizenship Amendment: A Threat to Equality*, 107 HARV. L. REV. 1026 (1994).

Note, *The Nationality Act of 1940*, 54 HARV. L. REV. 860 (1941).

Note, *Racial Violence Against Asian Americans*, 106 HARV. L. REV. 1926 (1993).

OKIHIRO, GARY, MARGINS AND MAINSTREAMS: ASIANS IN AMERICAN HISTORY AND CULTURE (1994).

Olivas, Michael, *The Chronicles, My Grandfather's Stories, and Immigration Law: The Slave Traders Chronicle as Racial History*, 34 ST. LOUIS U. L.J. 425 (1990).

OMI, MICHAEL, and WINANT, HOWARD, RACIAL FORMATION IN THE UNITED STATES: FROM THE 1960S TO THE 1980S (1986).

OMI, MICHAEL, and WINANT, HOWARD, RACIAL FORMATION IN THE UNITED STATES: FROM THE 1960S TO THE 1990S (2nd ed. 1994).

OSADA, MASAKO, SANCTIONS AND HORARY WHITES: DIPLOMATIC POLICIES AND ECONOMIC REALITIES IN RELATIONS BETWEEN JAPAN AND SOUTH AFRICA (2002).

Outlaw, Lucius, *Toward a Critical Theory of "Race,"* ANATOMY OF RACISM 58 (David Theo Goldberg ed., 1990).

PALANTE: THE YOUNG LORDS PARTY (1971).

Palmié, Stephan, *Spics or Spades? Racial Classification and Ethnic Conflict in Miami*, 34 AMERIKASTUDIEN—AMERICAN STUDIES 211 (1989).

Palumbo-Liu, David, *Los Angeles, Asians, and Perverse Ventriloquisms: On the Functions of Asian America in the Recent American Imaginary,* 6 PUB. CULTURE 365 (1994).

PASCHAL, JOEL F., MR. JUSTICE SUTHERLAND: A MAN AGAINST THE STATE (1951).

Peller, Gary, *Race Consciousness,* 1990 DUKE L.J. 758.

Piper, Adrian, *Passing for White, Passing for Black,* 58 TRANSITION 4 (1992).

Piper, Adrian, *Passing for White, Passing for Black,* PASSING AND THE FICTIONS OF IDENTITY (Elaine K. Ginsberg ed., 1996).

THE POLITICS OF LAW: A PROGRESSIVE CRITIQUE (David Kairys ed., 1982).

THE POLITICS OF LAW: A PROGRESSIVE CRITIQUE (David Kairys ed., revised ed. 1991).

Powell, T. R., *Alien Land Law Cases in the Supreme Court,* 12 CAL. L. REV. 259 (1924).

RACE, NATION, CLASS: AMBIGUOUS IDENTITIES (Etienne Balibar and Immanuel Wallerstein eds., 1991).

"RACE," WRITING, AND DIFFERENCE (Henry Louis Gates, Jr., ed., 1985).

RACE-ING JUSTICE, EN-GENDERING POWER: ESSAYS ON ANITA HILL, CLARENCE THOMAS, AND THE CONSTRUCTION OF SOCIAL REALITY (Toni Morrison ed., 1992).

RAWICK, GEORGE P., FROM SUNDOWN TO SUNUP: THE MAKING OF THE BLACK COMMUNITY (1972).

Reed, Adolph, *The Underclass as Myth and Symbol: The Poverty of Discourse About Poverty,* 24 RADICAL AMERICA 21 (1994).

REGION, RACE, AND RECONSTRUCTION: ESSAYS IN HONOR OF C. VANN WOODWARD (J. Morgan Kousser and James McPherson eds., 1982).

Richardson, Lisa & Robin Fields, *Latinos Account for Majority of Births in California,* L.A. TIMES, Feb. 6, 2003, at A1.

RINGER, BENJAMIN, and LAWLESS, ELINOR, RACE-ETHNICITY AND SOCIETY (1989).

Robinson, Amy, *It Takes One to Know One: Passing and Communities of Common Interest,* 20 CRITICAL INQUIRY 715 (1994).

Robinson, Reginald, *The Shifting Race-Consciousness Matrix and the Multiracial Category Movement: A Critical Reply to Professor Hernandez,* 20 B.C. THIRD WORLD L.J. 231 (2000).

Rodriguez, Gregory, *Mongrel America,* ATLANTIC MONTHLY, Jan./Feb. 2003.

Rodriguez, Gregory, *Dining at the Ethnicity Café,* L.A. TIMES, May 18, 2003.

RODRIGUEZ, RICHARD, BROWN, THE LAST DISCOVERY OF AMERICA (2002).

Rodríguez, Rey M., *The Misplaced Application of English-Only Rules in the Workplace,* 14 CHICANO-LATINO L. REV. 67 (1994).

ROEDIGER, DAVID, COLORED WHITE: TRANSCENDING THE RACIAL PAST (2003).

ROEDIGER, DAVID, TOWARDS THE ABOLITION OF WHITENESS (1994).

ROEDIGER, DAVID, THE WAGES OF WHITENESS: RACE AND THE MAKING OF THE AMERICAN WORKING CLASS (1992).

ROSALDO, RENATO, CULTURE AND TRUTH: THE REMAKING OF SOCIAL ANALYSIS (1989).

Rosaldo, Renato, *Others of Invention: Ethnicity and Its Discontents,* VILLAGE VOICE, Feb. 13, 1990, at 27.

Rosaldo, Renato, *Race and Other Inequalities: The Borderlands in Arturo Islas's* Migrant Souls, RACE 213 (Steven Gregory and Roger Sanjek eds., 1995).

Rose, Peter, *"Of Every Hue and Caste": Race, Immigration, and Perceptions of Pluralism,* 530 ANNALS OF THE AM. ACAD. 187 (1993).

Ross, Thomas, *The Rhetorical Tapestry of Race: White Innocence and Black Abstraction,* 32 WILLIAM & MARY L. REV. 1 (1990).

Rowell, Chester, *Chinese and Japanese Immigrants—A Comparison,* 34 ANNALS OF AM. ACAD. 223 (July–Dec. 1909).

RUSSELL, KATHY, WILSON, MIDGE, and HALL, RONALD, THE COLOR COMPLEX: THE POLITICS OF SKIN COLOR AMONG AFRICAN AMERICANS (1992).

Russell, Margaret, *Race and the Dominant Gaze: Narratives of Law and Inequality in Popular Film,* 15 LEGAL STUD. F. 243 (1991).

SAID, EDWARD, ORIENTALISM (1978).

SANDERS, RONALD, LOST TRIBES AND PROMISED LANDS: THE ORIGINS OF AMERICAN RACISM (1978).

SAXTON, ALEXANDER, THE RISE AND FALL OF THE WHITE REPUBLIC: CLASS POLITICS AND MASS CULTURE IN NINETEENTH-CENTURY AMERICA (1990).

Scales-Trent, Judy, *Commonalities: On Being Black and White, Different and the Same,* 2 YALE J. L. & FEMINISM 305 (1990).

SCHUCK, PETER, and SMITH, ROGER, CITIZENSHIP WITHOUT CONSENT: ILLEGAL ALIENS IN THE AMERICAN POLITY (1985).

Scott, Joan, *The Evidence of Experience,* 17 CRITICAL INQUIRY 773 (1991).

Sharfstein, Daniel, *The Secret History of Race in the United States,* 112 YALE. L.J. 1473 (2003).

SHIPMAN, PAT, THE EVOLUTION OF RACISM: HUMAN DIFFERENCES AND THE USE AND ABUSE OF SCIENCE (1994).

Shipman, Pat, *Facing Racial Differences—Together,* THE CHRONICLE OF HIGHER EDUCATION, Aug. 3, 1994, at B1.

Should the Census be Less Black and White? BUSINESS WEEK, July 4, 1994, at 40.

SICKELS, ROBERT J., RACE, MARRIAGE, AND THE LAW (1972).

Siegel, Reva, *Discrimination in the Eyes of the Law: How "Color Blindness" Discourse Disrupts and Rationalizes Social Stratification*, 88 CALIF. L. REV. 77 (2000).

Skrentny, John D., *Inventing Race*, 46 PUB. INT. 97 (Winter 2002).

SMEDLEY, AUDREY, RACE IN NORTH AMERICA: ORIGINS AND EVOLUTION OF A WORLDVIEW (2d ed. 1999).

SMEDLEY, AUDREY, RACE IN NORTH AMERICA: ORIGIN AND EVOLUTION OF A WORLDVIEW (1993).

Smith, Christopher, *Plea Bargaining Favors Whites as Blacks, Hispanics Pay the Price*, SAN JOSE MERCURY NEWS, Dec. 8, 1994, at A1.

SMITH, DARRELL HAVENOR, THE BUREAU OF NATURALIZATION: ITS HISTORY, ACTIVITIES, AND ORGANIZATION (1926).

Solomon, Joshua, *Skin Deep: My Own Journey into the Heart of Race-Conscious America*, WASHINGTON POST, Oct. 30, 1994, at C1.

SPANN, GIRARDEAU, RACE AGAINST THE COURT: THE SUPREME COURT AND MINORITIES IN CONTEMPORARY AMERICA (1993).

STANTON, W. R., THE LEOPARD'S SPOTS: SCIENTIFIC ATTITUDES TOWARDS RACE IN AMERICA (1960).

THE STATE OF ASIAN AMERICA: ACTIVISM AND RESISTANCE IN THE 1990S (Karin Aguilar-San Juan ed., 1994).

Stein, Judith, *Defining the Race 1890–1930*, THE INVENTION OF ETHNICITY 77 (Werner Sollors ed., 1989).

STEINBERG, STEPHEN, THE ETHNIC MYTH: RACE, ETHNICITY, AND CLASS IN AMERICA (2001).

STEINBERG, STEPHEN, TURNING BACK: THE RETREAT FROM RACIAL JUSTICE IN AMERICAN THOUGHT AND POLICY (2001).

Stepan, Nancy, and Gilman, Sander, *Appropriating the Idioms of Science: The Rejection of Scientific Racism*, THE BOUNDS OF RACE: PERSPECTIVES ON HEGEMONY AND Resistance 72 (Dominick LaCapra ed., 1991).

STEPAN, NANCY, THE IDEA OF RACE IN SCIENCE: GREAT BRITAIN, 1800–1960 (1982).

Stephenson, Gilbert, *Race Distinctions in American Law*, 43 AM. L. REV. 29 (1909).

STEPHENSON, GILBERT T., RACE DISTINCTIONS IN AMERICAN LAW (1910).

Strickland, Rennard, *Scholarship in the Academic Circus or the Balancing Act at the Minority Side Show*, 20 U.S.F. L. REV. 491 (1986).

Su, Julie Ann, *Race, Identity and Diversity at Harvard Law School: A Memo to the HLS Community* (1993) (unpublished manuscript).

Surro, Roberto, *Mixed Doubles*, AM. DEMOGRAPHICS, NOV. 1999.

TAKAKI, RONALD, IRON CAGES: RACE AND CULTURE IN 19TH-CENTURY AMERICA (1990).

TAKAKI, RONALD, STRANGERS FROM A DIFFERENT SHORE: A HISTORY OF ASIAN AMERICANS (1989).

Tehranian, John, *Performing Whiteness: Naturalization Litigation and the Construction of Racial Identity in America,* 109 YALE L.J. 817 (2000).

Terry, Robert, *The Negative Impact on White Values,* IMPACTS OF RACISM ON WHITE AMERICANS 119 (Benjamin Bowser and Raymond Hunt eds., 1981).

THEORIES OF RACE AND ETHNIC RELATIONS (John Rex and David Mason eds., 1986).

THERNSTROM, STEPHEN AND ABIGAIL, AMERICA IN BLACK AND WHITE: ONE NATION INDIVISIBLE (1997).

Torres, Gerald, and Milun, Kathryn, *Translating* Yonnondio *by Precedent and Evidence: The Mashpee Indian Case,* 1990 DUKE L.J. 625.

Treason to Whiteness Is Loyalty to Humanity: An Interview with Noel Ignatiev of Race Traitor *Magazine,* THE BLAST!, June/July 1994, *excerpted in* UTNE READER, Nov./Dec. 1994, at 82.

Tricario, Donald, *Guido: Fashioning an Italian-American Youth Style,* 19 J. OF ETHNIC STUDIES 41 (Spring 1991).

Trillin, Calvin, *Black or White,* THE NEW YORKER, Apr. 14, 1986, at 62.

TUAN, MIA, FOREVER FOREIGNERS OR HONORARY WHITES? THE ASIAN ETHNIC EXPERIENCE TODAY (2001).

U.S. COMMISSION ON CIVIL RIGHTS, THE TARNISHED GOLDEN DOOR: CIVIL RIGHTS ISSUES IN IMMIGRATION (1990).

U.S. DEPARTMENT OF JUSTICE, 1988 STATISTICAL YEARBOOK OF THE IMMIGRATION AND NATURALIZATION SERVICE (1989).

U.S. DEPARTMENT OF LABOR, THE RACIAL PROBLEMS INVOLVED IN IMMIGRATION FROM LATIN AMERICA AND THE WEST INDIES TO THE UNITED STATES (1925).

VAN DYNE, FREDERICK, A TREATISE ON THE LAW OF NATURALIZATION OF THE UNITED STATES (1907).

Vogel, Ursula, *Is Citizenship Gender-Specific?* THE FRONTIERS OF CITIZENSHIP 58 (Ursula Vogel and Michael Moran eds., 1991).

WARE, VRON, BEYOND THE PALE: WHITE WOMEN, RACISM AND HISTORY (1992).

Warren, Jonathan and France Winddance Twine, *White Americans, the New Minority?* 28 J. BLACK STUD. 200 (1997).

WATERS, MARY, ETHNIC OPTIONS: CHOOSING IDENTITIES IN AMERICA (1990).

WEBSTER, PRENTISS, THE LAW OF NATURALIZATION IN THE UNITED STATES OF AMERICA AND OTHER COUNTRIES (1895).

Welch, Susan, Gruhl, John, and Spohn, Cassia, *Dismissal, Conviction, and Incarceration of Hispanic Defendants: A Comparison with Anglos and Blacks,* 65 SOC. SCI. Q. 257 (1984).

WEST, CORNELL, RACE MATTERS (1993).

WHITE ETHNICS: THEIR LIFE IN WORKING CLASS AMERICA (Joseph Ryan ed., 1975).

Wigmore, John, *American Naturalization and the Japanese*, 28 AM. L. REV. 818 (1894).

Williams, Brackette, *A Class Act: Anthropology and the Race to Nation Across Ethnic Terrain*, 18 ANN. REV. ANTHROPOLOGY 401 (1989).

WILLIAMS, GREGORY, LIFE ON THE COLOR LINE: THE TRUE STORY OF A WHITE BOY WHO DISCOVERED HE WAS BLACK (1995).

WILLIAMS, PATRICIA, THE ALCHEMY OF RACE AND RIGHTS: DIARY OF A LAW PROFESSOR (1991).

Williams, Patricia, *The Obliging Shell: An Informal Essay on Formal Equal Opportunity*, 87 MICH. L. REV. 2128 (1989).

WILLIAMS, KIM, RACE COUNTS: AMERICAN MULTIRACIALISM AND THE CIVIL RIGHTS MOVEMENT (forthcoming 2006).

Williams, Kim, *Multiracialism and the Civil Rights Future*, 134 DAEDALUS 53 (2005).

Wilson, Pete, *Crack Down on Illegals*, USA TODAY, Aug. 20, 1993, at 12A.

WINANT, HOWARD, RACIAL CONDITIONS: POLITICS, THEORY, COMPARISONS (1994).

Wolf, Eric, *Perilous Ideas: Race, Culture, People*, 35 CURRENT ANTHROPOLOGY 1 (1994).

Wright, Lawrence, *One Drop of Blood*, NEW YORKER, July 25, 1994, at 46.

WRITING CULTURE: THE POETICS AND POLITICS OF ETHNOGRAPHY (James Clifford and George Marcus eds., 1986).

Wunder, John R., *Anti-Chinese Violence in the American West, 1850–1910*, LAW FOR THE ELEPHANT, LAW FOR THE BEAVER: ESSAYS IN THE LEGAL HISTORY OF THE NORTH AMERICAN WEST 212 (John McLaren, Hamar Foster, and Chet Orloff eds., 1992).

Yamashita, Robert C., and Park, Peter, *The Politics of Race: The Open Door, Ozawa and the Case of Japanese in America*, 17 REV. RADICAL POL. ECON. 135 (1985).

YANCEY, GEORGE, WHO IS WHITE? LATINOS, ASIANS, AND THE NEW BLACK/NONBLACK DIVIDE (2003).

YOUNG, ROBERT, WHITE MYTHOLOGIES: WRITING HISTORY AND THE WEST (1990).

Zackodnik, Teresa, *Fixing the Color Line: The Mulatto, Southern Courts, and Racial Identity*, 53 AM. Q. 420 (2001).

ZWEIGENHAFT, RICHARD L. AND DOMHOFF, G. WILLIAM, DIVERSITY IN THE POWER ELITE: HAVE WOMEN AND MINORITIES REACHED THE TOP? (1998).

Table of Legal Authorities

In re Feroz Din, 27 F.2d 568 (N.D.Cal. 1928).

In re Fisher, 21 F.2d 1007 (N.D.Cal. 1927).

Fong Yue Ting v. United States, 149 U.S. 698 (1893).

In re Gee Hop, 71 F. 274 (N.D.Cal. 1895).

United States v. Gokhale, 26 F.2d 360 (2nd Cir. 1928).

People v. Hall, 4 Cal. 399 (1854).

In re Halladjian, 174 F. 834 (C.C.D.Mass. 1909).

Hernandez v. New York, 500 U.S. 352 (1991).

In re Hong Yen Chang, 84 Cal. 163, 24 Pac. 156 (1890).

United States v. Javier, 22 F.2d 879 (D.C. Cir. 1927).

United States v. Jefferson County Bd. of Educ., 372 F.2d 836 (5th Cir. 1966).

In re Kanaka Nian, 6 Utah 259, 21 Pac. 993 (1889).

Kelly v. Owen, 74 U.S. 496 (1868).

United States v. Khan, 1 F.2d 1006 (W.D.Pa. 1924).

Kharaiti Ram Samras v. United States, 125 F.2d 879 (9th Cir. 1942).

In re Knight, 171 F. 299 (E.D.N.Y. 1909).

Korematsu v. United States, 323 U.S. 214 (1944).

In re Lampitoe, 232 F. 382 (S.D.N.Y. 1916).

Loving v. Virginia, 388 U.S. 1 (1967).

MacKenzie v. Hare, 239 U.S. 299 (1915).

In re Mallari, 239 F. 416 (D.Mass. 1916).

Mashpee Tribe v. New Seabury Corp., 592 F.2d 575 (1st Cir. 1979).

Mashpee Tribe v. Town of Mashpee, 447 F.Supp. 940 (D.Mass. 1978).

McCleskey v. Kemp, 481 U.S. 279 (1987).

Metro Broadcasting v. F.C.C., 497 U.S. 547 (1990).

In re Mohan Singh, 257 F. 209 (S.D.Cal. 1919).

Ex parte Mohriez, 54 F.Supp. 941 (D.Mass. 1944).

Montoya v. United States, 180 U.S. 261 (1901).

Morrison v. California, 291 U.S. 82 (1934).

In re Mudarri, 176 F. 465 (C.C.D.Mass. 1910).

In re Najour, 174 F. 735 (N.D.Ga. 1909).

Ex parte (Ng) Fung Sing, 6 F.2d 670 (W.D.Wash. 1925).

Oyama v. California, 332 U.S. 633 (1948).

Ozawa v. United States, 260 U.S. 178 (1922).

Plessy v. Ferguson, 163 U.S. 537 (1896).

In re Po, 7 Misc. 471, 28 N.Y. Supp. 838 (City Ct. 1894).

Porterfield v. Webb, 263 U.S. 225 (1923).

Presley v. Etowah County Commission, 502 U.S. 491 (1992).

In re Rallos, 241 F. 686 (E.D.N.Y. 1917).

Rice v. Gong Lum, 139 Miss. 760, 104 So. 105 (1925).

Richmond v. J. A. Croson Co., 488 U.S. 469 (1989).

In re Rodriguez, 81 F. 337 (W.D.Tex. 1897).

In re Sadar Bhagwab Singh, 246 F. 496 (E.D.Pa. 1917).
Saint Francis College v. Al-Khazraji, 481 U.S. 604 (1987).
In re Saito, 62 F. 126 (C.C.D.Mass. 1894).
United States v. Sakharam Ganesh Pandit, 15 F.2d 285 (9th Cir. 1926).
Sato v. Hall, 191 Cal. 510, 217 Pac. 520 (1923).
Shaare Tefila Congregation v. Cobb, 481 U.S. 615 (1987).
Ex parte Shahid, 205 F. 812 (E.D.S.C. 1913).
Terrace v. Thompson, 263 U.S. 197 (1923).
Terrace v. Thompson, 274 F. 841 (W.D.Wash. 1921).
United States v. Thind, 261 U.S. 204 (1923).
In re Thind, 268 F. 683 (D.Or. 1920).
University of California Regents v. Bakke, 438 U.S. 265 (1978).
Wadia v. United States, 101 F.2d 7 (2nd Cir. 1939).
United States v. Wong Kim Ark, 169 U.S. 649 (1898).
In re Yamashita, 30 Wash. 234, 70 Pac. 482 (1902).
Yameshita v. Hinkle, 260 U.S. 199 (1922).
In re Young, 198 F. 715 (W.D.Wash. 1912).
In re Young, 195 F. 645 (W.D.Wash. 1912).

CONSTITUTIONAL PROVISIONS

U.S. Const. art. I, sec. 8, cl. 4.
U.S. Const. amend. XIV.

STATUTES

Act of March 26, 1790, ch. 3, 1 Stat. 103.
Act of July 22, 1790, ch. 33, § 1, 1 Stat. 137.
Act of Feb. 10, 1855, ch. 71, § 2, 10 Stat. 604.
Act of April 30, 1855, ch. 175, § 2, 1855 Cal. Stat. 217.
Act of July 14, 1870, ch. 255, § 7, 16 Stat. 254.
Act of Feb. 18, 1875, ch. 80, 18 Stat. 318.
Act of July 9, 1884, ch. 220, 23 Stat. 115.
Act of May 5, 1892, ch. 60, 27 Stat. 25.
Act of April 29, 1902, ch. 641, 32 Stat. 176.
Act of April 27, 1904, ch. 1630, 33 Stat. 428.
Act of March 2, 1907, ch. 2534, § 3, 34 Stat. 1228.
Act of Feb. 5, 1917, ch. 29, 39 Stat. 874.
Act of May 19, 1921, ch. 8, 42 Stat. 5.
Act of Sept. 22, 1922, ch. 411, § 2, 42 Stat. 1021.
Act of Sept. 22, 1922, ch. 411, § 3, 42 Stat. 1021.
Act of March 20, 1924, ch. 394, 1924 Va. Acts 569.
Act of May 26, 1924, ch. 190, § 13(c), 43 Stat. 153.

Act of June 2, 1924, ch. 233, 43 Stat. 253.

Act of March 3, 1931, ch. 442, § 4(a), 46 Stat. 1511.

Act of Oct. 14, 1940, ch. 876, § 303, 54 Stat. 1140.

Act of Feb. 13, 1943, No. 47, §§ 1–2, 1943 Ark. Acts 75.

Act of Dec. 17, 1943, ch. 344, § 3, 57 Stat. 600.

Act of July 2, 1946, ch. 534, 60 Stat. 416.

Act of Oct. 2, 1965, 79 Stat. 911.

Chinese Exclusion Act, ch. 126, 22 Stat. 58 (1882).

Civil Rights Act of 1866, ch. 31, 14 Stat. 27.

Genocide Convention Implementation Act of 1987, 18 U.S.C. § 1093 (1988).

Immigration Act of 1924, ch. 190, § 13(c), 43 Stat. 162.

Immigration Act of 1990, §131, 104 Stat. 4978 (codified as amended at 8 U.S.C. §1153[c] [1994]).

Immigration and Nationality Act of 1952, § 101(a)(23), 66 Stat. 169 (codified as amended at 8 U.S.C. § 1101[a][23] [1988]).

Immigration and Nationality Act of 1952, ch. 2, § 311, 66 Stat. 239 (codified as amended at 8 U.S.C. § 1422 [1988]).

Nationality Act of 1940, § 201(b), 54 Stat. 1138.

Revised Statutes of 1873 (naturalization laws). Act of Feb. 18, 1875, ch. 80, 18 Stat. 318.

MISCELLANEOUS

Brief Filed by the Attorney General of the State of California as Amicus Curiae, Ozawa vs. United States, 260 U.S. 178 (1922).

Brief for Petitioner, Ozawa vs. United States, 260 U.S. 178 (1922).

Brief for Petitioner, Sipuel v. Bd. of Regents of the Univ. of Okla., 332 U.S. 814 (1947).

Brief for the United States, United States v. Thind, 261 U.S. 204 (1923).

Brief of Respondent, United States v. Thind, 261 U.S. 204 (1923)

H.R.J. Res. 129, 103d Cong., 1st Sess. (1993).

Illegal Aliens. Ineligibility for Public Services. Verification and Reporting. Initiative Statute, CALIFORNIA BALLOT PAMPHLET, GENERAL ELECTION, NOVEMBER 8, 1994, at 54.

Petition for Rehearing and Reargument, United States v. Thind, 261 U.S. 204 (1923).

Proposition 187: Text of Proposed Law, CALIFORNIA BALLOT PAMPHLET, GENERAL ELECTION, NOVEMBER 8, 1994, at 91.

Statement of Senator Cowan, 57 CONG. GLOBE, 42nd Cong., 1st Sess. 499 (1866).

Statement of Senator Hendricks, 59 CONG. GLOBE, 42nd Cong., 1st Sess. 2939 (1866).

Index

Before using this index, readers should be aware of a major idiosyncrasy. There is no entry here for "race" per se. Rather, I index race and related concepts in terms that reflect the thesis of this book, that race is constructed. Discussions about race are indexed primarily by reference to "racial attributes and descriptors," "racial categories," "racial categorization," and "the legal construction of race." These headings encompass, respectively, the characteristics often tied to race, for example criminality or innocence, the different groups often thought of as racial, for instance Black and White, the various categorical tools employed to construct and explain racial divisions, such as science and common sense, and the ways in which law adds to the social knowledge about race, including legitimization and reification. Though probably less susceptible to easy use, this approach seems best because it draws on, and emphasizes, the reconceptualization offered here of race as a social and legal construction which is unstable, ill-defined, and complexly woven back in on itself.

To illustrate how this index might work, imagine a reader interested in the discussion of Asians in this book. She will find no page numbers under "Asian." Instead, she will be referred to, among other entries, "racial categories." There, she will have to sift through the page references for not only what we might now consider obvious "Asian" entries, such as Chinese and Japanese, but also defunct or discredited racial groupings like Asiatic, Mongolian, and Hindu, as well as less clearly "Asian" categories, for instance Armenian and Syrian, and finally, she will also have to look over the racial groups now understood as clearly not "Asian," but which, nevertheless, have served in various ways to define the borders of that category, for example Black and White.

This indexical approach, though initially more difficult, seems likely to produce more nuanced readings of the book, thereby perhaps rendering this project more helpful to the reader. As a separate point, under this approach the index itself becomes a confirmation of the book's thesis. Reading through the entries associated with race demonstrates in startling ways the complexity and interrelatedness of racial categories and racial categorization. Perhaps the reader is best advised to use this index with patience (and hope), but also with a sense that, more than is usually the case, this index is itself an informative, substantive part of the book.

Multiracial. *See* Racial categories, mul-
  tiracial
Multiracialism, 145–46, 213 n1
  race mixing as part of, 146
Multiracial movements, in U.S., 144
Murphy, William, 90
Murray, Charles, 71
Muslim. *See* Racial categorization, reli-
  gion

NAACP (National Association for the
  Advancement of Colored People),
  27, 157
Nagurs. *See* Racial categories, Nagurs
Najour, Costa George, 48, 171
Narrative theory, 96
National Association for the Advance-
  ment of Colored People. *See*
  NAACP
National origin. *See* Racial categoriza-
  tion, national origin
National origin quotas, 27
Native American. *See* Citizen, Native
  Americans and; Racial categories,
  Indian (Native American); Racial
  categories, Native American; Racial
  prerequisite legislation, Native
  Americans and
Nativism, 2, 209 n31
  in U.S., 26, 101
Naturalists, 68
Naturalization laws, 30–34, 177,
  193 n32. *See also* Citizenship; Legal
  construction of race; Racial prerequisite cases; Racial prerequisite legislation
  definition of, 183 n2
  demographics influenced by, 82
  gender and, 33–34
  marriage and, 11
  racism in, xiii, 2, 11, 24, 60–61, 62–
  63, 82
  Revised Statutes of 1873, 177
  for South Asians, 31, 110
  state laws, 195 n15
Naturalization of citizens, 1, 30–34. *See*
  also Citizenship; Racial prerequisite
  legislation
  for African Americans, 35
  for Asian Indians, 64

for Chinese, 39–40, 193 n32
constitutional definitions for, 183 n1
data collection for, 1
in Germany, 32
legal requirements for, 2, 11, 24
in racial prerequisite cases, 18–19
racial restrictions on, 1, 11
in U.S. Constitution, 30–31
Naturalization of race, 18, 21, 30–34,
  41, 44, 64, 109–16, 136. *See also*
  Racial categorization; Social construction of race
  common knowledge and, 12, 19, 110,
  115
  cultural naturalization and, 114–15,
  116
  physical naturalization and, 112–14,
  115
"The Naturalization of the Japanese"
  (Kawakami), 106
Nature, 18, 65–68, 73. *See also* Racial
  categorization, nature and
Navy, U.S., 42
Nazism, 32
Nebraska, 83
Negroid. *See* Racial categories, Negroid
Negroization. *See* Racial categorization,
  negroization
Neuman, Gerald, 193 n25
New American Cyclopedia, 38
New Jersey, 201 n46
Newman, District Judge, 48–49
Newsweek, 71, 144
New York, 40, 42, 197 n34. *See also* City
  Court, Albany, (NY)
Ninth Circuit Court of Appeals, 62
Nixon, Richard, 149
Non-Hispanic White. *See* Racial cate-
  gories, non-Hispanic White
Non-White. *See* Racial categories, non-
  White
Nordic. *See* Racial categories, Nordic
North America, 25. *See also* racial cate-
  gories, North America and; (U.S.)
  United States
  colonialism in, 143
  first Africans in, 8
North American Review, 106
North Carolina, 83
North Dakota, 83

About the Author

Ian Haney López is a professor of law at the University of California, Berkeley, where he teaches in the areas of race and constitutional law. He has previously taught at the University of Wisconsin, Madison, as well as at Yale Law School, and was a Rockefeller Fellow in Law and Humanities at Stanford University. Haney López has published groundbreaking work in the study of the social and especially legal construction of race in two books, *White by Law: The Legal Construction of Race* and *Racism on Trial: The Chicano Fight for Justice*. His numerous articles have appeared, among other places, in the *Yale Law Journal*, the *California Law Review*, and the *Pennsylvania Law Review*; he has published opinion pieces in the *New York Times* and the *Los Angeles Times* and his work has also been featured in over two dozen anthologies and encyclopedias. Haney López's current research examines the emergence and operation of colorblindness in U.S. constitutional law as a harbinger of a new racial ideology aimed at legitimating and preserving the racial status quo.

Reserves Overdue / Replacement Policy

- $1.00 per HOUR LATE FEE
- NO CREDIT FOR BILLED ITEMS AFTER 30 DAYS